Studies in Economic Ethics and Philosophy

Springer

Berlin
Heidelberg
New York
Barcelona
Hong Kong
London
Milan
Paris
Singapore
Tokyo

Lorenzo Sacconi

The Social Contract of the Firm

Economics, Ethics and Organisation

With 10 Figures

 Springer

Prof. Lorenzo Sacconi
Centre for Ethics, Law & Economics (CELE)
LIUC – Università Cattaneo di Castellanza
Corso Matteotti 22
I-21053 Castellanza (VA)
Italy

"Originally published in Italian under the title:
Lorenzo Sacconi, Economia Etica Organizzazione"
© 1997 Gius. Laterza & Figli Spa, Roma-Bari. The English language edition
arranged through the mediation of EULAMA Literary Agency.

English language edition revised and translated by the author.

ISBN 3-540-67219-2 Springer-Verlag Berlin Heidelberg New York

Cataloging-in-Publication Data applied for
Die Deutsche Bibliothek – CIP-Einheitsaufnahme
Sacconi, Lorenzo: The social contract of the firm: economics, ethics and organisation /
Lorenzo Sacconi. – Berlin; Heidelberg; New York; Barcelona; Hong Kong; London; Milan;
Paris; Singapore; Tokyo: Springer, 2000
   (Studies in economic ethics and philosophy)
   ISBN 3-540-67219-2

Springer-Verlag is a company in the BertelsmannSpringer publishing group.
© Springer-Verlag Berlin · Heidelberg 2000
Printed in Germany

Hardcover Design: Erich Kirchner, Heidelberg

SPIN 10719481   42/2202-5 4 3 2 1 0 – Printed on acid-free paper

[...] At this moment the King, who had been for some time busily writing in his note-book, called out "Silence!" and read out from his book,

"Rule Forty-two. *All persons more than a mile high to leave the court.*"

Everybody looked at Alice.

"I'm not a mile high," said Alice.

"You are" said the King.

"Nearly two miles high," added the Queen.

"Well, I shan't go, at any rate," said Alice: "besides, that's not a regular rule: you invented it just now."

"It's the oldest rule in the book," said the King.

"Then it ought be Number One" said Alice.

The King turned pale, and shut his note-book hastily.

LEWIS CARROLL, *ALICE'S ADVENTURES IN THE WONDERLAND*

Preface

1.   A code of ethics, i.e. the set of moral rules governing an organisation, a firm or an association, may be implicit or explicit, tacit or recorded, either orally or in writing. It may grow up in an apparently spontaneous way or be deliberated by a formal process; it may be published and transmitted in an informal way or via formal procedures of communication and development. Obviously more or less formal ethical rules governing the running of the firm and business in general have always existed as principles leading the behaviour of the entrepreneur or values embedded in the corporate culture and in the beliefs of those who run the firm and work in it, as well as the ethical norms of the professions, arts and works. In the last twenty years, however, the phenomenon of corporate ethics has begun to grow up very fast and extensively. In large-scale multinational companies, business associations, public offices, universities and hospitals – all organisations with complex internal bureaucratic and hierarchical structures – the tendency to draw up and write down explicitly formulated ethical codes, formally decided by the management and communicated to employees via formal procedures and training programs and reported to external consumers or service-users, suppliers and public offices is not any more the exception but the rule. According to empirical research into the phenomenon of corporate ethical codes in the US – taking American firms classified by *Fortune* as the point of reference – the number of firms with a code of ethics grew from 8% in 1980 to 93% in 1990.

This is not the place for an empirical research into the phenomenon of corporate codes of ethics[1]. The scope of this study is, on the contrary, essentially theoretical, both in the explanatory and normative senses. The relevant question is, therefore: why has the phenomenon of corporate ethics spread so widely, beyond the contingent historical facts? In other words to find out whether there is an explanation in terms of the rise of institutional and governance structures of the firm, in accordance with the properties of efficiency

---

[1]   For empirical researches that first reported the phenomenon of ethical codes at an international level see Center for Business Ethics (1988,1994), Molander (1987), Benson (1989), Langlois and Schlegelmilch (1990). For a theoretical discussion of the subject, representing also the first stage in this study, see Sacconi (1991) ch.6, 7 and 9.

and stability generally called for by neo-institutional economics, from which we can predictively deduce the appearance of a code of ethics within a formal organisation which is usually based on hierarchical principles.

Unlike the law, a code of ethics is not enforced by legally binding sanctions (even though legal incentives for the adoption and setting up of a corporate code of ethics have recently been introduced in the US[2]). Thus a code of ethics must first of all have an endogenous explanation in terms of self-enforceability[3]. Our deduction of corporate ethical codes is both a potential explanation and a justification in the sense of Social Contract theories. Our hypothesis is that corporate ethics is a matter of transformation in the forms of corporate governance that involves evolutionary stability of norms, conventions and institutions and may be characterised in terms of behaviours mutually in equilibrium among economic agents. At the same time, it can be explained and justified as the result of fair and efficient partial social contracts between all the components of the firm and more generally those groups of agents (the stakeholders) who have an interest at stake in the running of the firm.

2. The title of this book – *The Social Contract of the Firm* –synthetically describes its content. Let us look at the main thesis to be discussed in the book: the logical premise for success and stability of the firm as an institution, capable of regulating and organising economic transactions, is its *Constitutional Social Contract*, even though implicit, among its stakeholders. This social contract *must* exist if the institution is to be justified, and *de facto* it exists if the firm is to be a stable institution, recognised as legitimate by those who work and transact with it and in it - given an economic and organisational context where every agent enjoys some degree of freedom of action and strategic decision-making[4]. A code of ethics is no less than the explicit, written or otherwise, manifestation of this constitutional social contract (an

---

[2] See US Federal Sentencing Guidelines, Ch.8, Sentencing of Organisations, November 1991; cf. EOA News (1996).

[3] Hayek (1986) vol.I speaks generally in these terms about rules of conduct; both Arrow (1986) and Sen (1993) speak specifically about the firms' codes of ethics.

[4] The idea of a margin of freedom and discretionary decision hold by any member of a formal organisation, notwithstanding his position into the hierarchy, was first introduced in the sociological theory of organisation by Michel Crozier (1963, 1986), but now it is a standard assumption in the economic theory of internal organisation, see for example Tirole (1986) and Aghion and Tirole (1997).

overview of the whole theory is given in ch.1). Its content is the set of constitutional principles that would be recognised as rational and hence acceptable in the agreed social contract amongst the stakeholders of the firm. As in any social contract theory, the Social Contract of the Firm is focused on two main problems:

(1) To find out the terms of the hypothetical agreement amongst the firm's stakeholders of the firm in an *ex ante* perspective, i.e. in the perspective of individuals who have to decide whether to enter a firm seen as a cooperative social venture amongst different stakeholders for their mutual advantage. They, from a hypothetical, impartial and impersonal stand point, ask the question of what agreement may be acceptable on the part of all those who cooperate *via* the firm (the answer is given by the normative model of social contract of the firm which is the subject of ch.1 and ch.2).

(2) To understand the endogenous mechanism generating appropriate incentives that induce to comply with the social contract itself, as seen in the *ex post* perspective, i.e. in the perspective in which agents can decide whether or not to comply with the social contract, which has been hypothetically agreed in the *ex ante* perspective. To take seriously the *ex post* perspective means that the decision by an agent to comply with the social contract has to respond to his rational self-interest (the answer to this problem, i.e. the theory of reputation effects, is presented in ch.3).

Solving problem (2), the social contract would prove to be self-enforcing. Thus it can be understood as a set of moral general principles, accepted by social conventions or by a code of ethics seen as a co-ordination equilibrium and not in need to be strictly enforced by the law. In the case of the social contract of the firm, however, this analysis is further complicated by two other aspects: *first,* the existence of *radical uncertainty* or lack of knowledge, ambiguity and vagueness, due essentially to the emergence of unexpected events, which escapes the usual treatment in terms of statistical uncertainty and constitutes the main source of contract incompleteness. *Second*, the latency of *abuse of authority,* which is related to the exercise of power by those who legitimately hold a position of *governance authority* within the firm, which in turn is inherently related to the solutions the theory of the firm suggests to contract incompleteness. As we shall demonstrate, the two problems are closely linked: radical uncertainty facilitates abuse of authority (see ch.1 and ch.4, were this point is raised on the basis of the path-breaking Kreps' contribution to the economic theory of *corporate culture*). All this makes the firm potentially unstable as a control structure, since the expectation of abuse of authority leads one to not respect or not enter into the hierarchical relationships that enable the firm to organise transactions efficiently. Radical uncertainty and the risk of abuse of authority within hierarchy creates more need to take a fair and efficient social contract as a reference point, in order to generate reciprocal expectations among the parties so as to back their cooperation. At the same time, however, they drastically complicate the compliance problem, that is the problem of conformity to norms, contracts and also to the moral constitution itself, which would guarantees justification and legitimacy. The joint solution to these problems is set out by the theory of the code of ethics as rational deliberative procedure which is the main constructive part of this book (see in particular chs.5, 7 and 8). To develop such theory we needed new technical tools for modelling incomplete contract and the deliberative ethical procedure, which we have found in some logic of limited reasoning: fuzzy set theory (see chs.6 and 8) and default logic (see chs.5 and 8).

Acknowledgements

This book is largely the English translation of the one I published in Italian under the title *Economia, etica e organizzazione* in 1997. In that book I acknowledged my debts toward a number of Italian colleagues, amongst whom let me at least remember here again Michele Grillo. After more reflection, I must also recognise some less direct debts to David Gauthier and Ken Binmore. In many senses the theory of the social contract of the firm, which elaborates on many ideas drawn form the theory of games, has grown up through explicit (in many occasions during the past years) and implicit (always inside my mind) confrontation with their own quite different (between them and also respect to the mine) contributions to the larger subject of 'game theory and social contract'.

Translating from Italian to English requires professional skills that I had not at the moment when the project was started. Those skill have been provided by Terry Bland, who helped me in preparing the basic translation on which I worked to improve the English version of the book. However this is not just a translation but in many points it is also a true improvement of the original text, and some of these are not only expositional but also – I suspect – theoretical improvements. I have got the suggestion to introduce them by the discussions following presentations of the basic ideas of the original book in many seminars and workshops. Let me remember only a few of them: the 5th Conference on Economic Ethics and Philosophy held in Mariernrode (Hannover) in 1997, the seminars at the Department of Economics of the University of Trento and at the Department of Economics of the University of Siena in 1998, a workshop at the 11th EBEN Conference on 'The Ethics of Participation' held at the Centrum Voor Economie en Ethiek, Katholieke Universiteit Leuven 1988, and the research group on 'Rationality, Norms and Organisation' at the Centre of Ethics, Law & Economics, LIUC University, Castellanza. The helping suggestions by all their participants is here collectively acknowledged.

Contents

CONTENTS

CONTENTS

Chapter 7

Chapter 8

Chapter 1

An Overview of the Theory: Hierarchies, Social Contract and Reputation

I. Introduction

Coase theorm, a well known result in economic theory, states that, when exclusive property rights are settled and transaction costs (i.e. the costs related to the negotiation and enforcement of contracts and property rights) are equal to zero, then for any configuration of the initial legal rights, market transactions – exchanges of rights, not only of goods – are always able to internalise all the costs, obtaining socially efficient outcomes (Coase, 1960). As often happens, the most interesting implication of this finding is represented by its negative complement. In other words, it suggests considering what happens when transaction costs are not equal to zero. In this case, in fact, property rights have to be optimally designed and - if necessary - enforced by means of an authority or a public choice mechanism, as they cannot be optimally transferred through costly market exchanges. Optimal designing of economic institutions and, in particular, of property rights is therefore a crucial task in the context of real economies, where transaction costs are effective[1].

It is the purpose of this book to suggest that the design of property rights may be not a sufficient condition to overcome the problem of transaction costs. Thus, the main idea of this book is not incompatible with Coase's result, but attempts also to enlighten the basic incompleteness of the *Law & Economics* approach based on it. There are distributive inequalities and efficiency losses (*less* than second best solutions) still asking to be accounted

---

[1] Sometimes it is assumed that the bulk of Coase theorem is the thesis of economic neutrality of the institutional framework with respect to the market's outcomes. This is completely mistaken however. In fact what Coase (1960) was wandering in stating without a mathematical proof his famous proposition, was a way for attracting the economists' attention on the real life economic world, where transaction costs are never absent, so that the comparative assessment of transaction costs involved by alternative institutional arrangement would become the main focus of economic policy-making. See Coase (1988) ch.1.

for, as they are generated by opportunistic behaviours that the property rights design exercise leaves unsolved. Moreover, these opportunistic behaviours can even destabilise the compliance with the same economic institutions of market societies. For these reasons, it seems necessary to integrate the efforts towards the optimal design of contracts and property rights with the study of a broader set of economic institutions.

One obvious line of argument at this point would be to consider legal constraints on the exercise of property rights, but this is not what concerns us in this book. One reason for looking elsewhere is that legal constraints are not self-sustaining and they need to be explained in terms of their acceptance as a part of an even broader constitutional order which has to prove to be stable and to stand up by itself- i.e. to satisfy an equilibrium condition (Buchanan 1975, Ordeshook 1992). This is also a way to say that enforcing legal constraints on property rights may be costly or simply doomed to be ineffective and perhaps contradictory with other parts of the constitutional arrangement. But I do not want to defer here the problem to the macro-constitutional level. Or – to say it differently – I choose to tackle squarely it by avoiding the infinite regress form one institutional level to another and by undertaking the somewhat new route of applying the 'constitutional-stability analysis' directly to the micro-level of the firm where these unaccounted transaction costs are born.

Thus, I focalise here on corporate ethical self-regulation, i.e. on the ever growing phenomenon of corporate codes of ethics, operating as a flexible mechanism to prevent opportunism by means of self-imposed patterns of behaviour. This can be done because, as the constitution expresses in formal language the set of commonly agreed upon general moral principles that links together the members of a society, similar principles surface also within the self-regulatory codes of ethics linking together the 'small society' of the stakeholders of the firm. The implicit idea being also that a constitution, made effective through these corporate self-regulatory norms of behaviours, can escape the breakdown of market institutions without letting these institutions being endangered by massive state regulations. Between the failures of the market's 'invisible hand' and those of the encumbering foot of Government, the importance of the visible - but discreet - hand of morality in the economy should be also acknowledged[2].

---

[2]   By this research program I also anticipate the obvious rebuttal that a partisan of Coase's theorem would make. He would say that in an imperfect world some

1. AN OVERVIEW OF THE THEORY

Codes of ethics can be seen as *rules of conduct* that are a necessary pre-requisite for rational calculations underlying the functioning of firms and the market. However, unlike as Hayek says - which is currently recognised as the major theorisation of rules of conduct sustaining the market order - these rules do not simply exist because of a spontaneous and evolutionary process (in socio-biological sense)[3]. They can also be the focus of *implicit social contracts* among firms and their stakeholders, who agree to delegate part of their sovereignty to those intermediate social institutions (firms), in exchange for expectations of well being. This is the interpretation of self-regulatory codes of ethics that I want to put forward here: they define the *fiduciary duties* the corporate governance has towards all the corporate stakeholders (clients, suppliers, workers, employees, shareholders, creditors and the public in general). It is because who governs the corporation bears these duties and responsibilities that he is entitled to exercise authority based on the property right over the physical assets of the firm.

In order to be complied with, however, these rules of conduct have to be 'incentive compatible' - or, in the jargon of game theory, must correspond to a Nash equilibrium. Although norms of conduct prescribe behaviours that would not be followed before their institution, and notwithstanding that they are not enforced by an exogenous mechanism, they are not 'cheap talk'. We will demonstrate that these norms play a basic role in the emergence of new equilibria, i.e. stable configurations of interdependent behaviours, that would be unimaginable without them. These configurations exhibit the stability properties required in order they can be understood as self-enforcing rules and conventions. At the same time, the typical rules and moral conventions underlying the economic institutions of capitalism cannot be insensitive to considerations of 'fairness' (as far as fairness is understood in the terms of a social contract for mutual advantage). In fact, if corporate ethical codes did

---

transaction costs are inescapable and we are doomed to accept something less than perfect efficiency (i.e. to accept *second best* efficiency), for seeking to get rid of these costs of the institutions of capitalism could result in even higher transaction cost as a whole. Of course I agree with the typically Coasian advise that State regulation would be introduced only when the transaction costs involved are less then those eliminated by means of a given intervention, but I'm looking to the role of economic institutions like self-regulatory codes of ethics that do not ask for heavy State regulation and enforcement.

[3] See Hayek (1982) vol.I. At present the evolution of social norms is the focus of a large literature on evolutionary games, see Sugden (1986), Weibull (1995), Samuelson (1997).

not embody some fundamental criteria of justice, the resulting level of trust towards the economic institutions of capitalism would inevitably be low, thereby endangering and representing a threat to their stability and efficiency. One could therefore affirm - *pace* the liberal-conservative Hayek - that 'social justice' is not a utopian dream for market economies. Distributive justice - at least in the sense of contractarianism - must be already embodied within the ethical code leading corporate conduct if economic institutions, such as property rights and corporate governance mechanisms have to work.

This chapter offers an overview of the theory I will develop throughout the entire book. At the beginning the basic concepts of the new institutional economic theory of the firm are given and the basic unsolved *abuse of authority problem* is made out of this literature. Hence a view point on corporate ethical codes is given, according to which they are designed to answer that problem. The basic functions played by the code of ethics are explained by means of two game theoretic models: social contract (in the terms of cooperative bargaining games) and non-cooperative games of reputation. The main point of the chapter is to introduce the idea that codes of ethics – seen as a 'micro-constitutional chart' based on the social contract amongst stakehoders of the firm – and moral norms in general, make possible to resort to the reputation effects mechanism in economic situations characterised by incomplete information and unforeseen events. I deal with this problem by developing an approach to rationality in the face of unforeseen events based on fuzzy sets and in particular on the concept of 'fuzzy reputation'. In this chapter, however, the reader can find only a sketch of the theory. I will come to the details in the following chapters.

II. The Firm as Hierarchy

The role of corporate ethical codes can be comprehensively understood by referring to the theory of the firm[4]. According to the new institutional approach, efficiency of the firm as a social institution is based on the virtues of the unified governance system for a wide range of exchanges and transac-

---

[4]   Some classic references to the literature of economic theory of the firm are Coase (1937), Simon (1951), Arrow (1974), Williamson (1975, 1988), Grossman and Hart (1986). Systematic presentations of this ever growing literature are Hölmstrom and Tirole (1987), Tirole (1988), Kreps (1990a), Eggertssom (1990), Buchley and Michie (1995).

tions, i.e. on the virtue of authority relationships that, in their turn, are based on the firm's ownership and control structure. I want to argue that this is only half an answer: the other half is that the firm is an efficient social institution because the authority relationship is legitimised by the agreement of all those who are subjected to that authority. Legitimisation, in turn, is not any longer generated by the ownership structure (which needs to be legitimised itself), but rather by corporate cultures and corporate ethical codes. In other words, an optimal control structure is not the sole key element to evaluate the efficiency of the firm's governance: we have to look as well at the corporate culture and ethical code, as they play the crucial role in promoting trust in those agents who are in a position of authority.

My argument will be presented by going through a sequence of analytical steps. To begin with, consider a hypothetical exchange situation, in which different 'patrons' (Hansmann 1988) rely on simple contracts to carry out separate transactions of goods or services, before any elaborate governance structure of transactions has been worked out.

Then add the typical assumptions of transaction-costs economics (Williamson 1986, Kreps(a) 1990, ch.20):

i)   *Specific Assets*. Different patrons make specific investments, that is

- *Labour*: the productivity of labour depends on the acquisition of specific technical skills for the given productive process, learning organisational codes and particular organisational routines, maintaining good working relations, environment and climates; much of these are highly specific assets.

- *Consumer's trust*: if the quality of goods is not observable, the consumer invests to acquire information not about the physical commodity, but about the producer. After having acquired enough information about her, if positive, he will trust her. Trust is a specific asset that loses its value outside the specific relation with the given producer.

- *Investors' trust*: supply of credit or financial investments are complex activity; being not able (or, simply, not willing) to exercise direct control, investors need to get information about the reliability of the producer to be financed. The value of such investment is, again, specific, as it can be only rewarded by the success of the producer about whom the relevant information has been gathered, but it is, however, useless with respect to trust in other producers.

Other typical assumptions are (Williamson 1986, Kreps(a) 1990):

ii) *Opportunism of the agents*, that is the usual utility maximising hypothesis plus the disposition to cheat any unenforced agreement.

iii) *Contract incompleteness* (or *bounded rationality* of the agents), which means that contracts cannot include conditional provisos for any possible event, as unforeseen or inconceivable events may occur.

To comment on the last assumption we may say that the problem lies in the fact that we cannot completely describe all the possible states of the world, i.e. we cannot give an internally coherent, mutually exclusive and jointly exhaustive description for every state of the world. Moreover, we cannot *ex ante* establish the set of possible consequences for each action belonging the set of each agent's choices. In decision theory terms, each event is a set of states of the world. Each action is a mapping from the state-set to the set of consequences - each of these being generated for a given state by an alternative action (Savage 1972). If some events have not been foreseen, because the states of the world belonging to them are non-conceivable or badly specified, then we are simply unable to figure out the consequences of our actions. This is to say that the real meaning of those actions escapes us. Then we cannot even say we have a specified set of action when we are lacking the representation of some states of the world. Note, incidentally, that this is the most radical characterisation of contract incompleteness. Some economic models – typically the *Grossman-Hart-Moore model,* which I assume as the main reference in the rest of this section - often tends to 'tame' contract incompleteness with notions that make it more manageable according to the standard maximisation techniques: for example, statistic uncertainty, linguistic complexity in writing complete contracts, and non-verifiability by a third part (Grillo, 1994).

From these assumption it follows that there is a risk that investments made in bilateral contracts are expropriated. In fact, agents have some *discretion*, due to the occurrence of unforeseen events. Once specific investments have created a dependency relationship (the *'lock-in'* effect) and unforeseen events have occurred, the agents may try to re-negotiate the contract in order to change the distribution of the transaction's surplus. The part holding the stronger position in re-negotiation will gain a rent to the detriment of the counterpart. The agent whose specific investments are put at risk, *ex post* will be forced to acquiesce in a certain amount of opportunism in order to avoid the risk of losing the entire value of the same investments. By forecasting the change - after investments - of the nature of interaction, and to minimise the costs of *ex post* re-negotiation, the latter will *ex ante* reduce his investments to a sub-optimal level.

1. AN OVERVIEW OF THE THEORY

Transaction costs economics defines the firm as a governance structure meant to solve this problem. This endeavour is accomplished by setting up authority relationships designed so that the party endowed with authority will have control upon the *ex ante* non-contractible decision variables. By 'authority' I mean the fact that one party receives from the others the right to control the actions' set physically belonging to those other parties. Hence, the agent in the authority position will command the action to be picked out from a given set of alternatives that other parties will perform at the proper time in the future. Consider, for example, the employees. By signing the labour contract they delegate to the firm's management or to the employer authority of establishing which actions they will perform, within the limits of their organisational role and working time specified in the contract (Simon 1951). However it is not required that a formal delegation of authority has taken place for the phenomenon of substantive authority to hold. Even though it is usually overlooked, the relevant aspects of an authority relationship also holds between firm on one hand and consumers, creditors and stockholders on the other hand, where they undergo specific investments but do not exercise control:

- *Authority towards consumers*: in the case of complex services, whose quality is not observable, the consumer accepts that his generic willingness to consume will be led by the services' supplier toward some particular object of consumption.

- *Authority towards investors and creditors*: financial resources invested or lent are possibilities of acting delegated to the controlling group (which appoints the management), who is entitled to establish how to use them, within the limits of its discretion.

According to the economic model of a firm's control structure, these authority relationships are established by allocating to a specific part - among all the parts participating in the exchange – the property right upon the physical assets of the firm. (This is a characteristic assumption in Grossman and Hart 1986, Hart and Moore 1988, see also Hansmann 1988). Consequently:

a) The agent who *ex post* will be in the state of best information for deciding, is given formal discretion about *ex ante* non-contractible variables, i.e. authority is assigned to the part that, after unforeseen events have occurred, will hold the relevant knowledge for choosing optimal allocation of inputs provided by the various stakeholders' specific investments.

b) Investments made by the party entitled with authority are safeguarded, as he can obtain the most advantageous solution in the case of re-negotiation threatening to exclude the counterparts.

c) If the choice of the party to be entitled with authority is optimal, a big amount of transaction costs are saved; in fact discretion is assigned to the agent who would have incurred the maximum loss due investments expropriation and at the same time would incur the lower costs for monitoring, controlling and - if necessary - sanctioning the opportunistic behaviours of the others.

This solution does not allow achieving a Pareto-efficient allocation of investments. A position of authority itself can be exploited by those who holds it in order to obtain a rent through renegotiation. Assume that specific investments related to an economic transaction are made by several parties - such as investors, workers, managers, consumers etc. Then those parties who are *not* safeguarded by the settlement of property rights against the risk of opportunistic behaviour - and, consequently, remaining subject to expropriation of benefits (that they consider unfair) - will not have *ex ante* adequate incentives to contribute to the joint production of the surplus. This will induce them to under-invest. Nevertheless, if authority is given to the party which is *more important* for producing the surplus, the constitution of the firm will, in any case, allow a positive shift towards Pareto-efficiency. Residuals will be large enough to allow the owner offering to the counterparts a margin not inferior to that which they would obtain under alternative contractual arrangements, in exchange for their acceptation of the control structure over the firm. The outcome will be what Transaction Costs Economics calls a *second-best* governance structure for the transactions at issue.

To be sure, there are several reasons to doubt whether this foundation of the concept of authority is really sound:

(i) There is a conceptual asymmetry between the content of claim implicit in the property right on the firm's physical assets and the content of claim implicit in the notion of authority. Property right implies a negative claim on forbearance from interfering in the use of the firm's assets held by the owner, i.e. the owner has the power to exclude others from every use of firm's physical assets he does not consent to. Authority, by contrast, implies a positive claim on compliance with commands put forward by the agent in the position of authority (typically, the management), i.e. the claim that those who are subject to authority should accept these commands as the premises of their own deliberation. Authority, therefore, includes a claim on positive ac-

1. AN OVERVIEW OF THE THEORY

tion, not only a claim on forbearance and exclusion. So we talk about *managerial* authority (Raz 1985, McMahon 1989) even if the management is not the firm; *political* authority even if the politician is not the owner of the public assets; *professional* authority even if the professional is not the owner of the resources the client employs to comply with the professionally recommended conduct.

(ii) A threat of exclusion is not a satisfactory explanation for the establishment of an authority. To be sure, any explanation of organisational authority uniquely focused on the power of inflicting sanctions, would result too superficial (Arrow 1974). Each time the possibility of enforcing sanctions is limited to a relatively small number of infractions. It would be impossible to sanction all the members of an organisation if everybody chose to disobey. At least compliance from those who are designed to enforce sanctions cannot be based on the sanctions themselves.

(iii) Any explanation of authority based on property rights is unsatisfactory, because it ultimately rests on compliance with the authority of law, i.e. on the decision to obey the law. But this, in turn, would require an explanation of the reason why members of the organisation decide to comply with the law, instead of resorting to forms of explicit disobedience or tacit defection.

These remarks concur to rise the main point I what to make here about the economic model of the firm grounded on the analysis of costs and benefits of ownership. One agent being in the role of an authority, in effect, does not prevent this same agent from resorting to the re-negotiation of the initial pre-investments contract. The assumption that whenever unforeseen events occur it is possible to share a surplus through re-negotiation remains unchanged. What makes the difference is the fact that authority based on property right settles the *status quo* for re-negotiating - through bargaining - the terms of exchange, in front of unforeseen events that was not provided for by the contract. That is what in fact allows discretionary decisions essentially by the owner. Given the power to settle the *status quo*, the owner will bargain according to his best interests. As a matter of fact, the owner has the authority to impose base-line conditions that may be quite unpleasant for the counterparts. Thus, re-negotiation will favour him. This means that the owner will be able to safeguard his earning expectations, making it possible not only to allocate an optimal level of investment, but also to exceed this level and gain a rent through the opportunistic exercise of authority. Grossman and Hart (1986) conclude that there will be a tendency to over-invest by the party enti-

9

tled with the authority - the owner - and a tendency to under-invest by the parties whose relationships with the firm are regulated by incomplete contracts. These two simultaneous incentives identify what I call *abuse of authority*.

III. Abuse of Authority

I define what has been identified at the end of the foregoing section the *abuse of authority problem*. It has not been tackled by the economic literature because of the appearance that it would only imply distributive effects, without affecting the *second-best* efficiency property of the economic solutions. Soon we will see that this is not the case. However, we may find two lines of argument that in the economic literature could be expected to answer this problem. The first employs the model of cooperative bargaining games. The second resorts to the model of repeated non-cooperative games.

1. Cooperative Bargaining Games

In Grossman and Hart's theory of ownership of the firm (Grossman and Hart 1986) an answer to the abuse of authority problem could be construed as follows. Effects of the opportunistic exercise of authority in the re-negotiation of contracts are anticipated and neutralised, before unforeseen events may occur, through a utility side transfer. *Ex post* a bargaining game will take place whose pay-off will measure the cost of re-negotiation to the players. But they can anticipate these costs by an *ex ante* contract upon the allocation of property rights. This will prescribe the utility side-payment to the players forgoing control. Due to this utility transfer, one party agrees to delegate ownership to the other i.e. the control upon all the *ex ante* non-contractible decision variables. In such a way the problem of fairness would be reabsorbed by a preventive *ex ante* compensation. What can be obtained is a second best efficiency solution, because incentives under any control structure cannot accomplish the first best allocation of idiosyncratic investments. However this answer underestimates the difficulties arising from contract incompleteness. *Ex ante* the parties will fail to negotiate the value of the side transfer that *ex post* they would recognise as the proper compensation for any opportunistic exercises of authority that will eventually occur. In fact, as it is impossible to establish *ex ante* all the decisions that will prove to be available and relevant when unforeseen events have occurred, neither the limits to discretion nor their price can be explicitly defined. It being impossible to specify exactly the sphere of exercise of authority, it is also impossible to exclude opportunistic behaviour when the time for re-negotiation comes. That is what, in effect, Grossman and Hart model explicitly predicts, as it proves that each governance structure implies some incentive distortions. What is at fault with this theory, however, is that the amount of these distortions cannot be predicted. The amount of costs that abuse of authority would impose upon the damaged parties will result to be contingent on *ex ante* non even conceivable events.

To give an example, the labour contract could define the set of orders X that A, the owner of a firm's physical assets, can legitimately give the employee B. However, some of the orders $x_i \in X$ may, under some circumstances, represent a heavy cost or damage for B, who has not already been compensated for that. In fact this cost or damage only occurs under a particular state of the world s_i that was not included within the description of all the possible states of the world when B signed the labour contract. Therefore, the abuse of authority in the re-negotiation setting is possible. Why, then, should I not suppose that the property right itself could be denied and re-negotiated when unforeseen events transpire? Why, moreover, should I not consider that the parts that can be subject to abuse of authority could even choose to not enter the authority relationship?

2. Repeated Non-Cooperative Games

An attempt to answer the abuse of authority problem within the theory of repeated non-cooperative games rests upon the concept of *reputation effects*[5]. The reference situation is a game in which one long-run player B - for example the management of the firm - meets an infinite sequence of short-run players $A_1,...,A_n$ ($n \to \infty$) - for example consumers - each staying in the game only one play (Fudenberg and Levine 1989). (See figure 1.1 for the stage game).

---

[5]   The standard explanation of this theory can be found in Fudenberg and Tirole (1991), part IV.

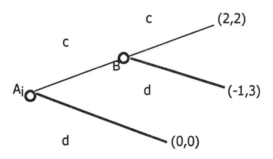

Figure 1.1. *The strategy combination (d,d) is the sole Nash equilibrium and it is in dominant strategies.*

In each stage game, first a consumer chooses whether to buy or not; afterwards, the management chooses whether to supply high or low quality services. Each time decisions are taken in sequence, but only communicated after both of them have been taken. In the one-shot game the dominant strategy for the management is always to supply low quality services. This induces the consumer's best reply, i.e. not to buy, leading to the sub-optimal equilibrium solution (d,d) of the stage game. Nevertheless, the infinite repetition of the stage game allows us - except for an initial finite sequence of periods - to obtain an infinite sequence of co-operative exchanges (solution (c,c) in figure 1.1). This requires the assumption that each short-run consumer A_i is not sure about the 'type' of player B, i.e. he puts a positive probability p on the possibility that A is not the standard fully rational, strategic utility maximiser, but a non-strategic follower of a code of honesty, that is a code asking its holder to always supply high quality services. The probability p measures the reputation of B as 'honest' player in the eyes of the A_i players. Assume that the initial p is positive but very small. The idea is that each A_i chooses on the basis of his expected utility, given the current probability that B is an honest player. This probability inductively increases every time a short-run player A_i observes that player B at the immediate foregoing repetition supplied high quality services. At any time player B were seen to be choosing d, her reputation would become zero, because this move would be incompatible with she being the 'honest' type. On the contrary, if B were seen to be supplying high quality services from the beginning on, then, however small the initial p might be, after a certain number N of repetitions, in which the various A_i have not bought, the expected utility of buying would increase enough - together with the p - that the following A_i would find more advantageous to buy. Assuming for simplicity only two possible types of player B, this means that $2p + (-1) \, 1-p > 0$.

Therefore, if player B is patient enough (i.e. she does not excessively discount future utilities), even if she is a strategic rational 'type', then she has an equilibrium strategy consisting of 'sustaining her reputation' of being an honest player, always offering high quality services. Assume she has been employing this strategy for a number of times, beginning from the first play of the game, then the consumers will eventually begin to buy and later on the payoffs (2,2) will become accessible each time. To sum up, there exists an entire set of equilibria of the game supporting some co-operation among a number of players A_i and player B. The upper boundary of this set consists of an equilibrium point such that both players co-operate all the time but the N first times, where players A_i still not co-operate but player B nevertheless invests in her reputation (Fudenberg and Levine, 1989).

It is quite problematic, however, to apply this result to hierarchical transactions taking place within the firm, that is when the player B is in the role of an authority. *Ex ante* the optimal decision cannot be identified because of unforeseen events. Otherwise *ex post* - after some unforeseen event has occurred - player B has real discretion. Nothing prevents her from undertaking some action, given that the decision taken is drawn from the set of actions that are under her control after the delegation of authority. To be sure, whether one of these decisions constitutes to an abuse cannot *ex post* be identified unambiguously on the basis of the content of the contract. This only determines a set of action the authority can order to be performed, no provisos or constraints being settled conditionally upon the occurrence of unforeseen events. Nevertheless the party suffering hardness may guess he has been abused. Lots of fuzziness and dissent can be expected after a single player in the position of a A_i reports having be abused by the counterpart B.

Let's consider the following game situation: an infinite number of workers (short-run players) $A_1,...,A_n$ have to decide, through an infinite sequence of identical iteration of the same stage game, whether to enter a dependency relationship with the long-run management A. The management, dealing with unforeseen events, will take a discretionary decision concerning the tasks it wants the workers to perform. Some of these decisions constitute - *under some circumstances* - an abuse of authority, as they take away the workers a part of the fair share of the surplus generated - among other things - by their

13

own investments in human capital (Grossman and Hart, 1986; Hart and Moore, 1988). I assume that the strategy 'to abuse' is dominant for the management in the stage game (see Fig. 1.1). However, it is not possible to recognise as abusive these decisions on the basis of the labour contract. Due to the labour contract incompleteness, player B is free to take *ex ante* non-contractible decisions at her discretion.

In other words, in the game described in figure 1.1 the action *d* has a unique description (to '*defect*') and a well specified meaning (i.e. to offer low quality services). In the context of hierarchical transactions however the action *d* may represent an act that in normal circumstances belongs to the set of admissible behaviours but, under unforeseen circumstances, constitutes an abuse. In standard terms of economics, the player A's action not only will be *ex post* not verifiable by a third party, it will also be not 'observable' by the players themselves. This is so not because they cannot observe *ex post* the acts performed *per se*. But because *ex post*, in the face of unforeseen events, these acts do not have clear meaning, that is players are not able to specify without ambiguity which consequences are associated with those acts. This amounts saying that under unforeseen events actions become *vague*. Therefore, being impossible to unambiguously identify the abusive actions, the basis itself for assessing player's A reputation is lacking. But this would imply that A has no way to establish a positive reputation that could induce the various $B_1,...,B_n$ to enter into the authority relationship. Consequently, relationships of trust, that should back the constitution of the firm, will breakdown, endangering both the emergence and the stability of the firm as an institution.

IV. Codes of Ethics

Corporate ethical codes are the main tool for implementing ethics within firms and organisations. In the United States there has been a rapid diffusion of written documents clearly recognisable (in spite of their differences in form and structure) as ethical codes of conduct, promulgated and periodically revised by the firm's top management and aimed to incorporate ethical values and concerns about the way firms do business. According an empirical survey by Cressy and Moore in 1980 only 8% of American largest companies (the *Fortune 1000* list of industrial and service corporations) had an ethical code. Afterward many studies illustrate that rapid expansion of the phenomenon in the US. For example, the *Center for Business Ethics* of the Bentley

1. AN OVERVIEW OF THE THEORY

College reports that according to surveys performed in 1985/86 and 1990/92 on the *Fortune*'s first 1000 US firms, those endowed with a code of ethics were respectively 77% and 93%. Usually, a well structured code of ethics clearly reflects the idea of corporate responsibility towards all the firm's stakeholders, and is divided into different chapters defining the corporate duties towards customers, employees, suppliers, government agencies, competitors, local communities, political representatives etc. The same *Center for Business Ethics* stressed that the managers of the companies where a code was adopted recognised that the aims of the code were to increase social responsibility of the firm toward its stakeholders, to state impersonal and impartial guidelines for employees conduct and to improve the level of compliance with the law, but at the same time they linked any development of the company reputation to the implementation of an internal 'policy for ethics'. Consequently the code was seen as the basis for and ethical infastructure and concrete organisational measures such as ethical training, ethical auditing, ethics committee or ethics officer etc [6].

Although it is less extensive, nevertheless the phenomenon is clearly recognisable also in Europe. A research performed by Langlois and Schlegelmilch in 1988 – the CEOs of the 600 largest industrial companies in RFT, GB and France was asked to answer a questionnaire and the level of acceptance was around 30% - concludes that at that time code of ethics was present in 51% and 41% of the RFT and GB companies respectively. The very fast development of the filed of business ethics in Europe in the last decade allows us to say that these levels has certainly grown in the meantime. Moreover it seems clear that the different levels and timing of the spreading process of code of ethics throughout US and European companies can be correlated to the different levels of legally and bureaucratically enforced social protections of the workers and the other stakeholders and to the trends of liberalisation and privatisation of various national economies, which is obviously related to the empowerment of business in society and to the discretionary power exercised by corporate governments of the firms.

---

[6] Some examples are the following companies' codes of ethics: *Guide to IBM Business Conduct, Ethics in Business of TI, Helwett Packard Statements of Corporate Objectives, Code of Conduct of Colgate-Palmolive, Integrity: GE Code of Conduct.* Examples that strictly fit the explanation given in this book are the Italian League of Co-operatives and Mutuals *Codice Quadro per le imprese cooperative* (Model code for co-operatives firms), the *Codice etico* ('Code of ethics') of GlaxoWellcome Italy, and the *Codice etico* of ENI.

1.4 CODES OF ETHICS

This apparent success of the self-codification option suggests an interpretation in terms of 'evolutionary stability': corporate ethical codes are an advantageous 'mutation' in the corporate governance systems that tends to spread over the population of companies. My suggestion is that this is so because of the abuse of authority problem. In fact, what is the function of a corporate ethical code? My answer is that it allows us to solve the above-described risks of breakdown of trust relationships that makes authority within the firm unstable. To ensure stability of the firm's authority relationships a common pre-understanding of the limits to legitimate exercise of authority is needed. This implies that (i) such limits have to be designed so to earn enough consensus and acceptance to start transactions and that (ii) they make a focus of mutual expectations possible, revolving around the belief that those limits will not be exceeded by any party in the organisation. It has been suggested that the underlying corporate culture, rather then the firm's legal structure, is the key element favouring this common pre-understanding of mutual commitments, establishing the rational expectation by each party that others will comply with those same commitments (Kreps, 1990; Tirole, 1987; Simon, 1991). I want to argue that the corporate ethical code, even more than the generic corporate culture, is what gives shape to such a pre-understanding.

Analytically, the purposes of corporate ethical codes are:

a) To clarify, by means of very general but not void moral principles, the criteria that would be used to identify the abusive exercise of authority. These principles give a common understanding of the constraints limiting each stakeholder's prerogatives and legitimate claims with respect to many ill defined situations, as these constrains cannot be *ex ante* specified by particular statutes, contracts and regulations. I call this the *cognitive role* of the ethical code.

b) To guarantee that rights and duties stated in the code may be accepted and could rationally be agreed upon by all the organisation participants, including both those who exercise and those who are submitted to corporate authority. How the code can achieve this purpose can be explained by resorting to the model of the Social Contract as a hypothetical agreement on the fair constitution' of the firm. I call this the *justificatory role* of the code.

c) To provide incentives for compliance with the code itself, which thus becomes a self-enforcing system of norms. A code is self-enforcing if under it the relevant organisation participants and stakeholders cal-

16

culate that their best response to the expected behaviours of the counterparts is compliance with the commitments embodied in the code itself. The achievement of this purpose can be explained only if we add to the model of reputation effects a specific account of how a moral code may constitute a parameter for reputation within incomplete information contexts. I call this the *incentive role* of the code.

I shall explain how an ethical code can favour the achievement of the goals (b) and (c) in the following two sections of this chapter. A complete explanation of how ethics works according to the goals (a) is deferred to later chapters (ch. 5-8). However, before going through these subjects, a remark is in order to anticipate the kind of cognitive function (point a) that is provided by the social contract model of an ethical code (point b), it being instrumental also to the incentive nature of the code (point c). The social contract model works as a *default reasoning system*. It provides agents with a hypothetical agreement model from which they can infer a set of normative statements for every state of the world, also the *ex ante* unforeseen one. These statemets have already proved to be sound within the domain of states of the world the agents are able to describe and account for. However, reasoning by default logic the agents assume it is legitimate to extending the validity of this normative system also to states of the world that they cannot accurately describe. They draw some additional statements from the system and assume that these statements are valid by default, i.e. until a contrary proof has been given (Reiter 1980). Validity of these inferences is not warranted against mistakes. In fact, validity of the extensions of the model to situations not accounted for before, is no proved by an effective procedure answering yes or not the question whether these sentences hold in all the logically conceivable worlds.

Thus, these extensions are fallible. However they are not at all irrational. Can we really be sure of reasonably believing only sentences that we have effectively ascertained to be true by means of a recursive procedure of decision? On the contrary, these extensions express that we are doing our best in outlining our beliefs in the light of consistency with what we positively know about the situations we are able to figure out. They transform the absence of any negative answer into the provisory statement that a given sentence does positively hold.

The cost for these extensions of our beliefs system is the 'non-monoticity' of the system itself: it may change without retaining the entire old beliefs set under the after-change system. Of course the logic of default reasoning im-

17

plies that we have to be ready to correct our systems of normative beliefs as an unforeseen contingency transpires in which a given normative sentence clearly does not hold. A good normative system (a good 'Constitution') can be defined as a set of norms requiring, as time goes by, minimal contractions in terms of renunciation of a body of sentences and postulates in order to keep coherence and soundness of the remaining part. The better the normative system, the larger the set of default extensions which do not have to be 'contracted' in the light of more information (Gärdenfors 1988). The social contract model employs default reasoning to provide instructions for behaving in the presence of incomplete contracts. So it can also be defined as a *filling gap* rule, i.e. an abstract model of hypothetical rational agreement from which instructions can be drawn for filling the holes of contracts (Coleman 1992).

V. The Constitutional Contract of the Firm

The first function of ethical codes can be explained by referring to the typical social contract model in political philosophy: the firm is understood as an institution endowed with a formal organisation. Under it transactions are governed *via* authority relationships. This institution, in turn, is based on a social contract among all the agents participating in the transactions. Through the social contract they establish the 'constitution' of the firm. The social contract provides, therefore, a hypothetical model of ideal agreement that can constitute the criterion for assessing real economic institutions. The definition of 'abuse of authority' therefore does not rely on a real contract, but on an implicit contractarian ideal of fairness. This ideal is based on the hypothetical model of impartial agreement, negotiated by the parties in absence of power and fraud and without the dependency effects generated by specific investments. Thus, social contract defines the ideal benchmark for identifying the non-abusive exercise of authority. It provides for participation of each member of the organisation in a joint co-operative strategy in exchange for an efficient, fair share of the surplus. The code can then be seen as the 'constitutional chart' that makes the implicit social contract explicit. This way a general notion of fairness is set up, affirming the criterion of sharing costs and benefits in the case of re-negotiation due to unforeseen events.

1. AN OVERVIEW OF THE THEORY

There is, in fact, a strict analogy between the firm, understood as an institution, and the idea of the State underlying the theory of social contract[7]. According to contractarianism, the starting point to explain and justify any institution (the State as well as the firm) is an hypothetical situation of choice ('state of nature') where rational, self-interested agents have to face the risk of undergoing reciprocal opportunism if they enter the mutual advantageous co-operative relationships. Were a constitutional order not established, in the above described situation no particular agreement or commitment would be complied with, because each agent would find it individually rational to cheat. If he thinks the other will cooperate, he will try to take advantage of the others' co-operation, without doing his part in the agreement. On the other hand, the fear of suffering the other's opportunism will also drive each agent to find it rational to protect himself and choose a non-co-operative strategy as well. Game theory formalises this situation as the well-known Prisoner's Dilemma, a game where distrust, cheating and mutual non co-operation represent the sole equilibrium - while robustness of this solution is underlined by the fact that it is an equilibrium in dominant strategies. (See Figure 1.2).

Market relationships, characterised by contracts under incompleteness and information asymmetry, are instances of a 'quasi-state-of-nature' situation, where no appropriate constitutional order has yet been agreed upon and, consequently, a non co-operative equilibrium tends to prevail. Protagonists of the 'state of nature' are, in this case, the patrons of the firm who really hold specific investments (workers, stockholders, consumers, and suppliers). We equate here the term 'patrons' - used in the 'Law & Economics' literature (Hansmann 1988, 1996) - with the term 'stakeholders' - used in managerial sciences, the idea being that they hold stakes on the firm's outcome *because* of the specific investments they do. At the same time, due to contract incompleteness, they undergo the risk of expropriation.

---

[7]   We refer in general to the family of contractarian political theories that originates form Hobbes, Locke and Rousseau. Amongst contemporary theorists the renaissance of contractarianism is due mainly to Rawls (1971). However in order to enlighten the parallelism between the State and the firm it is more useful to refer to the hobbesian tradition as it has been renewed by Gauthier (1968, 1986), Buchanan (1975), Hampton (1986) and more recently, by approaching the contractarian view in the perspective of game theory, Binmore (1994, 1998).

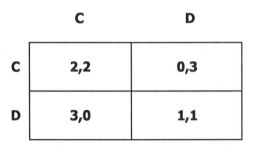

Figure 1.2 *The strategy combination (D, D) is the sole Nash equilibrium, but sub-optimal.*

According to contractarianism, escaping the mutually destructive outcome of the 'state of nature' requires the agents to set up, by unanimous agreement, a central authority entitled to disincentive opportunistic behaviours and protect each agent's ownership. A similar interpretation can be given the decision of calling an agent, external to the group of workers, to carry out the role of 'guard' of Pareto efficiency (Alchian and Desmetz 1972, Hölmstrom 1982). Similarly, we can give a 'social contract' interpretation of the delegation of authority upon *ex ante* non contractible decisions to the party able to minimise transaction costs (Williamson 1975, Grossman and Hart 1986). However, unlike the typical transaction-costs model, contractarianism does not explain the emergence of authority simply by comparing the aggregate costs and benefits of each institutional governance structure. *Aggregate* efficiency – or transaction costs minimisation – does not matter *per se,* but as one of the components of the fair/efficient agreement. Authority arises only if all the holders of specific investments rationally accept a governance structure by a constitutive agreement, in the perspective of a mutual advantage. Legitimacy follows from the unanimous acceptance of the establishment of an authority by 'social contract'. This does not exclude the fact that authority might be allocated to the owner of the physical assets of production. But in the contractarian view authority does not rest simply on the prerogative implicit in the property right. As already said, a property right on goods and assets is a *negative claim* that simply forbids transfer without consent of the owner. On the contrary, the holder of hierarchical authority in the firm lays a *positive claim* on employees' compliance with his directives concerning the use of firm's assets.

1. AN OVERVIEW OF THE THEORY

Why should the holders of specific investments sign the social contract? Given the utility level of the *status quo* - what each part gets if the attempt to reach an agreement fails - the additional product of the joint activity can be defined as *cooperative surplus*. Participants will rationally bargain about how to split the co-operative surplus, taking the agreed outcome of bargaining as the necessary pre-condition for their participation in the joint activity. This approach naturally leads to the theory of Bargaining Games. This theory proves that social contract will be signed on a joint action plan allowing the production of a *socially efficient* co-operative surplus. The optimal additional amount (with respect to the status quo) will be shared in such a way that each agent will have the highest possible share given the share obtained by the counterpart. Several bargaining solutions can be calculated as outcomes of different bargaining processes. Under any of these each part makes rational claims and concessions in response to the rational claims and concessions carried out by the counterpart - i.e. each bargaining model ends up with the reaching of a bargaining equilibrium. However, most celebrated bargaining solutions - namely Nash (1950), Kalai-Smorodinsky (1975), Harsanyi (1977) and Gauthier (1986) - have in common that, if the payoff space of the game is a symmetric bargaining set - i.e. the set of possible bargaining outcomes is invariant under the permutation of the players' names - they share the surplus in equal parts.[8]

---

[8] Some theorist have suggested to approach the theory of the firm and formal organisations in terms of the Social Contract model. In the Business Ethics literature, after a first formulation (Donaldson 1985), this approach gained considerable attention (Dunfee and Donaldson 1995). Dunfee and Donaldson theory however cannot be considered genuinely contractarian, as it is evident its comunitarian element, which is incompatible with the contractarian point of view that construes norms as the artificial output of an agreement amongst a multiplicity of individuals. On this see *Business Ethics Quarterly*, special issue, n.5.2, 1995. Amongst organisation theorists Keeley has suggested to adopt the Social Contract model and the theory of rights drawn from contractarian political theory as opposed to the prevailing organicist and functionalist theory based on the biological analogy, in order to deduce the goal of the organisation from the goals of the individual members the constitute the organisation itself (Keeley 1988). James Coleman (1990) employs the concept of a 'constitution' to address the system of norms by means of which rights and authority are transferred within formal organisations seen as those 'corporate actors' (firms, public companies, bureaucracies etc.) which populate modern complex societies, so that these societies have a very different structure than simpler societies populated by 'natural actors'. In his *Foundation of social theory* Coleman (1990) resorts to the

1.5 THE CONSTITUTIONAL CONTRACT OF THE FIRM

Identifying the *status quo* suitable to the extent of a social contract theory is quite a controversial matter[9]. I follow here Gauthier in assuming that suitability of the bargaining model for ethical theory requires the identification of the *status-quo* with the baseline of a hypothetical bargaining situation between rational agents who negotiate *before* any social interaction could have advantaged or disadvantaged one party over the other. A fair *status quo* must therefore forbid outcomes depending upon force and fraud, free riding and parasitism that could take place only in unfair transactions (Gauthier 1986). It can be identified only by imagining a joint productive venture that begins at a starting point from which all these distortions have been erased. Turning back to the firm context, this hypothesis means that the situation resulting in specific investments and characterised by contract incompleteness cannot be taken as the appropriate baseline for measuring the co-operative surplus. Nor can the re-negotiation situations, where one or both parties in the contract are locked-in, due to the cost of their specific investments, be a fair *status quo*.

Rawlsian model and to Social Contract theory to account how corporate actors are constituted as rational solution to problems of strategic interaction amongst individuals, according to a scheme traceable back to the Pricipal (the constituencies) – Agent (the corporate actor) relationship. More recently Viktor Vanberg (1992) has outlined a theory of the firm as a constitutional order, according to the view of constitutional contractarianism within the Public Choice approach. A common limitation to many of these theories is that they fail in giving an adequate formulation of the social contract theory as it is allowed by the modern theory of bargaining games (Harsanyi 1977) - as on the contrary has been suggested by a few scholars (Gauthier 1986, Binmore 1988, 1994). If the code of ethics expresses the norms, legal and moral, that constitute the implicit or explicit 'Constitution' of the firm, and if moreover we want to give a contractarian account of it, both in explanatory and normative senses, then it is to the theory of bargaining games that we have to resort. For an exposition of the bargaining games theory see Sacconi (1986), for its first use for the social contract of the firm see Sacconi (1991) and in general for the cooperative game theory of the firm see Aoki (1984).

[9]   Quite well known are the contrary views set out by Sen (1970) and Rawls (1971) against the use of bargaining games as a tool for the theory of social justice, turning around the point that the bargaining solution would be dependent on a morally arbitrary *status quo*. A favourable view has been put forward by David Gauthier (1986) who suggests a moralised *status quo* that departs quite sharply from Buchanan's position (Buchanan 1975) according to which the bargaining *status quo* identifies with 'natural equilibrium'. For a different idea of moralised *status quo* see Sacconi (1986, 1991).

1. AN OVERVIEW OF THE THEORY

The appropriate baseline is the situation coming *before* the cost of any specific investment having been paid.

We can find a rationale for this assumption: the parties anticipate that they will undergo the burden of specific investments if they enter the joint co-operative venture. Consequently they want to be assured that their payoffs will be at least neutralised with respect to these costs. Each of them legitimately claims as *status-quo* payoff at least the amount of utility he had before entering the effort of the joint co-operative production. Therefore the co-operative surplus must be calculated at the *net of all* the costs of specific investments.

I shall now consider how the social contract model applies to the decision of establishing the firm. The world of economic institutions (firms and markets) is an imperfect world. In fact, property rights on a firm's assets held by agents who carry out the most important investments, gives them an advantage. They are not only permitted to protect themselves, but allowed to seek a rent through re-negotiation - i.e. abuse of authority. From the point of view of contractarian ethics, this solution is arbitrary. In order for the constitution of an authority and the allocation of property rights on the firm's assets to be justified, each patron - who waives the firm's control on behalf of the one who will be entitled with the authority role - has to be compensated with a fair share of the surplus net of any specific investment cost. 'Fair' means that shares must correspond to what they can expect on the basis of the rational bargaining game solution, calculated from the appropriate *status quo*. For example, take the case of the surplus generated by a co-operative joint action between a single capitalist and a single worker, where the feasible set of outcomes is symmetric. Then, each of them will make a rational claim on half of the expected surplus, calculated on the basis of the value (in terms of expected utility of risky prospects and their certain equivalents) of the return net of all specific investment costs that at minimum has to be repaid if each of them is to ready to enter the joint venture. The patron waiving control - let it be the worker or the capitalist depending on case specific governance costs - holds a legitimate claim on a fair share of the benefits generated by the firm. In this sense he is a 'stakeholder': he holds a legitimate claim independently of the fact that this claim is not protected by the property right - i.e. in spite of the fact that he is not a 'stockholder'.

A social contract is an impartial agreement. Firstly, as far as the *status quo* is concerned, nobody may complain that a failure of the agreement would represent a more serious threat to him than his own refusal to agree with the others. What each is entitled to before co-operation takes place, is not subject to the moral requirements of fair co-operation. However, each party is guaranteed that she will not be put under duress by an agreement failure due to the lock-in effects of *ex ante* investments. Secondly, surplus is shared in such a way that anyone, putting himself in everybody else's shoes, would recognise the rationality of her claim to the share she effectively gains. The solution (the agreed upon outcome that distributes shares of surplus) is rational according to everybody's view. In fact rational acceptance of the shares of surplus each agent gets under the bargaining solution is invariant with replacement of each agent in the position of anybody else. Therefore, it satisfies requirements of anonymity and universalisability.

From this construction a scheme for the 'constitutional chart' of the morally justified firm follows, i.e. the set of rights and duties governing transactions within and outside the firm. This 'constitutional chart' would provide for

1. the owner's the legitimate residual claim and exercise of authority, this including authority on *ex ante* non-contractible decisions and on the choice to exclude anyone form the use of the firm's physical assets. At the same time, it allows the owner to delegate monitoring and control to the manager, with the aim of disincentivate opportunistic behaviours, thereby maximising the value of co-operation among the patrons/stakeholders.

2. the owner's responsibility towards other stakeholders: to respect their legitimate claims to fair shares of the surplus - as fixed by the hypothetical social contract.

If the management of the firm is so constrained by the constitutional contract (and if the constraint is made explicit by a corporate ethical code) then all the stakeholders would willingly enter co-operative relationships with the firm.

VI. A Parameter for Reputation Effects

The foregoing explanation is not sufficient in the *ex post* perspective. Once the firm's stakeholders have entered the constitutional contract that allocates discretionary power to specific parts, why then should the holders of such discretion respect their duties of responsibility? If this expectation cannot be supported, why should the stakeholders trust the institutions that assign discretionary power to that party? This problem refers to the second purpose of a corporate ethical code: how can it create the incentives to comply with the code itself?

In the economic literature 'corporate culture' (Kreps, 1990) is explained in the light of the theory of 'reputation effects' (Kreps and Wilson, 1982; Kreps, Milgrom, Roberts and Wilson, 1982, Fudenberg and Levine 1989. Fudenberg and Tirole 1991). I extend this explanation to corporate ethical codes arguing that this application of the game theoretical analysis to explain corporate ethical norms is even more appropriated than the one resting on the somewhat obscure notion of 'culture' (Sacconi 1991, Sacconi 1994, Sacconi 1997). This theory can be traced back to Hume's moral conventionalist view, a typical example of rational choice ethics. I will not consider here other approaches that would explain ethical codes as rationally chosen – by means of sort of meta-choice – dispositions or rules of choice constraining the base-level decision-making wherein the agents face social interaction dilemmas (Gauthier, 1986; McClennen, 1990), as they do without any reference to reputation effects which is my focus in this section[10].

I showed in section 3 that some difficulties arise in applying the theory of reputation effects within hierarchical contexts. Essentially, what generates these difficulties is the discretionary nature of decisions taken by the agent endowed with authority. Given the set X of allowable decisions, some of them may turn out to be abusive *ex post*, without the possibility to provide for them *ex ante*. Nevertheless, whether abuse were identifiable at least *ex post*, it could be argued that reputation effects as such are able to discourage abusing because of the threat to the prospective abuser of losing his face forever (i.e. in the following repetitions of the game). This is not the case however. Neither the contract, nor the law provides a unique criterion to identify these abuses. *Ex post* there will be a large amount of dissent among the players entering the game after the abused one. Apparently this problem also prevents us from resorting to the hypothetical social contract as a parameter to identify abusive actions. If, in fact, an agreement is signed in the *ex ante* hypothetical constitutional phase, *ex post* the contract may not account for unforeseen costs or benefits, which have not been agreed upon *ex ante*. Nevertheless, we can resort here to the difference between *ideal* and *real* contracts and more generally between moral/constitutional general principles on the one hand and detailed regulations on the other. This possibility relates to the

---

10   See however ch. 3 *infra* and Sacconi (1995c).

general nature of moral language used in 'writing' the social contract and embodied within the corporate moral code.

By definition, the social contract model (a general ethical model of fair/efficient agreement) is not intended to regulate each specific and concrete case. It addresses strategic interactions as a whole, characterised by only a few structural features. Taking the social contract point of view, players put themselves under the *Archimedean point*: any rational agreement will be assessed independently of any personal, historical, empirical features about the participants and the contexts - the only salient features being the few characterising the abstract bargaining interaction. One could say that the social contract is a cognitive device to focus only on a few ethically relevant variables among the many that could be considered in a more concrete account of the same situations. This enables us to abstract from many details of the concrete bargaining situations in which the structural features focused by the social contract are embedded. Thus, the validity of the social contract is not limited to the occurrence of *ex ante* known cases in point. Situations presenting cases that we were not even able to figure out, can then be subjected to the social contract machinery, because they display at a significant level the pattern of its structural variables. Indeed, it works as a device for 'pattern recognition'.

Moreover the social contract, and the code incorporating it, specify which procedures the firm must adopt every time an event occurs that calls over a principle - that is when the event displays the same pattern of the concerned structural variables. It is not necessary to have already provided exactly for that event. It is enough that it satisfies the criterion of belonging to the class of cases to which the given procedure applies, even if the elements of this class are not entirely *ex ante* known. In other words, the code of ethics provides a standard procedure of behaviour which is not conditional upon the occurrence of specific events. Instead it depend on the occurrence of situations whose borders are not univocally determined in set theoretical terms. These are situations that, at a certain level of approximation, display the pattern of a given ethical principle. An incomplete description of the world is enough to recognise that an unexpected events belongs to the class of cases morally relevant in the light of a given principle (this is exactly what we termed before as the 'pattern recognition' function of social contract). Thus, moral language applies to *ex ante* unforeseen events.

For instance, the corporate ethical code may request 'safeguarding the job of a worker every time he is in conditions of real need and is not responsible for wrongs to the firm', where the conditional is wide enough to include a range of situations *ex ante* impossible to specify. Or it can request 'sharing gains in equals parts, every time an unforeseen advantage can be achieved thanks to the investments both of the client and the supplier, or both of the worker and the employer'. 'Being co-responsible for the production of the surplus' is a characteristic that can be found in several situations whose *ex ante* description is not complete. Once principles settle pattern of the morally relevant events, again it becomes possible to exploit reputation effects. Compliance with commitments announced, i.e. implementation of a settled procedure, can be verified and judged by all the subordinate agents and stakeholders. On that basis they will update probability assigned to the owner types ('honest' vs. 'opportunistic'). Then it will become rational again for the agent endowed with authority to support his reputation by acting according to the norms of the code. This, in turn, will lead the subordinate to accept her authority and invest within the firm.

VII. Code of Ethics, Rationality and 'Fuzzy Reputation'

The crucial but very problematic point of Kreps' theory of corporate culture (Kreps 1990c) is the suggestion that we treat 'general principles' of a given corporate culture (i.e. what I mean by the principles of a corporate code of ethics) as a way of *ex ante* defining the behaviours to be implemented *ex-post*, when unforeseen events have occurred. This requires a model of rationality under unforeseen contingencies. This section gives a sketch of this model.

If rationality would be unbounded, the players would have all the complete alternative descriptions of the possible states of the world at their disposal. Consequently, there would be no unforeseen events any longer. Unfortunately human rationality is bounded, and we do not have all the complete alternative descriptions of the states of the world at our disposal. To explain, imagine that we want to describe a set of alternative state of affairs given a language endowed with n individual constants and m monadic predicates. We could describe, for example, a state of the world where the individual i is white, not black nor yellow, the individual j is black, not white nor yellow, the individual k is white... another state where the individual i is black, not white, nor yellow, the individual j is yellow, not white, not black, the individual k is black...etc. We would like that these alternative and mu-

27

tually exclusive descriptions of the state of the world to prove to be exhaustive as a whole. But, as a matter of fact, the language in use could not be rich enough to express every possible property that would transpire through time and experience.

Now assume that we discover a state of the world in which a surprising property occurs. It can be seen as an unforeseen event occurring only in that state of the world. This property is not accounted for by the repertory of predicates included in our current language. Accordingly, the individual showing the 'new' property is not properly white, not properly black, not properly yellow....but nevertheless it is in some sense both white, black yellow etc... In other words we are unable to establish for this state of the world whether each predicate has to be affirmed or denied with reference to the relevant individual. Consequently this state will not be clearly specified, in the sense that we may not be able (in this state of the world) to understand whether some event occurs or not, simply because under that description the relevant characteristic is not clearly specified with reference to the relevant individual constant. My suggestion (in a very exploratory way) is that a code of ethics works as the appropriate tool to prescribe behaviours in situations like these.

A moral code can be seen as the settlement of general principles and statements announcing that the firm will perform some pre-defined procedure when (generic) events satisfying morally relevant characteristics occur. Consider for instance the general sentence 'the firm A follows the principle of compensating any loss or damage suffered by the client/employee when it realises that a client/employees is in conditions of real need'. Assume that, if it is the case, the firm will apply the aid procedure Y without request for compensation. The problem, of course, is that the event 'the client/employee is in conditions of real need' is a *vague* event. Therefore we are *ex ante* unable to say exactly in which states of the world this event occurs. This situation can be expressed in terms of *fuzzy set theory* (Zimmerman 1991). Considering a reference set W, composed by n elements, a fuzzy sub-set E of W is given by a set of membership functions that are defined for each element belonging to W. Each function defines the degree of membership of a single element of W to E and takes its values in the ordered set [0,1]. In other words, the set E is a set of elements of W which are members of E at a certain degree x ($0 \leq x \leq 1$). The set E is therefore a set with fuzzy or vague borders that can be used to deal with vague concepts like 'to be near', 'to have a reddish colour' etc. - i.e. defining the set of things having these vague characteristics[11].

This definition can be used to give an account of unforeseen contingencies in terms of their impact on the level of vagueness of our description of *ex post* possible events. Some events are *vague* because their occurrence is not clearly defined in some state of the world and this typically happens for the unforeseen ones. Consider Ω as the all encompassing set of states of the world that happens to be possible in the *ex post* perspective. Given the resources of our current language (the language we had in the *ex ante* perspective) Ω will be constituted by all the alternative accurate descriptions of the state of the world *relative to that language*. Nevertheless Ω will also include some *ex ante* unforeseen states that *ex post* we cannot accurately describe by means of the existing language. Thus as a whole we have only a superficial and incomplete description of the states set Ω. We may know their number n (this is not a painless assumption) but have only a partial description for them. Then a *fuzzy event* is defined as the set of membership functions that associates each of the n states of the world to the degree to which the given state belongs the event in point – the degree to which the characterising property of the event does occur in the given state. For example, the event 'a client is in conditions of real need' is the set of states in which for at least one individual constant (a client) the property 'to be in need' is predicated. Then the state ω_1 may be a state for which we are able to describe exactly an individual constant with the relevant characteristic (degree of membership 1, i.e. the state of the world ω_1 unambiguously belongs the event in question). On the contrary the state of the world ω_2 may be a state in which we are unable to describe an individual who clearly displays the characteristic in point. In this case it is impossible a sharp assignation of ω_2 to the domain of membership of the event 'a client is in conditions of real need'. Nevertheless we may assign *a grade* of membership of ω_2 into the event. The resulting event is a *fuzzy event*, to which the state ω_2 belongs only to a certain degree. A fuzzy event expresses the idea that we may be unable to clearly define the states of the world in which a given event occurs and, consequently, it corresponds to incomplete descriptions of states.

---

[11]   For an introductory exposition of the basic concepts of fuzzy sets theory see ch.6 *infra*. More complete presentations of the theory can be found in Kaufmann (1975) and Zimmerman (1991), while a suggestive overview is given by Kosko (1993).

1.7 CODE OF ETHICS AND "FUZZY REPUTATION"

Let us come back to codes of ethics. A conditional strategy - according to standard decision theory - is a rule that provides an action conditional upon the occurrence of each non fuzzy event, i.e. upon the occurrence of events with respect to which the relation of being a member for different states of the world is clearly defined (0 or 1). Events like these are, however, quite artificial and their semantic content is very poor. Moral language, on the contrary, refers to 'open' worlds, in the sense that *ex ante* we do not have for each of these states a complete description enabling us to say whether any event occurs in it. That is, we do not know every mode in which a given event can take place. However a fuzzy event, that is the situations belonging to the domain of a moral norm at a certain degree, asks for less than so. By mean of this sort of events we express that some *ex ante* unexpected situations ('worlds') belong to the relevant badly specified moral category to a vague but nevertheless quantifiable degree. An ethical code provides for the firm's behaviour in relation to fuzzy events like this.

We call these events *moral events* and intend them as sets of situations ('worlds') belonging to the domain of a given moral principle. Notice that the prescriptive meaning of the command embodied in a moral principle may be perfectly clear-cut (for example the following: 'in any interactive situation satisfying the definition of a co-operative game, share payoffs according to the *Nash Bargaining Solution*'). Where vagueness comes about however is in the descriptive characteristics required in order to make the inference that the situation falls into the domain of the principle, for example if a given situation satisfies properties such as 'co-operative games'.

Assume that the degree of fuzziness associated to any given state of world, when it occurs for the first time, is common between any two players entering at immediately adjacent times the game in the role of the short-run player (see section 3.2 this chapter). This means that for any value of n the membership functions do not undergo dynamic changes during the time lags between the repetition n - when the n-ary player learns the outcome of the game, and the repetition $n+1$ - when the $n+1$-ary player is called to participate in the game. Assume moreover that the firm (i.e. the long-run player) is able of capturing the fuzziness degree assigned by the two adjacent short-run players. Thus an ethical code will guarantee that, for all the states of the world in which the event E (showing the morally relevant characteristic C) occurs at a degree not less than α - i.e. for all the states that belong to E with a membership degree $\mu(\omega_i) \geq \alpha$, with $\alpha \in [1,0]$ - the firm *will adopt the procedure* Y. Define this as a *fuzzy (default) commitment*. Given the same degree of fuzziness between the two adjacent short-run players assumed above, the stakeholders will be able to recognise, as well as the firm, the degree z to which any given state belongs to the event. If the degree is $z > \alpha$ but the firm still does not apply the procedure Y, then the stakeholders will be able to update their beliefs down-rating the firm's reputation. This implies that in the continuation game each player who will match the firm in the role of a A_i (i = 2,...,n, where n goes to infinitum) will punish the player B not entering the relation. I call *fuzzy reputations* those reputations whose variance is a direct function of the compliance with the fuzzy (default) commitments defined above.

Chapter 2

Economic Theory and
the Social Contract of the Firm

I. Theory of Property Rights and Control on the Firm

In order to work out more precisely the case for the social contract of the firm the basic reference is the economic theory of the firm, particularly in the versions of Grossman and Hart (1986) and Hart and Moore (1990). These theories examine the inter-temporal structure of transactions in which specific investments take place and which are regulated by incomplete contracts.

At time $t = 0$ it is assumed that the parties decide on the contractual structure of rights and control under which they will transact for goods or services. It is therefore assumed that at time $t = 1$ at least one person must carry out an action. This action is in the nature of a specific investment, such that the well-being of the individual who has carried it out comes to depend upon the evolution of the transactional relationship with the other parties. That is, he has taken on sunk costs for investments which have no value outside the relationship with the subjects involved in the particular transaction; however, these investments offer the prospect of a surplus if the transaction with the given parties is successfully completed in the future. Specific investments create the typical 'lock in' situation, where the party engaged in it becomes dependent on some action of the counterpart in order to benefit from the result of its own investment. Assume that specific investments are decided on independently of the initial contract by which the parties promise one another to provide services, where the value of such services however depend on the specific investments made by the parties. In principle at time $t = 0$ they could attempt to write down a detailed contract regulating all the concrete aspects of their transaction, or on the contrary they may only shape the control structure of the assets by means of which they will carry out the transaction. Assume however that any contract will be incomplete since it cannot include provisos either about the specific investments or about unforeseen events that may occur in the future.

2.1 PROPERTY RIGHTS AND CONTROL ON THE FIRM

At time $t = 2$ decisional variables appear which are unforeseen and therefore not contractible *ex ante*. The way in which such decisional variables are resolved *ex post* influences the level of return which can be made to correspond to the specific investments made at time $t = 1$. It is therefore possible, at time $t = 2$, to negotiate the distribution of the benefits made possible by the specific investments. The negotiation is influenced by the control structure chosen at time $t = 0$. In Hart and Moore's version of the theory this is equivalent to the structure of the property rights which allows the possibility of excluding certain individuals from the use of certain physical assets. Let us assume that all the investments are in human capital and that in order to carry out these investments it is necessary to use a given set of physical assets. The person who controls these physical assets has an advantage in the bargaining game that will take place at time $t = 2$, since he can threaten to exclude the other parties who carried out specific investments at time $t = 1$, leaving them with the burden of an unrecoverable cost.

This analysis, although insufficient for a complete account of the concept of authority, is nevertheless an explanation of the *de facto* authority held in the firm by one party, who owns the firm, over the others (once the efficiency of an economic constitution, which grants this party the property right, has been established). It furthermore explains how something such as an opportunistic use of authority can occur: the party who owns the firm can at time $t = 2$ use ownership to renegotiate the solution and extract a rent.

Let us consider a situation with two agents A and B. Given a contractual structure of rights chosen at time $t = 0$, A can carry out an action x, i.e. a specific investment in human capital at time $t = 1$, with the cost c(x). At time $t = 2$, if A has done x, and only in that case, the possibility appears for B to decide on an action **d** whose cost is c(**d**), but which generates a surplus of benefits, so that the benefit of the transaction is a function of x, V(x). However, this happens only if in the meantime favourable events have occurred, which could not be specified *ex ante* in the contract (since their details cannot be foreseen). Furthermore, even if it were possible, **d** would be useless if A had not done x at time $t = 1$. Suppose that the detailed description of the decision **d** changes substantially on the basis of the occurrence or otherwise of events that could not be foreseen *ex ante*, so that the decision **d** cannot be included, even conditionally, in the conditions of the contract. We can say therefore that the decisional variables **d** are not contractible *ex ante*, at time $t = 0$ (we cannot say which specification of **d** should be undertaken in the various contingencies), and that they remain discretionary decisions for whoever *ex post* effectively controls them, by means of the structure of the rights of property and control of the firm which nevertheless was established *ex ante*. *Ex ante*, in the contract agreed at t = 0, it is however possible to assign the probability p that a *generic* decision about innovation **d** (conditional upon the occurrence of generic events, which are not well specified) generates a surplus if A has undertaken the specific investment x^1. If A decides to invest at time t = 1, the return on the investment (which we shall here regard as net benefit) at time t = 2 will be

$$W(x) = V(x) - c(d) - c(x) > 0$$

Consider the effects of the different contractual structures established at time t = 0 and imagine at first an ideal contract C in which, however the structure of control over **d** is defined, there is no risk of opportunism at time t = 2. A can always decide the level of the investment x in the socially optimal way. In fact A expects (with probability p) to obtain the return on his investment, net of costs, and considers the effect of the control structure over **d** to be negligible, due to the negligibility of bargain opportunities at tine t = 2. Given the hypothesis of linearity of the utility with the monetary payoffs, he will have the following expected payoff for his decision to invest:

$$U_A(C) = p[V(x) - c(d)] - c(x)$$

Consequently his decisions to invest will follow the rule of equating marginal costs with the marginal returns expected from the investment, which makes the level of the returns (or of net benefits) W(x) socially opti-

---

[1]   The hypothesis we are making serves to introduce probabilistic considerations where they would in principle be excluded, since unforeseen events do not even form part of the support for the players' distributions of probability. The idea is that the event 'a decision to innovate produces a positive result' is too generic to be inserted in the contract as a binding provision, but can nevertheless be the object of an assignation of probability. Conversely the detailed description of a particular decision to innovate and of its effects could be introduced into the contract but it would require knowledge of unforeseen events, which therefore do not have an assignation of probability.

mal. Consider on the other hand a contractual context influenced by the structure of rights at time $t = 2$, which means that negotiation is therefore possible. Take the contract C' in which B has ownership of the physical resources to which A's act x is applied. He is therefore able to control the decisional variable **d** which could not be contracted for *ex ante*. After A's investment the *status quo* is $[-c(x), 0]$. B can now reopen the negotiation *ex post* and ask that part of the return, which is attributable to A's specific investment x, be given to B. In this case the payoffs anticipated by A and B, considered at time $t = 1$ respectively will be:

$$U_A (C') = p [V(x)-c(\mathbf{d})] / 2 - c(x)$$

$$U_B (C') = p [V(x)-c(\mathbf{d})] / 2$$

In fact B asks for a portion of the surplus which becomes possible if he takes the decision **d**, considering as the *status quo* of the negotiation the state in which A has already carried out the action x and $c(x)$ is therefore an unrecoverable cost for A. The particular bargaining theory used here is *Nash bargaining solution*, which under the hypotheses of linearity of utilities in the monetary payoffs and symmetric payoff space, requires a division into equal parts of the surplus calculated with respect to the *status quo*[2].

---

[2]   Nash's solution (1950, 1953) for co-operative bargaining games between two players provides that, under the hypothesis of individual rationality, Pareto efficiency, invariance to independent, affine positive transformations of the individual payoff functions (therefore irrelevance of interpersonal comparisons), independence of irrelevant alternatives, the rational outcome of the bargaining should coincide with a single point of the compact and convex payoff space made up by the utility representation of the set of joint strategies of the players. This point is where the Nash product is maximised, i.e. maximise $\Pi_i (u_i - d_i)$, where u_i is the payoff of player i (with $i = 1,2$) for one joint strategy while d_i is the payoff of the same player for the *status quo*. The meaning of this solution is that the product of the cooperative surpluses that the players obtain from the negotiation has to be maximised and that the rate of substitution of the players' utilities does matter for finding the solution on the utility frontier.

2. ECONOMIC THEORY AND THE SOCIAL CONTRACT

In contrast, let us consider the contract C'' in which the individual A is the owner of the physical assets on which he applies his investment x, and therefore he also controls the decision **d**, which constitutes a cost for B. The *status quo* of negotiation in this case is given by the fact that A can threaten to order B to take the decision **d** in any case and therefore to bear the cost c(**d**), even in the circumstances in which the decision **d** would not offer the surplus $V(x) - c(\mathbf{d}) > 0$. It is to be supposed that if **d** produces a benefit, its cost is always reimbursed by A to B. However if **d** does not produce any benefit, A can deny B any payoff to cover the additional costs c(**d**) (for example in the case of a piece rate contract by which A, the owner of the physical resources on which the pieceworker B works, pays only for the result). In this way A can obtain an income in return for giving up this threat. The *status quo* therefore assigns to A $p[V(x) - c(\mathbf{d})] - c(x)$, while it assigns to B $(1 - p) [-c(\mathbf{d})]$. It is therefore possible to obtain the following expected payoffs (seen at the time t =1) for the contract C'' by means of bargaining. For A

$$U_A (C'') = p[V(x) - c(\mathbf{d})] + (1 - p)[\tfrac{1}{2}\, c(\mathbf{d})] - c(x)$$

while for B

$$U_B (C'') = (1 - p)\, \tfrac{1}{2}[-c(\mathbf{d})]$$

In Grossman and Hart's analysis (1986) the comparison between what investor A expects, if he can obtain the return on the investment without renegotiation (the socially optimal contract C) and what he may expect at time $t = 1$ if he has property rights (contract C''), or if he does not have them (contract C'), indicates the tendency to under- or over-invest. In the case C' in fact he equalises the marginal costs of the investment to half the marginal returns on the investment, and therefore he under-invests. On the other occasion – C'' - on the other hand, he equalises the marginal costs with the marginal variation of the linear combination between the return on the investment and 'income' from opportunistic use of the property right, and therefore over-invests.

Since, under any arrangement of property rights, giving control over the variables not contractible *ex ante* influences the social efficiency of the transaction, what the parties can do to prevent the outcome from being sub-optimal in one way (A under-invests because he fears being expropriated by B) or the other (B does not participate in the transaction or does so at higher initial costs, since he fears that A will impose unfavourable decisions *ex post*) is to agree *ex ante*, at time t = 0, on the most efficient arrangement of the structure of property and control. The decision about the arrangement of the rights to be preferred from the normative point of view is taken on the basis of which contractual arrangement permits the closest approximation to the *first best*) case in which the individual A makes his investments in the socially optimal way (case C), that is equalising the marginal costs of the investment with the expected marginal return[3].

Hart and Moore (1990) offer a generalisation of this theory. We shall present the model of the social contract by referring to this reformulation. It uses the idea of a coalition S of individuals whose characteristic function, that is the joint value of the co-operation between the individuals in the coalition, is superadditive. That is, the value of S is always greater than the sum of the value of the two sub-coalitions that make up S. It is therefore possible to consider the effects of the control structure, and therefore of the *ex post* bargaining, on the incentives to invest on the part of members of the coalition.

---

[3]   This decision *ex ante* is the point at which economic theory approaches most closely the theory of the social contract: imagine an original decision in which property rights have not yet been established, or at any rate have not been definitively established, and which precedes the start of the transaction of goods and services between A and B. In this original situation it is hypothesised that the parties, anticipating the effects in terms of social efficiency (approximation to the social optimum) that the best allocation of property rights will have over the transaction can agree *ex ante* not about the details of the transaction but about the institutional arrangement of rights which will subsequently regulate discretionary decisions, so that their choice will fall on that arrangement which will permit the greatest gain in social efficiency. This interpretation is not, however, the prevailing one among theorists of the firm, in the approach of organisation theory and *Law & Economics*, including Grossman, Hart and Moore, who think rather of spontaneous adaptations of the control structure of firms through voluntary transfers of property rights in a suitable financial market, taking for granted that this market and these property rights exist.

2. ECONOMIC THEORY AND THE SOCIAL CONTRACT

Given that bargaining under various control structures causes inefficiency, the different allocations of the rights of control are in general *second
best* with respect to the situation in which there is no contractual incompleteness. Control structures can however be chosen so that they minimise
inefficiency and approximate as nearly as possible the socially optimal result
(*first best*).

According to Hart and Moore, the most significant rules for defining the
second best structure of control and allocation of property must respond the
following questions:

(a) how *important* action or investment is; if an individual has to make the
only specific investment or action which will generate the surplus, he should
have the property right;

(b) how *idiosyncratic* an asset is; if the benefit of all the members of the
coalition S except one particular individual is indifferent to a certain asset,
then this resource is said to be specific to the individual i; then the individual i should have the property right over this asset;

(c) how *indispensable* an agent is; if an asset has positive effects on the production of a surplus by the coalition only if individual i participates in the
coalition, then i is indispensable to the resource. But if individual i is indispensable for a given asset, he should have property rights over it.

The notion of an *indispensable agent* highlights the fact that, in allocating ownership, it is not only the people who have investments to make that
are important, but also those who are good business partners. If, for example, an individual A has a specific investment to make, on which his welfare
depends, but the realisation of the welfare depends on the co-operation of a
second individual B, without which A's investment will not bear fruit, then
the rule admits that ownership of the resource on which A makes his investment might also be given to B.

The notion of indispensability is important for the theory of the social
contract. In general the contractarian argument maintains that in order for
the investment of resources (generic liberties or possibilities of action) in cooperative rather than aggressive activities to have value for the members of
society, it is necessary that each of the individuals in a state of nature should
participate in the social contract; that is, that they should be part of the coalition between all those who make the above-mentioned investments. If some
individual remains outside the coalition, the fear will arise that they will
suffer the opportunism of those who remain in a state of nature and the

39

whole coalition will lose value. Consequently, the social contract assigns to every individual the right of collective sovereignty, that is the possibility of prohibiting the formation of co-operative coalitions which he dislikes. This is the same as saying that the social contract is a criterion of unanimity of choice.

II. Constitutional Contract of the Firm and the Theory of Justice

The contractarian model for the choice of the *constitution of the firm* is made up of the following elements[4]: N individuals; for every given productive activity A, S of these constitute a coalition whose characteristic function is superadditive. Of these m make high specific investments and l are indispensable as partners in the transaction. $S - (m + l)$ members of S on the other hand carry out unspecific actions. These may be useful to add value to the coalition S, but they are not strictly *locked-in* to the coalition in order to realise the value of their investment, nor are they strictly indispensable in order for the investments in human capital of the other investors to produce their positive differential benefits. The three groups of members of S allow us to distinguish between those $(m + l)$ who are candidates for the exercise of authority and those who are not $(S - (m + l)$. The choice within the $m + l$ will obviously depend on effects of comparative efficiency. The remaining $N - S$ individuals are indifferent to the activity A in question. That is they do not participate in this small economy (the 'firm').

The model is intended to take account of a problem of collective decision making in three phases among potential members of the coalition S. At time $t = 0$ the allocation of rights is decided (rights not only of ownership and control but also of redress and compensation) which determines the structure of the social contract. At time $t = 1$ the right-holding individuals take investment decisions in view of the carrying out of transactions. At time $t = 2$ a bargaining game begins, defined for each allocation of rights and for every

---

[4]   In developing the theory of the social contract of the firm we mix ideas form the just described economic model of the firm with some formal modelling of the Social Contract worked out in the filed of Constitutional Political Economy, see in particular (Brock 1978, 1979, Sacconi 1986, 1991).

set of investment decisions, which follows the occurrence of events that could not be foreseen in a contract hypothetically agreed *ex ante* (at time $t = 0$). The problem of sequential decision-making is modelled by a compounded game G, whose intuitive idea is that at time $t = 0$ a set of strategies for each player is chosen by means of which a subsequent game can be played at time $t = 2$, but – please note this point – this set of strategies of the second game is a subset of the strategies available in the initial game.

In order to clarify the background, consider a non-cooperative game G_N ('state of nature') characterised by a set of pure strategies $B_1 \times ... \times B_n = B$, where N is the cardinality of the colaition S and each B_i is the set of pure strategies of the i-th player (which expresses his unlimited freedom of action) and by a space of payoffs $U_1 \times ... \times U_n = U$, where U_i is the payoff function of the i-th player defined on the outcomes of the game. Let us assume, as is typical of PD-like games, that this game has a non-cooperative equilibrium solution d^* which is inside the frontier of the payoff space U, and therefore not efficient.

Given G_N let the game of the constitutional choice G_C be defined as the co-operative game characterised by (a) the set of strategies $\underline{B}$ that can be generated by all the joint strategies that can be constructed from $B_1,...,B_n$, and from their joint randomisation; (b) the payoff space P which, due to the continuity of the payoff functions and the nature of the strategy set $\underline{B}$, is the convex and compact hull of all the possible payoff vectors in U.

Like all cooperative games, G_C is preceded by a bargaining session. The peculiarity of this special bargaining game is that the players do not have to choose one particular joint strategy to be implemented in G_C, but rather they have to choose an entire subset of the set B of the pure strategies of G_N. Let $I_1,...,I_n$ be the various subsets of B. Since every set of pure strategies I_i is a limitation on the possibilities for action compared to those allowed in G_N, every subset I_i can be seen as a Constitution, that is, as a set of institutions that limits the freedom of the various players.

For every subset I_i, a particular cooperative sub-game G_i can be defined, by generating it from all the pure strategies of G_N included in the particular subset I_i, including all the probabilistic joint combinations between vectors of pure strategies in I_i. Since for every choice of I_i, the resulting set of strategies includes the convex combination of all the elements of I_i, every sub-game G_i has a compact and convex payoff space P_i. Thus the set of strategies of the cooperative sub-game G_i is a subset of $\underline{B}$ and its payoff space is a subset of P. This follows simply from the fact that $\underline{B}$ and P are nothing more

41

than the intersection of the sets of strategies and the payoff spaces defined for the various co-operative sub-games G_i. Each particular G_i will be a cooperative game, preceded in its turn by an imperfectly cooperative bargaining game.

At time $t = 0$ in G_C the players agree upon a 'social contract' regarding the Constitution and then at time $t = 1$ they decide how much to invest given the hypothesis that a non-contractible decision variable conditional on unforeseen future events may transpire, which might influence the cooperative outcome of the following sub-games. In fact, at time $t = 2$ an event unforeseen by the contract occurs, then a new bargaining game G_i ensues about how much is produced and how to share the surplus fruit of the second phase cooperation. In any G_i the parties are assigned payoffs according to the Shapley value for cooperative games of coalition[5]. The agreement that ends the second bargaining game is effectively implemented in the particular sub-game G_i chosen. That the outcome agreed at time $t = 2$ belongs to the set of joint strategies of the sub-game G_i indicates that the Constitution influences the outcomes of the second phase of negotiation, constraining both the number of joint strategies at the disposal of the players and the exit option (*status quo*) to which they can resort in each particular game of negotiation G_i.

Players participate in a sequential game which they resolve by backwards induction. First, given hypothetically every possible sub-game G_i and every vector of investment decisions for every G_i, the players calculate the ex-

---

[5]   The Shapley value calculates the payoff for each player as the linear combination of all the contributions that an player can make by entering into each subcoalition of S, which includes him, as marginal member including the contribution that the individual can give to the value of S, where each contribution is weighed with the probability that the particular coalition will be formed

$$v_i(a|x) = \Sigma_{S' \subseteq S}\, p(S')[v(S', a|x) - v(S' - \{i\}, a|x)]\lambda$$

the criterion with which the probability $p(S')$ is assigned that each coalition will form, in which player i is the marginal component, is given by the coefficient $(s - 1)!(n - s)!/n!$ which multiplies the difference
$v(S', a|x) - v(S' - i, a|x)$
for each coalition S', where the symbol k! stands for $k \times k - 1 \times ... \times 3 \times 2 \times 1$, and $0! = 1$.

pected payoff assigned to them by the Shapley value for the coalitional bargaining game that follows every chosen level of investment. Second, moving backward they therefore choose the level of investment that enables them to obtain the highest Shapley value, given that the others also choose the level of investment which will give them the highest Shapley value. In other words, every sub-game G_i is resolved by the distribution of the payoffs according to the Shapley value, which is associated with the equilibrium investment decisions (that is, which equalises the marginal costs of the investment to the marginal variation in the Shapley value). Thus for every G_i there exists a univocal solution in terms of a precisely defined vector of payoffs.

How is the game G_C dealt with? Still moving backwards, each player knows that the choice of a subset of strategies I_i corresponds to the choice of a particular solution for the associated sub-game G_i. The set of payoffs P can also be considered as the set of solutions for all the possible games G_i. Therefore the game G_C can also be treated as a co-operative bargaining game in which the players must agree on a particular vector of payoffs in P, corresponding to the solution of a specific sub-game G_i.

Among the other points belonging to P, there is one in particular corresponding to the solution in the case of $I_i = B$. In this case the special hypothesis is made that, in the absence of any restriction on B, it is not possible to transform the set of strategies I_i into a set of joint strategies, typical of a co-operative game, and that therefore the game selected remains G_N with the same solution d*. Intuitively this corresponds to the idea that if the players cannot set any restriction, they cannot either establish a Constitution and therefore their interaction remains the same as that described in G_N. Therefore we can take the point d* as the *status quo* of the cooperative bargaining game G_C.

To resolve G_C is it therefore necessary to specify the bargaining rules leading the selection of any particular point in P. Let us assume that the result of G_C is different from d* if and only if the players establish a unanimous agreement on a particular vector of strategies corresponding to a point in P which Pareto-dominates d*. In other words, only co-operation among all the players, or the formation of the total coalition S, is worthwhile. Given what we said before, let us make d* = (0,...,0) and let us assume (for the sake of simplicity) that the form of the space P is symmetrical (this is the basic case of Nash's theory which provides a postulate exactly for this case). Nash's bargaining solution (see note 2) under this hypothesis selects the point on the *Pareto surface* of the bargaining game payoff space, which offers equal quantities of surplus to all the players. This point corresponds to a Constitution on the basis of which the particular game G_i, which is initiated once the admissible strategies have been selected, distributes an equal cooperative surplus among the parties (under the above hypotheses). Evidently such a Constitution distributes the rights of property and control within the firm according to the egalitarian rule, once the coalition S has been set up, amongst all the members of the coalition. Consequently it does not assign to any of them a favourite bargaining position at the moment of negotiating *ex post* any coalition formation within the particular game G_i chosen.

What interpretation can we give to the solution of the game G_C in terms of the theory of distributive justice? The solution for every game G_i according to the Shapley value can be interpreted as an application of the principle of *remuneration on the basis of relative contribution* (Brock 1979, Sacconi 1986a,b). The Shapley value is in fact the linear combination (equiprobabilistically calculated) of all the marginal contributions that an individual can give to all the possible coalitions. From the fact that the distribution according to the Shapley value follows the opening of negotiation at time 2 after the occurrence of unforeseen facts, it does not follow that we have to give up the interpretation of the solution as a distribution in accordance with the above-mentioned ethical principle. In fact at the moment of making their investment choice at time $t = 1$, all the players know that their payoffs will depend on a bargaining game in which the importance of the players as members of the various sub-coalitions of S is measured. Thus each one contributes to the investments, taking into account the value that his co-operation, according to the existing constitutional rules, can have for the specific sub-coalitions of S (including S) in which he is a member.

On the other hand it has been shown that Nash's bargaining solution can be interpreted as an equivalent solution to distribution on the basis of relative needs, that is to the relative intensity of the variation in preference at the point where the solution falls (see Brock 1979, Sacconi 1986a, b)[6].

---

[6]   What counts as a measure of relative needs is the ratio between one's player marginal variation of utility and the marginal variation of the utility of the other $-\partial U_1/\partial U_2$ at each point on the *Pareto frontier*. This means that in order to distribute the surplus in proportion to relative needs it is necessary to choose the distributive proportion a_1/a_2 represented by the straight line starting from the *status quo* point which intersects the Pareto frontier in the exact point

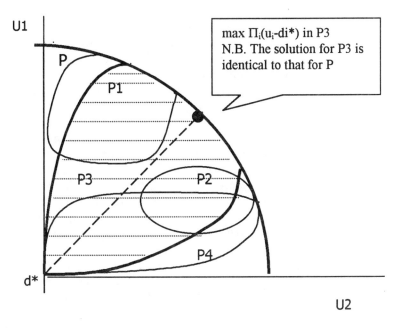

Figure 2.1 *The constitutional choice in a case of two players: the spaces P1, P2, P3, P4 – subsets of P – refer to sub-games Gi resulting from the restrictions imposed on the strategies of game Gc.*

where the two ratios are equal but opposite in sign $(-a_1/a_2 = -\partial U_1/\partial U_2)$. There is only one place on the boundary where this condition is satisfied and it coincides with the point where the Nash product is maximised. It should be recalled that the measurement of relative needs only makes sense if the utilities are interpersonally comparable and this introduces an additional assumption to Nash's traditional bargaining theory. However, this does not restrict the field of application. Nash's solution is in fact invariant with respect to separate affine positive utility function transformations. This means that a valid solution for the constitutional choice for every choice of utility functions units and zeroes will also be valid for the particular choice under which the unit and zero are interpersonally calibrated. Obviously, only under this choice of the utility functions are we able to appreciate its meaning in terms of distributive justice.

2. ECONOMIC THEORY AND THE SOCIAL CONTRACT

The double ethical characterisation of the two-step solution is adequate to the diverse nature of the problems of collective choice modelled by every single sub-game G_i and the game of constitutional choice G_C. The solution of the various sub-games distributes benefits, to the production of which the various players have contributed, both by means of their investment decisions and through the decision to participate in the various sub-coalitions of S.

In the case of the constitutional bargaining game G_C no-one yet has desert-based claims to advance, since no-one has yet made a contribution. In G_C a Constitution is chosen that will shape the following investment decisions, but no-one can yet advance claims based on what they have contributed. Rather, what the various players will be able to contribute derives from the choice of the Constitution. For this reason an appropriate criterion for a solution will be based on relative need or relative substitution ratio of the parties' utilities .

Thus the solution to the game of constitutional choice consists of allocating rights proportionally to the relative need which the players have for these rights, in view of the effects of these over the final distribution of benefits. On the other hand, since the solution is found on the Pareto surface of the payoff space, the fair criterion for the constitutional choice is also efficient.

To sum up, the solution to the game of constitutional choice (see fig.2.1 for the illustration of the case for two people) consists of the following *rule for constitutional choice:*

(i) *select* an efficient constitution in Pareto's sense, calculated on the basis of the particular status quo (0,...,0), which

(ii) *distributes* the surplus generated by the co-operation among the members of S in *proportion* to their *relative needs,* if the distribution is seen in the context of the constitutional choice (with respect to the space of the payoffs P for the game G_C),

(iii) but also *proportionally* to the *relative contributions,* if seen in the context of the post-constitutional choice which occurs in any particular game G_i.

46

III. Economic Constitution, Ownership, Compensation

Until now we have considered the most abstract case in which every Constitution is possible. In this case every point on the Pareto surface of the game G_C, whose payoff space is the convex hull of the outcome of G_N, can be reached by means of an appropriate restriction of the strategies at the players' disposal in the state of nature G_N. This would be a world of perfect efficiency, which would not be subject to the *second best* results typical of the theory of the firm. This is not however the most natural situation.

It should therefore be assumed that only a certain number of restrictions I_i on the set of strategies B is *institutionally feasible*. We shall regard as institutionally feasible a Constitution under which a relationship of authority can be established and which consequently can ensure that any contracts made between the parties can be enforced. Typically these conditions will be satisfied only by limitations of the original set of strategies to the subsets for which there is an unequal allocation of the rights of property and control. These subsets will consist of particular games G_i, whose payoff spaces constitute the convex and compact hull of only some discrete regions P_i of the payoff space of the original game G_N.

In particular let us allow that only exclusive allocations of the property rights over the whole of the physical assets of the firm are institutionally feasible. To this is linked the possibility of assigning all the authority to one party or another, but no intermediate stages (as happened in the egalitarian solution found previously). Let us therefore allow that the available arrangements of property on the physical assets, allowed by the possible Constitutions, are such as to bias ex post bargaining power heavily in favour of one or other subject. The salient aspect of this situation is that Nash's bargaining solution with respect to the payoff space P of the game G_C may now not coincide with the solution of any of the sub-games G_i that are institutionally feasible. A plausible assumption in this case is that the sub-games allowed by the institutionally feasible subsets I_i also have payoff spaces P_i which are completely internal with respect to the payoff space of the constitutional choice game G_C. We shall therefore say that the initial game G_C is a purely ideal model of the constitutional choice, that is, it contains 'Utopian' institutions. 'Utopian' is here to be understood in the sense that, given the Constitution chosen at time t = 0, the contract signed at time t − 2 cannot be enforced. Typically, Utopian institutions do not include the establishment of authority relationships that, within the given order, guarantee the enforcement of the set of rules belonging to the particular constitution chosen.

How should we deal with the constitutional choice in this imperfect world? The criteria proposed by economic theory are based on the importance of investments and on indispensability. If one party being endowed with ownership were able to ensure a higher surplus, then he would also acquire the property right by buying it from the other party by means of a conditional contract. Let us take the arrangement of rights under which one party holds ownership as the *status quo*. Then it can be verified that the alternative arrangement of property rights is more efficient if it is possible to find a utility side payment that enables the second party to induce the first to cede to him the property right itself. That is, the ownership is allocated to the party who has more important contributions to make to production, or who is indispensable in making the investments of the others productive because this will allow the required side payments to be made. This implies choosing the sub-game G_i whose solution is closest to the Pareto surface of the payoff space.

However, the rational consent of the other agents also has to be accounted for in the context of the constitutional bargaining model. They may accept that the player who makes the most valuable investment or who is most indispensable in realising the value of these investments should be given property rights. Nevertheless making the constitutional choice requires the consent of all the players whose membership of the coalition ensures the super-additivity of the value of S (whether these make specific investments, are indispensable agents with respect to some assets or ordinary members of S who add some value to the coalition). This requirement implies that the proceeds of the actions will reward all parties fairly.

Fortunately we are still able to calculate the fair distribution that defines the rational expectations of the parties. The initial position is 'without rights'. The appropriate *status quo* is therefore $(0,...,0)$. Desert or contribution based claims are not relevant here because in G_C the contributions have not yet been made. Investments come into play only in G_i. Distribution according to the criterion of relative need can be calculated by taking the convex combination between the payoff spaces defined by the institutionally feasible games and the origin $(0,...,0)$ of the Cartesian axes representing the players' payoff functions. Within (on the boundary of) this convex set of points Nash's bargaining solution permits calculation of the required payoff distribution (a linear combination of the payoffs the players obtain under the solutions of the single institutionally feasible games G_i).

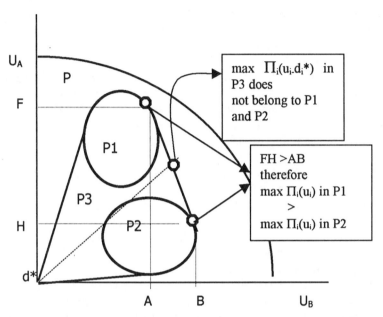

Figure 2.2 *P1 and P2 are payoff spaces for the institutionally feasible Constitutions G1 and G2, the solution to P3 is the constitutional contract which can be reached only by a utility side payment.*

This solution is clearly different from the constitutional contract in the Utopian context, since in general the convex combination of the two or more payoff spaces P_i relative to institutionally feasible games (constitutions) G_i is still itself a proper subset of the payoff space P of the Utopian game of constitutional choice G_C so that its solution too falls on a boundary (the linear combination of the efficient solutions relative to the games G_i) which is 'internal' with respect to the Pareto frontier of the space P relative to G_C. Furthermore the proportion according to which the surplus will be distributed may also change in relation to the asymmetry of the space resulting from the convex combination of the two (or more) feasible spaces P_i. On the other hand the resulting constitutional contract will in any case be an approxima-

49

tion to the Utopian one. In fact the larger the region of P covered by the pay-off spaces relative to institutionally feasible Constitutions, the greater the approximation of their convex combination to P. If by chance an institution-ally feasible sub-game G_i had a payoff space P_i inclusive of the valid solution with respect to P in G_C, then such a solution, due to independence of irrele-vant alternatives axiom, would also be valid in P_i.

A problem arises for, as we know, no actually feasible constitutional so-lution corresponds to this distribution. The solution we can suggest is therefore based on a side utility payment. In order to get from the *status quo* $(0,...,0)$ to the solution of the particular sub-game G_i nearest to the Pareto surface of G_C, the player who would obtain a position of advantage must un-derwrite a side utility payment. Even though, under the particular arrange-ment of property rights, he is able to obtain a larger portion of the surplus than the other parties, according to this side payment model the payoff allo-cation will conform to the criterion of distribution proportional to relative need. We can therefore say that payoffs of those who after the social contract do not own property take the form of compensation for giving up their quo-tas of control. For example, consider the case of two players (fig 2.2). If A is a more efficient owner (because his investment is more important), this means that there is one feasible Constitution G_1 which gives the property right to A, with a payoff space P_1 whose solution is more efficient than that of the alternative Constitution G_2 which assigns the property to B, with pay-off space P_2. Thus, due to reasons of incentive, ownership must be given to A.

However, this does not change the fact that in order to obtain ownership A must take account of B's expectations and compensate him. The social contract establishes that the distribution must correspond to the constitution in which the various members of the co-operative coalition will be paid in proportion to their relative needs. This solution is calculated within the pay-off space P_3, generated by the convex combination of the outcomes associ-ated with the actually feasible I_1 e I_2 Constitutions and the *status quo* of G_C. This requires utility side payments, by which the party who makes the most efficient use of ownership compensates those who would be less efficient and consequently have to give up control. Compensation will last until the cooperative surplus is divided up according to the constitutional criterion.

Take the case of two people considered in section 1, in which A makes a specific investment but the decision of B, if by chance it is made available, is also indispensable. Let us suppose that allocating authority to agent A is more efficient, in the sense that the outcome under A's ownership, when he has a incentive to over-invest, is less far from *first best* efficiency than the outcome under B's ownership, when A has a incentive to under-invest. This will happen when the cost $c(d)$ is small compared to the value of the investment x. Let us suppose that both agents A and B are risk neutral. How large must the utility side payments be? To put it simply, since Nash's solution is calculated from the *status quo* $(0, 0)$, the surplus expected from the action x must be divided into those portions y and z (with both y and $z \geq 0$ and $x + z = 1$) that reflect the inclination of the boundary of the payoff space (resulting from the convex combination of the payoff spaces relative to the two feasible Constitutions plus the *status quo*), where it is cut by the straight line starting from the status quo and having the same inclination as the boundary itself in the tangency point (which happens only where the Nash product is at its maximum). Under the hypothesis of symmetry of the payoff space it is well-known that $y = z = \frac{1}{2}$, but it is clear that this hypothesis does not correspond to the case under consideration. In fact if one player is more efficient than the other in the exercise of property, then the solution ensured under the Constitution which gives him ownership will be asymmetrical with respect to the opposed solution which gives ownership to the other party. Thus the convex combination resulting from the respective payoff spaces is also asymmetrical and provides for an asymmetrical distribution, that is to say the solution does not lie on the 45° straight line starting from the origin. Furthermore, it is clear that the solution is not *first best*, since the convex combination of the spaces relative to the two feasible Constitutions is a proper subset of the space P, and this is reflected on the level of x and on the value of $V(x)$ which will normally result to be lower than under the Utopian constitution. However also for the non-Utopian constitutional contract C* the payoffs will take the form

$$U_A(C^*) = y \{p[V(x)\text{-}c(d)] - c(x)\}$$

$$U_B(C^*) = z \{p[V(x)\text{-}c(d)] - c(x)\}$$

and then the side utility payment T must be such that the payoff for B is

$$(1\text{-}p) [- \tfrac{1}{2}c(d)] + T = z \{p[V(x) - c(d)] - c(x)\}$$

while that for A

$$p[V(x) - c(\mathbf{d})] + [\tfrac{1}{2}c(\mathbf{d})](1 - p) - c(x) - T = y \{p[V(x) - c(\mathbf{d})] - c(x)\}$$

or to put it another way

$$T = z \{p[V(x) - c(\mathbf{d})] - c(x)\} + (1 - p) [\tfrac{1}{2}c(\mathbf{d})]$$

In other words the payoff calculated *ex ante* at time $t = 0$, must reward B with the portion z of the expected surplus on the hypothesis that the decision $\mathbf{d}$ is possible, and insure him against the possibility that if $\mathbf{d}$ is not possible A will nevertheless order B to bear its cost. The hypothesis of risk neutral players implies that the side payment T can be regarded as a sum which A pays B in exchange for the acquisition of property rights at time $t = 0$. Alternatively we may suppose that at time $t = 0$ A endorses the commitment to pay B the portion z of the surplus with probability p and half the cost $c(d)$ with the probability $1-p$ (supposing that the exercise of authority necessarily brings abuse with it). The system of rights ensuring this compensation at this point should be clear: it is a *Constitution of the firm* providing both for property rights and for a constraint on their exercise, that is, a duty to compensate the other party with the portion of the surplus established by the hypothetical constitutional agreement in the non-Utopian context which has to be complied with once the surplus has been generated.

Before concluding this section, we should make one further remark. Up to now we have proceeded on the basis of the constitutional contract as a theoretical stratagem for justifying a given arrangement of economic rights. We have therefore been able to assume that the choice of a set of institutions is the object of a co-operative game, the game G_C. This involves ignoring the compliance problem of the social contract and concentrating on the question relative to which of the available constitutional arrangements the players would be ready to enter once the problem of the possibility of co-operation has been taken as resolved. This approach is adequate only insofar as we stick to the moral perspective that considers an institutional arrangement justified when it is based on a unanimous agreement.

Obviously, the assumption that the social contract is a co-operative game is a problem in itself, since no explicit explanation has been given for the passage from the basic game G_N to the hypothetical game G_C. However, an additional problem arises if we consider the compensations. These are side payments of utility which do not belong explicitly to the actions included in the particular possible Constitutions. In the compensation case players in fact make a double choice by constitutional contract: on the one hand they choose the feasible Constitution which most approximates social efficiency (on the hypothesis that these rights are enforced at a later date), on the other hand they make the commitment that they will later carry out a side utility payment through which the parties who are placed at a disadvantage by the Constitution will be compensated, so that payoff equity is restored. However, in general we cannot take for granted that the party endowed with authority/property rights will endorse ex post simply to compensate the parties who will be under his authority. In fact *ex post* he will not have enough incentives to do it. But, by anticipating that, the other parties will have no reason to sign up to the constitutional contract.

Chapter 3

Games of Reputation and Compliance with the Social Contract

I. The Compliance Problem

An explicitly formulated code of ethics, or one that is implicitly shared by the parties making up a firm or any kind of organisation, must logically come before the firm or the organisation itself in that it expresses the constitutive social contract, which is the true underlying agreement of the firm that makes co-operation possible between all the organisation's *stakeholders*. This constitutional or moral agreement logically precedes and is more fundamental than the corporate contract itself in the legal sense (see for example any civil code where the corporation is defined as a *societas* based on the 'social contract' among *associates*), expressed by the statutes of the firm - usually intended to establish the reciprocal rights and duties between the partners or *shareholders* (holders of shares of ownership). In other words, regardless of the firm's legal ownership and governance structure, the parties (in the moral sense) of the firm's constitutional social contract are its *stakeholders*, who may be more numerous than the legal owners (*shareholders*) of the firm itself.

From the point of view of economics the ethical code - inasmuch as it is distinct from the law or the legally binding contract - constitutes an endogenous mechanism, capable of making its rules stand up for themselves. The ethical code must thus essentially be self-binding, that is it must generate the reason of compliance with the code itself, without relying - except in occasional circumstances - on an external power of enforcement. This property is typically required of moral norms, as their effectiveness does not depend on some external legal or political authority providing for their enforcement, but on a form of spontaneous adhesion. In fact this is required also of the *social contract* as moral foundation of legal and political authority: insofar as it plays the role of the fundamental justification, it cannot be based on a superior authority that enforces compliance with it, given that the ultimate basis of any authority is represented by the social contract itself. What constitutes an authority is that some individuals, forgoing part of their own

55

freedom of action, transfer that freedom of action to a third party, the latter being placed in a position of authority as a consequence of the acceptance of that position by the former. Thus, until this transfer is effective - in terms of practical acceptance of orders the authority puts forward - the authority cannot be said to be effectively established. Consequently, if there is no compliance with the social contract, it cannot be said that acceptance of authority has practical effectiveness. It therefore follows that there is no subject with properly established authority who could be asked to impose the norms set out by the social contract itself.

Contractarianism thus embodies the idea of a self-supporting system of norms. But this is also the paradox of the contractarian program. We assume as starting point a situation of anarchic interaction, structured as the well-known *Prisoner's Dilemma* (PD) game (see fig.3.1). This is a game where every participant has an individual 'opportunist' strategy, consisting of failing to respect any pact or promise as far as it is practically possible to do that, and avoiding any cooperative effort towards others, while attempting to take advantage of any cooperative effort of others (call this strategy D: *defection*). This strategy dominates over another individual strategy consisting in undertaking and complying with the commitment of 'doing one's part' in a joint plan (call this strategy C: *cooperation*). This Hobbesian 'natural state' is a situation of interaction with a single equilibrium (moreover in dominant strategies) that is clearly socially sub-optimal but nevetheless individually rational: for each party to defect from any agreement that could help the parties in planning a joint cooperative venture.

	C	D
C	2,2	0,3
D	3,0	1,1

Figure 3.1 *Prisoner's dilemma*

This interaction structure rationally justifies the idea of a social contract that establishes a constitutional framework of rights and a legal system that allows for positions of authority whose role it is to enforce the fundamental framework of rights. The idea is that the constitution of rights and the legal system of authority set up to protect it should be able to modify the interaction structure between the participants in the social interaction by discouraging non-cooperative behaviour and rewarding the cooperative. However, as long as the anarchic interaction has the PD structure, this structure will generally prevail in making ineffective the compliance with any pacts and promises, including that special pact or promise that constitutes the 'social contract'. This means that defection from the social contract, as well as from any other contract, will prevail in this situation. On the other hand we know that until the social contract is not able to elicit the spontaneous compliance of the majority of subscribers, it cannot be said that an authority relationship, where individuals transfer a share of their natural liberty to those placed in positions of authority, has been effectively accepted.

What I am saying is that the authority of the law comes from its acceptance on the part of the subscribers to the social contract, which is made manifest by their effective willingness to comply with norms and regulations. But in a PD interaction structure, the parties do not cooperate, that is they do not respect pacts or promises, and thus - even if they have nominally subscribed a social contract - they do not respect the obligation of obeying the law. In a PD interaction, thus, the strategy of defection being dominant for each participant in the game means that nobody will cooperate with the others in a joint action consisting in supporting or merely conforming to the constitution and the legal system of authority embodied in it. In essence, the paradoxical nature of the *Prisoners' Dilemma* (not from the point of view of the mathematical theory - in that there is no paradox and the solution is uniquely determined as rarely happens in non-cooperative games, but from the point of a rational choice theory of social institutions) consist in that it appeals to a solution via the social contract, but at the same time it contradicts the contractarian solution itself, at least as long as we accept the hypothesis that anarchic interaction is fully represented by a PD-like interaction structure. On the other hand, were this hypothesis made to fall, the paradox of the social contract would disappear, but the urgency of the contractarian solution would also no longer apply, inasmuch as it has been worked out as a construction tailored to the problem of the 'self-defeating' (or simply inefficient) character of 'natural' anarchic interaction. Thus, to speak by analogy with a well known paradox in logic, if the formal theory of PD-games is a *complete* description of the game the players play when they interact in the pre-institutional setting, then the social contract solution cannot be *coherent*, and if it has to be *coherent* then the PD theory of the game cannot be *complete*.

An apparent answer to this problem would be one where the agents, in adhering to the social contract, put themselves in an *ex ante* perspective, from which they can appreciate the social benefits of establishing a legal system without having the disposition to consider (thanks to some form of 'impartiality') the incentives to defect. If they adhere, the authority of the legal system is thus *constituted* and *consequently* the constituted authority would be effective in discouraging opportunistic behaviour. But this justification does not stand up. It identifies the rationality of *adhering* to the social contract, and thus the rationality of *effectively* accepting the authority of the legal system – guaranteeing the compliance with the stated obligations– simply with *ex ante* rationality, i.e. rationality of *entering* into the social contract. The rationality of *adhering* to the social contract requires, however, two conditions which must both be satisfied: *first* the rationality of *entering*, or *ex ante* rationality, which considers the social benefit of the passage from anarchic interaction to a constitutionally well-ordered society. *Second* the rationality of *respecting*, or complying with the contract, i.e. *ex post* rationality, which involves evaluation of the *individual incentives* to respect or not respect the obligations laid down by the legal system. It is erroneous to believe that one implies the other: they follow from *two* distinct sets of conditions. One coincides with the conditions for a *Pareto efficient* outcome, the other with the conditions for an *equilibrium point* – i.e. individual rationality of compliance for each player, given the expectations of what the other players will do[1].

If the rationality of respecting is not satisfied, it cannot be said that, although the parties recognise the *ex ante* rationality, they have effectively adhered to the social contract and that, thus, they are effectively willing to accept the consequent authority and obligations. But if they have not effectively adhered, i.e. they have not effectively transferred the exercise of part of their freedom of action to the authority - provided for in the legal system - then the authority is *empty* and cannot in anyway be effective in enforcing the law.

---

[1] For similar conceptualisation of the decision of adhering to the social contract cf. Gauthier (1969) and Gauthier (1986). Moreoever see Sacconi (1993a).

3. GAMES OF REPUTATION AND COMPLIANCE

In order to better explain the double nature of the *ex ante* and *ex post* perspectives, we can distinguish between *justification context* and *implementation context*. The first is concerned with reasons justifying the social contract, including impartial considerations such as social efficiency and equity, the second is concerned with an individual's decision to respect a duty on the basis of the real motivation the agent has. The first perspective is impartial, whereas the second is agent-relative, i.e. it concerns the reasons the agent has, in that he is *that particular* individual, characterised by *his* preferences and beliefs.[2] We assume here that agent-relative individual motivations are described by some theory of rational self-interested choice. Thus the aim of a theory of implementation is to work out the conditions which ensure that real motivations of the agent converge with justification in upholding justified norms. This convergence cannot be assumed from the outset however, but must be appropriately demonstrated. The problem is that in an implementation context, characterised as PD, self-interested reasons do not naturally converge towards the goal of upholding justified norms.

II. Approaches to the Compliance Problem

This problem is not new in the social contract tradition. John Rawls, for example, in *A Theory of Justice* (1971) looks at it in dealing with the subject of the *ex post* stability of the two principles of justice, that are to be chosen behind the "veil of ignorance" (i.e. *ex ante*). He concludes honestly that the choice is not stable *ex post* if we analyse individuals' behaviour in terms of a theory of self-interested rationality. Then he suggests the development of moral sentiments: from infancy to maturity a sense of justice is developed, enabling individuals, who are thus appropriately motivated, to respect the principles of justice inasmuch as they are impartially justifiable. It is fairly clear from Rawls argument that the sense of justice does not come from the development of rational self-interest, but from the growth of the sphere within which we can cultivate primitive sentiments of altruism and love. It is evident, however, that this solution tames the compliance problem rather than solving it. If we start with an 'implementation' theory in which indi-

---

2   See Nagel (1986) ch.9.

vidual motivations are originally not self-interested, it is fairly clear that they will eventually converge with the upholding of *ex ante* justified principles (in fact the use of the *ex ante* rational choice model in Rawls' original theory proves to be no more than a purely deductive stratagem).

If, on the other hand, we adhere to the view that a theory of social contract or ethical code implementation has to be based on the assumption that the parties respond to self-interested incentives, there are two lines of thought in the literature, which both attempt to demonstrate the rationality of taking on commitment within PD-like situations:

a) the theory of *rational moral constraint* (Gauthier 1986, McClennen 1990a 1990b, Danielson 1992); this theory holds that a rational player will be ready to submit to a moral constraint of conditional cooperation, since a morally constrained player will exploit the opportunity of cooperating with other morally constrained players, while he would not be bound to undergo exploytation by unconstrained opponents without protecting himself by symmetrical non-cooperation.

b) The theory of repeated games of *reputation* (Kreps and Wilson 1982, Kreps, Milgrom, Roberts and Wilson, 1982, Fudenberg and Levine 1989, 1992). This is based on the intuition that players have an incentive to respect commitments from the beginning of a repeated game, because of their interest in keeping their reputation high in view of future transactions. That is they will act in such a way to confirm the opponents' belief that the player is in fact committed to follow a cooperative strategy – a strategy compatible with mutually advantageous outcomes.

The two lines of thought appear to follow a common approach: compliance with the social contract (the respect of the commitment to act in accordance with it) is motivated by the individual advantages that each player will gain from reciprocal cooperation if commitments are respected. The theory of agent's motivation is in both cases apparently realistic and agent-relative. However there are more differences than similarities. The theory of rational moral constraint - which does not concern us here[3]- suggests *first* to investigate a meta-decision problem where rules of rational behaviour are to be chosen and *then* to consider how, by means of the decision rules chosen, a one-shot PD-like interactive decision problem may to be faced. It says that, by considering the effects on the second step, it is rational at the first move to substitute the rationality rule that leads to an inefficient

---

[3]   See Sacconi (1995) where this theory is analysed and at the end rejected.

solution of the PD with an alternative rationality rule – i.e. 'constrained maximisation' - which would prove to be a better approach to deal with the one-shot game finally faced . This implies changing the pattern of practical motivation according to which the single PD is faced, and – let me insist – this is accomplished via a meta-choice, i.e. a choice about rules or dispositions for dealing with the PD. Although this choice must always satisfy the request of maximising the overall player's utility, it no longer needs to identify with straightforward maximisation of payoffs. Notice that no repetition of the game is involved in this approach. On the contrary, for this approach to be successful *psychological moral dispositions* must already exist, i.e. patterns of behaviour that do not incorporate strategic reasoning in their own operating and that can constrain behaviour *at distance*. This must be assumed in order to make sense of a decision between alternative dispositions. Only after this independent assumption - about the pre-existence and the power of dispositions in determining later behaviour - has been made, can the decision to enter such dispositions be rationally justifiable.

Thus compliance in the real sense is not dealt with by Gauthier and other theoreticians of rational moral constraint, because it is guaranteed at the outset by the binding nature of dispositions. Once the rule has been chosen, given that compliance is guaranteed by the corresponding disposition, there is practically no choice to be made about whether to follow the rule or not. The rule is put into practice in the circumstances called for by its conditional formulation, not because of a decision about the opportunity of respecting or not respecting it, but only because acting accordingly corresponds to a disposition that says *to do that*. Thus, in a strict sense, Gauthier does not succeed in solving the compliance problem. All his theory is, in a sense, a theory of *ex ante* choice: *first*, the choice of the terms of agreement according to some cooperative bargaining principle and *second*, the individual choice of whether to develop a disposition encouraging compliance with those terms of agreement or not. Contrary to what Gauthier himself says, his theory of *external rationality* answers the question about which disposition it is more rational to endorse and develop, not the question of whether it is rationally worthwhile to respect *ex post* the choice taken within the *ex ante* perspective. After having entered the appropriate disposition, in fact, this choice simply vanishes.

The second line of thought - which we will be looking at in this chapter - shows that the rationality of honouring commitments depends on the existence of a series of games still to be played, in which reputation is deemed by the players to be an important asset, in that it encourages both the sides to adopt a behaviour that is the most advantageous for the players themselves. The rationality rule, which leads us to reason in this way, is the same as the one that in the one-shot PD game leads the players to use the strategies making up the single (dominant, although inefficient) Nash equilibrium. Motivational assumptions are kept to a minimum and do not require any deviation from the 'best-reply' game theoretical logic. Rather, the most important assumptions cover the beliefs of the parties about their reciprocal rationality. This view does not therefore presuppose the effectiveness of any moral psychology, seen as independent of strategic calculation. It seems thus capable of facing squarely the compliance problem within implementation contexts where the reasons of the players are assumed to be genuinely agent-relative and self-interested.

This point was anticipated by David Hume in his *Treatise on Human Nature* when, having stated that conformity to rules of justice could initially be based only on selfish interests[4], he tries to resolve the apparent contradiction between this statement and the other in which he states that selfishness in the natural state gives rise to inefficient results, which are inescapable if you keep only to the natural forces of self-interest[5]. Hume gives a solution in terms of the rise of artificial social conventions, or regular patterns of behaviour constituted by systems of reciprocally consistent actions, that are based in their turn on common knowledge of the common interest, in the light of which everyone is better off conforming to rules under the hypothesis that others do the same[6]. It is important to underline that in this way, according to Hume, a convention is not necessarily based on binding promises, since the system of reciprocal expectations is a sufficient condition to induce conformity to the convention, as long as the convention itself represents an equilibrium behaviour of all the agents[7]. However, awareness of such com-

---

[4]   Cf. Hume (1976) p.479-483.
[5]   Cf. ibid. p.486. As a comment on Hume's theory of conventions see also Magri (1994).
[6]   Cf. Hume (1976) pp.490-491.
[7]   "This convention is not of the nature of a *promise*: For even promises themselves, as we shall see afterwards, arise from human conventions. It is only a sense of common interest, which sense all the members of society express to one another, and which induces them to regulate their conduct by certain rules: I observe, that it will be for my interest to leave another in the possession of his goods, *provided* he will act in the same manner with regard to me. He is sensi-

mon interest cannot come from the narrow perspective of a single act or a one-shot interaction. It requires a wider perspective or what we could call the perspective of long-run interaction:

"A single act of justice is frequently contrary to public interest; and were it to stand alone, without being follow'd by other acts, may, in itself, be very prejudicial to society [...] Nor is every single act of justice, consider'd apart, more conductive to private interest [...] When therefore men have had experience enough to observe, that whatever may be the consequence of any single act of justice, perform'd by a single person, yet the whole system of actions, concurr'd in the by the whole society, is infinitely advantageous to the whole and to every part; it is not long before justice and property take place. Every member of the society is sensible of this interest: every one expresses this sense to his fellows, along with the solution he has taken of squaring his act by it, on condition that others will do the same. No more is requisite to induce anyone of them to perform an act of justice, who has the first opportunity. This become an example to others. And thus justice establishes itself by a kind of convention or agreement; that is, by a sense of interest, suppos'd to be common to all, and where every single act is perform'd in expectation that others are to perform the like".[8]

In another point Hume also introduce the idea of a system of reciprocally consistent expectations based on repeating the game and learning trough repetition:

"[a convention] arises gradually, and acquires force by a slow progression, and by our repeated experience of the inconveniences of transgressing it. On the contrary, this experience assures still more, that the sense of inter-

---

ble of a like interest in the regulation of his conduct. When this common sense of interest is mutually express'd, and is known to both, it produces a suitable resolution and behaviour. And this may properly enough be call'd a convention or agreement betxit us, tho' without the interposition of a promise; since the actions of each of us have a reference to those of the other, and are perform'd upon the supposition that something is to be perform'd on the other part. Two men who pull the oars of a boat, do it by an agreement or convention, tho' they have never given promise to each other", ibid, p.490.

8 Ivi. pp.497-498.
9 Ivi p.490.

est has become common to all our fellows, and gives us a confidence of the future regularity of their conduct".[9]

To sum up, Hume admits that if compliance with social convention is to be self-enforcing, that is the behaviour required by the rules is to be put into practice simply on account of reciprocal interests to conform, the agents must take a long run perspective and consider the repetition of a basic situation that does not have conformity as its immediate equilibrium outcome. Moreover, he holds that reciprocally consistent expectations are the result of an inductive learning process by means of which we repeatedly observe others' behaviour and progressively build up reliable beliefs about the fact that behaviour of others conforms to the same rule we also conform to.

III. Strategic Rationality and Endogenous Sanction of Contractual Commitments

The idea behind the theory of reputation effects in repeated games is that, although the given commitments in a single game need not be binding or irrevocable and although in any single game there may be prevalent incentives to not respect the given commitments, thanks to the repetitive nature of the game respecting commitments in the single stage games may become part of an equilibrium path of the general repeated game. Thus the choice of repeated game equilibrium strategies upholds conformity to commitments in any single stage games.

The concept of reputation is implicit in all solutions where it is shown that the possibility of cooperation arises out of the repetition of a basic game (call it the stage game) having PD structure. The idea behind all these solutions is that, if the game is repeated several times, a player who suffers from opportunistic actions of another player in one period is in a position to punish the other player in the next by adopting in turn opportunistic behaviour. At the same time this same player may decide to choose in each repetition of the stage game actions having reciprocally advantageous outcomes ('being cooperative' in the DP game) making this decision conditional on the absence of opportunistic behaviour of the opponent along all the repetition of the stage game. In this way we may ask whether the existence of an endogenous sanction, i.e. a sanction decided by the player himself via the use of strategies that make up the repeated game, can induce an equilibrium of cooperation in the repeated game.

3. GAMES OF REPUTATION AND COMPLIANCE

The *Tit for Tat* strategy (cooperate in the first period and thereafter replicate the same strategy as that used by the opponent in the previous game) is a typical example of a strategy that *first* incorporates a sanction conditional on the opponent's behaviour in the stage immediately preceding the stage game at hand, and *secondly* offers the possibility of cooperating in the future if the opponent also cooperates. Intuitively a player who is known to have adopted a *Tit for Tat* strategy is one who has the reputation of punishing any defection by the opponent with a defection in the next period and rewarding any cooperation by the opponent adopting a cooperative action in the next period.

The threat implicit in a repeated game strategy is nevertheless not enough to demonstrate that compliance with a pact or a promise is supported by an equilibrium path in the repeated game. If in fact the horizon within which the game is played is not long enough, the threat of endogenous sanction is not strong enough to disincentive recourse to unilateral defection. If the horizon is finite and known to the players, they will be faced in the last stage game with a strategic interaction situation which is identical to the typical one-shot Prisoners' Dilemma; thus in the last period, with no future perspective that can make a threat of punishment to a player defecting in the present game, the players will inevitably fall back on the dominant strategy of the stage games, i.e. reciprocal defection. But then in the second-to-last stage game, they will know that there is no benefit to be gained or punishment to be avoided by adopting a cooperative strategy (in other words there is no credit or reputation to be gained in view of the final repetition). Thus, in the second-to-last stage game too each player's dominant strategy of the stage games will prevail. In this way, however, in the third-from-last stage game the perspective facing the players is identical to that described for the second-to-last. This reasoning can thus be passed by *backwards induction* back to the first period of the game. The only equilibrium path throughout the entire game is ever defecting at any stage game.[10]

One condition for Humes's intuition to be valid is, then, that the horizon of the repeated game should be infinite. But the absence of a horizon that is sufficiently long to make endogenous punishment strategy effective results even if the horizon is actually infinite (i.e. if the game is repeated *ad infini-*

---

[10] A delightful proof of this result may was first given by in Luce and Raiffa (1957). Cf. ibidem pp.97-103

tum) but anyway future gains do not have sufficient value for the players. Players may be short sighted devaluing too much the benefits of future coooperation compared to those of immediate defection, due to an excessive discount rate of utility over time. Thus the second (more general) condition to guarantee the existence of a set of repeated game equilibria where the players adopt strategies of sanctions and cooperation conditional on previous opponent's behaviour, is that the discount rate of utility over time (the *impatience* rate) should not be too high.

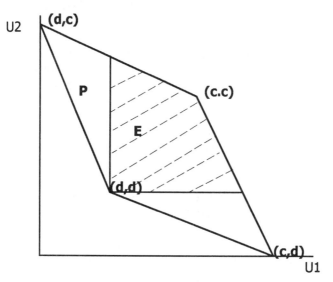

Figure 3.2 *Points (d,d), (c,d) , (d,c) and (c,c) correspond to the four payoffs of the stage PD game and are avarage payoffs of players gaining in each stage game the corresponding payoff. Their convex combination generates the space P.*

---

[11]   To be precise, in repeated PD games the relevant relationship is the ratio of the two payoffs differences of unilateral successful defection less that of reciprocal cooperation, and of unilateral successful defection less that of reciprocal defection, i.e in our case the discount rate must be

$$\delta \geq u_i (d,c) - u_i (c,c) / u_i(d,c) - u_i (d,d) = \frac{1}{2}.$$

For a general proof of a series of Folk Theorems see Fudenberg and Maskin (1986).

3. GAMES OF REPUTATION AND COMPLIANCE

In fact 'common sense' in game theory tells us that if repetitions are infinite and the discount rate of utility over time is not excessive in terms of the parameters of the game - and here I mean the ratio amongst the difference between payoffs of the different outcomes of the stage game - then there are repeated game equilibria which the players can play maintaining reciprocal cooperation throughout he whole game or part of it[11]. For example the *Tit for Tat* strategy is a repeated game equilibrium strategy, in that it is a best reply against itself (Axelrod 1984): then if a player adopts *Tit for Tat* his opponent's best reply is to adopt *Tit for Tat* himself.

The case for the existence of equilibria that are very different to the one requiring the adoption of the defection strategies in every stage DP game is, however, very general. Indeed, a variety of results that make up what is known in game theory as *Folk Theorem*, show that, having established the lowest payoffs that players can expect to obtain by adopting an equilibrium strategy, there is a large multiplicity of equilibria that offer a higher payoff than this. Applying *Folk Theorem* to the repeated PD is immediate. The strategy combination that requires both players to defect for the whole duration of the repeated game identifies an equilibrium point and in particular the equilibrium corresponding to the maximin strategy of each player. The average of the maximin payoffs throughout the repetition of the game is what the players manage to gain in the worst possible case. This equilibrium identifies the lower boundary of the equilibrium set of the game: every equilibrium must guarantee the players at least an average payoff equal to the average maximin payoff assured by the equilibrium of permanent reciprocal defection.

We shall now look at the region of utility space within the positive *hortant* of the cartesian axes U_1 e U_2 where the payoffs associated with the four outcomes of the Prisoners' Dilemma stage game are represented (see fig.3.2). Let's create the space P by the convex combination of the four payoff pairs of the PD stage game and say that the points enclosed in that space represent all the average payoffs associated with possible ways of playing the repeated game by two players. This means that on average the players may get every time the payoffs of one of the four outcomes (d,d), (c,d) (d,c) (c,c) or any combination of some of them. In this space the average payoff of reciprocal defection (d_1, d_2) sets the lower boundary of the average payoffs in the equilibrium set of the game. We can then generate the area E inside space P (shaded in fig.3.2), representing the average payoffs of all the equilibrium strategies combinations of the two players in the repeated game.

Folk theorem says that every point in the area E of space P corresponds to a pair of average payoffs that the two players can obtain if they play an equilibrium strategy against the equilibrium strategy adopted by their opponent. Hence the most interesting and problematic aspect of *Folk Theorem* is not the existence of repeated game equilibria other than that of repeated defection but rather, the fact that these other equilibria are an infinite set and consequently the solution to the game, unlike in the one shot game, is indeterminate - unless we are able to work out an appropriate theory of equilibrium selection[12].

IV. Explicitly Modelled Reputation Effects

Up to now reputation has been treated as a notion implicit in the solutionsf to the PD structured problem of cooperation. Reputation becomes an explicit notion when a peculiar form of uncertainty about players behaviour is introduced. In particular, the players, or some of them, may be uncertain about their opponent's *type*. By *type* we mean a rule of behaviour that the player might automatically follow; the player belonging to a certain *type* follows certain rules of conduct that add up to a repeated game strategy, determining which action will be taken in any single stage game.

---

[12] We have to turn then to theories of equilibrium selection which may be *eductive* (i.e. based on the simulation inside the players' mind of a process of outguessing regress and reciprocal adaptation of the players' beliefs, until that a system of mutually consistent expectations emerges that justifies a given equilibrium as the solution of the game) or *evolutive* (i.e. based on a mechanism of natural selection of the fittest strategies: short-sighted players play strategies during the course of repeated random encounters scoring the relevant payoffs; the process evolves until that only players adopting the fittest strategies remain in the game as a function of their cumulative payoffs). For this distinction see Binmore (1887/88). Eductive processes originated with Harsanyi (1975) - see also Harsanyi and Selten (1988), and its first application to the theory of social contract can be found in Sacconi (1993b). For evolutionary game theory and the evolutionary selection of equilibria see Sugden (1986), Weibull (1995), Samuelson (1997). Applications to the theory of social contract are found in Skyrms (1996) and Binmore (1998).

3. GAMES OF REPUTATION AND COMPLIANCE

We can envisage *types* by characterising them with the hypothesis that they follow invariably one specific strategy within those logically possible in the repeated game. Some of these may coincide with playing every time an equilibrium strategies of the basic game. Others may be totally idiosyncratic and irrational from the point of view of strategically rational behaviour as it is defined when the game is seen without the kind of uncertainty described here. In other words, *types* can be seen as alternative forms of commitment and rule following behaviour: a specimen of player who is committed to follow some strategy independently of any sophisticated strategic reasoning about the game. It is usual in this literature that types are divided into two classes: 'the rational' that commits the player to adopt actions corresponding to the equilibrium strategies of the stage game and the 'irrational' that commits the player to adopt acts that as such do not correspond to equilibria[13].

Notice that all this uncertainty concerns only the state of information that one player has about the other - for example player 1 about player 2 - while the second player must not actually be identified by any *type*. As a matter of fact, player 2 is a strategically rational player and as such he will act on the basis of an equilibrium strategy, i.e. a best reply to the behaviour adopted by the other player – given his state of information. On the contrary player 1 believes that player 2 may effectively be with very high probability 1-p a type whose behaviour is that of a rational and strategic player, as he in fact is, but at the same time he also believes that player 2 might be an idiosyncratic *type*, following a predetermined rule in a non-strategic and stereotyped way, possibly with small but positive probability p. Thus the strategy choice player 1 will adopt during the course of the repeated game must reflect this state of uncertainty, i.e. it is built up of the choices he makes in each stage game in order to maximise his expected *payoff*, given the probability distribution on the opponent's actions which at each stage game is induced by the probability of *types*. The uncertain player, given the prior probability of the opponent's *types*, gets some evidence from observation of the opponent's behaviour during the repeated game and updates his probabilistic beliefs about *types*. Then he defines in each repetition the rational

---

[13] The beginning of the reputation effects models literature dates at the publication of three connected papers by Kreps and Wilson (1982), Milgrom and Roberts (1982) and Kreps, Milgrom, Roberts and Wilson (1982) which made for the first time these typical assumptions. Nowadays it is a flowering field; for a systematic view see Fudenberg and Tirole (1991) ch.9.

behaviour to be adopted for the remaining part of the repeated game (and consequently the action for the current stage game) in terms of his subjective best reply, given the current probability of each of the opponent's actions in the light of the probability of *types*.

Now, player 2 is assumed to be aware of player 1's uncertainty and reasoning. The calculation of her rational behaviour cannot ignore the hypothesis about player 1's uncertainty. She will decide her behaviour during the game in such a way as to confirm the opponent's beliefs that will give him the incentive to choose the action that offers higher *payoffs* to player 2 herself. Thus, player 2's best reply must be defined in the light of the beliefs it induces given the form of uncertainty about *types* on the part of player 1. This approach makes it possible to find a 'cooperative' solution to the PD game even if it is repeated a finite number of times, i.e. it is capable of providing a proof for the statement that there is an equilibrium path of the repeated game along which players cooperate reciprocally at least a certain number of times from the beginning, which is determinable on the basis of the value of the parameters of the game, except for a final period that is independent of the length of the repeated game[14].

The most useful reputation effect theory for our purpose is that defined for a special class of repeated games based on the hypothesis that there is one constant (long-run) player (throughout all the repetitions) who plays against an infinite series of single period (short-run) players, who take turns in repetitions of the stage game. This class of games has been studied by Fudenberg and Levine (1989, 1991). They can be understood as formal

---

[14] The result shown by Kreps, Milgrom, Robert and Wilson (1982) is however much more general than that outlined here. To give a simple intuition, we can say that for probability $p > 0$ but as small as you like, assigned to the player 2's *type*, constrained to use Tit for Tat, if the game is repeated a finite but sufficiently large number (N) of times (N>M) and if the utility discount rate is near to 1, there is a sequential equilibrium under which for a number of periods the two players will use 'cooperative' actions of the stage game and these periods last for the entire repeated game (N-M) except for a final number of periods M, where M is independent of the global duration of the game (and depends on the *payoff* and p). This equilibrium allows the total players' *payoff* to approximate that which they would obtain if the rule of the game were such that the players were able to undertake binding commitments to use a strategy of conditional cooperation.

models of situations where an institution or organisation which is stable over time, for instance a firm, an hospital or a university, interacts with single individuals in turn – one workers or consumers, an individual patient or student at a time. These interactions are repeated with an infinite series of workers or consumers, patients or students who are different each time, while the institution or the organisation last for the entire repetition of the basic game.

The interpretation that most interests us here is that of the firm, under-stood as the institutional player who remains stable over time, and a series of individual stakeholders whose interaction with the firm may be for a single period. We will look at the theory with reference to a typical stage game ('the game of trust')[15] in which any short-run player at the time when he is called over to play, must decide whether to enter or not (**e** or **non-e**) in rela-tions with the permanent (long-run) player (for example enter his shop to purchase goods or enter his employment) and the long-run player must de-cide whether to abuse his trust or not (**a** or **non-a**), for example by offering a high or low quality good, or whether to abuse or not his power of decision. Let's assume that the short-run player must move first, thus enabling the long-run player to make the second decision. We must also assume, how-ever, that the two players learn the result of the game together with the rela-tive payoffs simultaneously at the end of each stage game, so that the normal form of the game in fig. 3.3 represents the same game as the extended form of fig.3.4.

	a	non-a
e	-1,3	2,2
non-e	0,0	0,0

Figure 3.3 *The game of trust – normal form.*

---

[15]   This is the name of the game after Kreps (1990c)

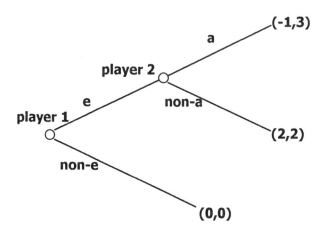

Figure 3.4 *The game of trust - extended form.*

In the stage game the pair of actions (**non-e, a**) is the only Nash equilibrium feasible but it is sub-optimal given that the outcome (0,0) is Pareto dominated by (2,2). Under this equilibrium the first (short-run) player does not enter for fear of suffering the non-cooperative action **a** of the second player. Thus, the stage game turns out to be an adaptation of the Prisoner's Dilemma from the idea that the initiative of opportunistic behaviour may be one-sided (under player 2's control), but the first player may nevertheless have an anticipatory and defensive strategy to escape his opponent's opportunism and end the game with a failure of cooperation.

V. The Repeated Game between One Long-run Player and an Infinite Series of Short-run Players

We will now consider the repeated game between a single long-run player and the infinite succession of short-run players.[16]

---

[16] This presentation is based largely on Fudenberg (1991) and Fudenberg and Tirole (1991), see also Fudenberg, Kreps and Maskin (1990), Fudenberg and Maskin (1986).

3. GAMES OF REPUTATION AND COMPLIANCE

Strategies Let h^t be the history of the repeated game where t is the number of repetitions of a stage game which has been played up to repetition t. Each history describes one possible sequence of actions the long-run player and the various short-run players may have taken up to repetition t. We can then define the set of possible histories of the game up to repetition t by H^t.

A long-run player *strategy* is defined as a function that for each history $h^t \in H^t$ determines which action of the stage game will be used by the long-run player from repetition t+1 on, where t has any value (from 1 to infinity). Obviously, since a short run player participates in a single repetition of the stage game, a strategy will be a function that, for all the possible histories of the game up to the repetition before the one he takes part in, determines the action he will choose in the current stage game. The length of the history of which the short-run player's action is a function obviously depends on the point at which the player enters the game.

Payoff functions Since his *payoff* depends only on the stage game he takes part in, the short-run player is interested in the outcome of that game only. He is thus *short-sighted* and tries to predict only the action that the long-run player will take in the game he is involved in, ignoring any predictions about the further development of the game.

The long-run player, on the other hand, has a *payoff* function which is built up as the infinite sum of the *payoffs* received from all the stage games; the *payoff* received from each stage enters into the sum multiplied by a discount rate which is 1 at the first repetition and δ (between 0 and 1) at the second repetition, δ^2 at the third, δ^3 at the fourth, δ^4 at the fifth, etc. The discount rate is the value the long-run player attaches to future utility or, if you like, his "impatience" level (of course the greater the value of δ, the greater the value of future utility for the player). Unless his impatience makes him evaluate positively only the *payoffs* from the nearest repetitions, the long-run player is *far-sighted*, in that he is interested in predicting how the various future short-run players will act, in terms of the various strategies they will adopt. Consequently his game strategy is chosen not only as a result of the current game, but also in terms of the effect this strategy will have on the short-sighted behaviour of the short-run player in any further repetitions of the game.

73

3.5 THE REPEATED GAME

Initial beliefs   We will now introduce the typical assumption of all reputation effects models: all short-run players believe it possible to meet more than one *type* of long-run player, where a *type* can be defined as a particular idiosyncratic way of playing the repeated game. Thus, we can identify a *type* with a commitment to use a particular strategy all through the game. In the stage games the presence of a particular *type* is revealed by the fact that in each repetition the player's action is decided by a given predetermined rule. To illustrate this we will describe three possible *types* of long-run player:

$\theta 1$, the *ethically constrained type*: $\theta 1$'s strategy is to always use **non-a** from the first repetition to the last, independently of the game history;

$\theta 2$, *the rational stage game type*; $\theta 2$'s strategy is to always use the dominant strategy of the stage game with respect to all the game histories;

$\theta 3$, the *unpredictable type*: $\theta 3$ uses a mixed strategy with 0.75 probability of choosing the dominant strategy in each stage game, and 0.25 probability of choosing the **non-a** strategy.

In actual fact the third *type* is only a sample of a family of *types* whose typical strategies use some combination of the two pure actions during the repeated game, according to either a deterministic mechanism (e.g. use **non-a** for the first M times and the dominant strategy of the stage game thereafter) or a random mechanism, as in the mixed strategy described above. In order to simplify the analysis, $\theta 3$ is the only *type* explicitly considered here. In a more general analysis it is, however, reasonable to assume that the short-run player takes a number of different *types* like $\theta 3$ into consideration. In fact, there could be various attitudes to strategic behaviour behind the decision to adopt a mixed strategy: for example, making it difficult to predict the player's choice, or pretending to be a cooperative player for a certain number of repetitions to induce error in the short-run player. The short-run players express their beliefs about the actual *type* of long-run player by assigning subjective probabilities to the *types*. We assume that the prior probability of $\theta 1$ is $q°$ before any observation, and that the remaining *types* share the remaining probability $(1-q°)$. In fact, it can be seen that admitting only a slight initial probability of the "ethically constrained" *type* is sufficient for cooperation to emerge amongst the players.

74

3. GAMES OF REPUTATION AND COMPLIANCE

Updating rule In the light of the game history the short-run players update their beliefs about *types*: for every observed outcome of the short-run game, i.e. the action of the long-run player in each stage game, they calculate the conditional probability of each *type* according to Baye's rule. For example, after a history h^t. in which only **non-a** actions have been observed, and given the **non-a** observation of the most recent repetition, the conditional probability of *type* $\theta 1$ will be

$$q(\theta 1|\textbf{non-a}, h^t) = \frac{\text{prob}(\textbf{non-a}|\theta 1, h^t)\, q(\theta 1|\, h^t)}{p(\textbf{non-a}|\, h^t)}$$

where

$p(\textbf{non-a}|h^t) = \text{prob}(\textbf{non-a}|\theta 1, h^t) \times q(\theta 1|h^t + \text{prob}(\textbf{non-a}|\theta 2, h^t) \times q(\theta 2| h^t) + \text{prob}(\textbf{non-a}|\theta 3, h^t) \times q(\theta 3| h^t)$

Let's say that the probability of the first *type* after the history h^t has reached $q(\theta 1|h^t) = 0.1$ and that, in the light of the past history, the probabilities of the other two *types* are 0.45 and 0.45 (to be sure if the history h^t includes only **non-a** observations, *type* $\theta 2$, who never uses **non-a** should have zero probability; but we may then take $t = 0$ or decide that *type* $\theta 2$ may be more sophisticated than thought and modelling it with a strategy meant to confuse the short-run player by using **non-a** actions in the first t repetitions and using the dominant stage game action from t+1 onwards). In this case, the likelihood functions of evidence for the various *types* are

$\text{prob}(\textbf{non-a}|\theta 1, h^t) = 1$ (*type* $\theta 1$ must always use **non-a**);

$\text{prob}(\textbf{non-a}|\theta 2, h^t) = 0$ (*type* $\theta 2$ never uses **non-a**, or never uses it after t repetitions);

$\text{prob}(\textbf{non-a}|\theta 3, h^t) = 0.25$ (*type* $\theta 3$ uses **non-a** one fourth of times)

thus the conditional probability of *type* $\theta 1$ will be $q(\theta 1|\textbf{non-a}, h^t) = 0.1/0.212 = 0.47$. By a similar calculation the conditional probability of the other two *types* will be $q(\theta 2|\textbf{non-a}, h^t) = 0$ (in fact the observation **non-a** falsifies the hypothesis that player 1 is *type* $\theta 2$) and $q(\theta 3|\textbf{non-a}, h^t) = 0.53$.

Reputation   The reputation of the long-run player is defined as the distribution of probability of possible *types*. In other words the long-run player has the reputation of being *type* $\theta 1$ with probability q_1, *type* $\theta 2$ with probability $q_2 = x(1-q_1)$ and *type* $\theta 3$ with probability $q_3 = 1-x(1-q_1)$, for $1 \leq x \leq 0$. Regarding the "ethically constrained" *type*, reputation reduces to nil if any short-run player witnesses the long-run player using action **a** just once. Similarly the reputation of being *type* $\theta 2$ is cancelled if the short-run player witnesses one occurrence of **non-a** action. Other *types* of reputation, e.g. *type* $\theta 3$, however, can be compatible with both **a** and **non-a**. It is the presence of these other *types* that lends the model the form of a continuous process of updating of probability and reputation. In fact, there were just $\theta 1$ and $\theta 2$ *types*, the short-run players would be in a position of absolute certainty about the *type* of the long-run player after a single observation.

Players' rational choices   How do the short-run players make their decisions? Given that they are rational but short-sighted, they simply calculate the expected utility of choosing **e** or **non-e** in the stage games in the light of outcome probability deriving from the conditional probability assigned to the various long-run player's *types*. Thus in our example, after the observation of **non-a**, the short-run player (with payoff function noted U_{t+1}) who takes part in the repetition $t+1$ will choose **e** if

$$EU_{t+1}(\textbf{e}) = U_{t+1}(\textbf{e}, \textbf{non-a}) [q(\theta 1|\textbf{non-a}, h^t) + 0.25q(\theta 3|\textbf{non-a}, h^t)]$$
$$+ U_{t+1}(\textbf{e}, \textbf{a}) [\theta 2|\textbf{non-a}, h^t) + 0.75 q(\theta 3| \textbf{non-a}, h^t)] > 0$$

Given the prior probabilities $p(\theta 1) = 0.1$, $p(\theta 2) = 0.45$, $p(\theta 3) = 0.45$, the short-run player's best choice for the hypotheses made is still **non-e**, whereas, in fact, for the conditional probability given by one further **non-a** evidence (given any h^t history in which no **a** evidence were been never seen), the best choice becomes **e**, since $2 \times (0.47 + 0.25 \times 0.52) - 1 \times (0.75 \times 0.52)$ is greater than 0. What counts is obviously the combined probability p of the **non-a** action that derives from the probability that any *type* uses action **non-a**. As long as the combined probability of action **non-a** does not increase up to a critical level $p^* = 0.33$, where expected utility of the two strategies **e** and **non-e** are equivalent, expected utility is insufficient for the choice **e**. When conditional probability of θ1 increase up to 0.47, however, in our example the combined probability of action **non-a** becomes p = 0.6 that already exceeds the critical level p*. Thus the best choice for the short-run player, given the probability distribution of outcomes, becomes the same as the best reply to the characterising strategy of *type* θ1 in the stage game (i.e. given p* < p = 0.47 + 0.25 × 0.52, the short-run player's optimum choice in the current stage game is **e**).

We will now look at the reasoning of the long-run player. He is not committed and can freely choose a strategy from those available. However, if he chooses a strategy that is identical to one characterising a *type*, he simulates that *type* and the short-run player will come to believe he is in fact that *type*. He must therefore reason strategically about which strategy to adopt, on the basis of the effect it will induce in the beliefs of the short-run players. He can use a strategy that aims to generate a certain distribution of probability about *types*, to obtain a certain reputation (read it 'to invest in reputation').

The result Thanks to this construction we get the following result: if the long-run player is not too impatient, there is a repeated game equilibrium path in which the long-run player's strategy enables him to obtain almost the *payoff* that he would obtain if in every stage game he could effectively adopt a binding commitment to use **non-a** action when the short-run player chooses **e**, in other words, the long-run player could obtain the *Stackelberg payoff* in almost all the repetitions of the game. We recall that a *Stackelberg* game is one where a *leader* can announce an irrevocable commitment to use a given strategy, i.e. he first states the chosen strategy in such a way as to make it perfectly predictable for the opponent (the *follower*), and then proceeds to use it, so that the *follower* only needs to choose the best reply to the irrevocable commitment announced by the *leader*, taking for granted that this will also be the best reply to the strategy *effectively* used by the *leader*. Obviously a *leader* chooses ex ante his irrevocable commitment to be announced optimally, that is for each strategy he might commit himself to, he considers the *follower*'s best reply and consequently chooses to announce first the strategy that, given the best replies of the *follower to each announcement of the leader*, maximises his *payoff*.

This can be expressed in more technical terms: take first all the possible announcements of commitments by the *leader* and all the best replies by the follower to some of those announcements; for each *follower*'s best reply, corresponding to any of the *leader*'s possible commitments – if there are more than one – the commitment with greater utility for the *leader* is selected. That is the *leader* calculates any pair of strategy made up of one *leader's* commitment and one *follower's* strategy which are reciprocally best replies to one another. Then, from all the commitments satisfying the property of being optimal against the follower's best reply, the one which above all maximises the utility for the *leader* is chosen. If the game in normal form of fig. 3.1 were a *Stackelberg* game, then the corresponding extensive form would be the inverse compared to that presented in fig. 3.2. In fact the long-run player would first have to choose between **a** and **non-a** and then, in a state of perfect information, the short-run player would decide whether to enter or not. In other words (according to our representation) the game would be played out according to the *Stackelberg* solution if the long-run player (the would-be *leader*) could irrevocably state his commitment to use one of the two strategies, **a** or **non-a**. Against the commitment to **a** the best reply of the short-run player (the would-be *follower*) would be **non-e**, while against the commitment to **non-a**, the best reply would be **e**. Moreover, against the two best replies of the short-run player, the long-run player anticipates one best-reply-commitment each, respectively **a** and **non-a**, which produces the two pairs of mutual best replies (**a, non-e**) = (0,0) and (**e, non-a**) = (2,2). Clearly the second is the *Stackelberg* solution to the stage game and the would-be leader would choose it at the outset of the game. Fudenberg and Levine's result thus shows that there is a long-run player equilibrium strategy that allows him in almost all the repetitions of the stage game to obtain *payoff* 2 (and thus almost all the single-run players obtain 2).

Fudenberg and Levine's result is however more general than this. It says in fact that in the game just described, assuming non-zero probability for at least one *type* acting in each stage game according to the *Stackelberg* stage game solution, there is a discount rate $\delta < 1$ such that the *payoff* that the long-run player can get in every Nash equilibrium of the repeated game is (i) *at the most equal to* an approximation of the sum of the *Stackelberg payoffs* (as they were gained in each repetition) and (ii) *at the least equal to* the sum of *payoffs* that he would get if in all the repetitions he obtained the *maxi-min payoff*, by playing always the stage game dominant strategy.

The result thus characterises the set of equilibria of the repeated game, with an upper boundary and a lower boundary to the *payoff*s that the long-term player could obtain using any of the equilibrium strategies available to him. This tells us that in the most desirable equilibrium he will approximate the sum of *Stackelberg payoffs* and in the least desirable equilibrium he will approximate the sum of maximin *payoffs*, i.e. the *payoff* that any rational player can obtain in every repetition by choosing his optimal action given the hypothesis that for each of his actions the short-run player's response makes only minimum *payoffs* feasible to him (that in fact coincides to the stage game equilibrium (0,0)).

Sketch of the proof If the global *payoff* of the long-run player is to be an approximation to the sum of *Stackelberg payoffs*, then in almost all the stages the *payoff* of the stage game for the long-run player must be a *Stackelberg payoff* except in an identifiable number of stages. The demonstration of this proposition is intuitive here, given our simplifying assumptions on the game's parameters[17]. If the long-run player is patient (i.e. does not discount his future payoffs very much) and if he uses the strategy corresponding to the *type* θ1, which prescribes the use of **non-a** in each repetition (i.e. the 'would-be' *leader* plays the Stackelberg strategy), then (enumerating the periods from the first one on):

(i) N periods are needed for the conditional probability of *type* θ1 to become high enough to induce the short-run player to use action **e**; i.e. short-run player's best choice in each stage game - given the conditional probability of *types* and the probability distribution thus generated of the long-run player's actions and the outcomes of the game – after N periods will become the short-run player's strategy belonging to the stage game *Stackelberg* solution. We have seen in our example that, if the probability of **non-a** increases over p*, which happens very fast – for example at p = (0.47+ 0.25 × 0.52) – then from that time on the short-run players will choose action **e** as the best choice in the stage game. This is also the best reply to the action used by *type* θ1 in every stage game and together with **non-a** makes up the *Stackelberg* solution in the stage game studied here. On the other hand, given the q° it is easy to calculate how many observations of **non-a** are needed to make the conditional probability assigned to *type* θ1 (and to *type* θ2) generate the critical level of probability p* for the **non-a** action. In our example if q° = 0.1 (given the other probabilities of *types*) only one period is enough to obtain this result!

---

[17] For a general proof of the proposition cf. Fudenberg and Tirole (1991), pp.380-381.

(ii) up to period N the long-run player will have built up unadvantageous partial *payoff* $(0 \times N)$. However since there are an infinite number of repetitions to play after N, at repetition N+1 he can choose whether to obtain all at once payoff 3 or look for an infinite number of times *payoff* 2. Thus, if the long-run player does not excessively discount future utility, a continuation *payoff*, made up just of discounted *Stackelberg payoffs* from period N + 1 to infinity, compensates for the null *payoff* of the initial N periods and exceeds that of the alternative continuation *payoff*, made up of the stage game dominant *payoff* 3 for a single time and an infinite series of zeros. It should be noted that all the alternative continuation *payoff*s from period N have the form 2M + 3 (discounted for the appropriate parameters), where M ≥ 0 is the finite number of additional periods after the first N, in which the long-run player can continue to 'simulate' *type* $\theta 1$ before defecting, so that if the above is true, it must also be true that 2M + 3 (multiplied by the appropriate discount rates) is lower than the continuation *Stackelberg payoff* for infinite periods. This is so because if in our simplified example at time N+n, for any number n, the long-run player decides to abuse, the sole *type* that remains possible is then the one that plays the stage game strategy **a** with probability 0.25 and **non-a** with probability 0.75. But for our choice of the parameters value this *type* is incapable to induce cooperation on the part of the short-run players at any stage, as it is obvious that $(0.25) \times 2 + (0.75) \times (-1) < 0$. Thus the continuation payoff after N for the long-run player is necessarily the discounted $(n - 1)2$ plus $3\delta^{M+n}$. Following the typical strategy of *type* $\theta 1$ is then a long-run player's Nash equilibrium strategy for the repeated game that approximates the sum of *Stackelberg payoffs* for each stage game and also the equilibrium with the maximum total *payoff* for the long-run player. That this is an approximation is implied by the fact that the total *payoff* of this equilibrium for the long-run player differs from the infinite summation of *Stackelberg* payoffs by discounted 2N, i.e. by the cost (think of it as an investment cost) of the periods spent in convincing the short-run players of the reliability of his reputation.

Notice however that this is not the sole equilibrium point of the repeated game[18]. Assume for example that from the outset of the repeated game the long-run player plans to simulate *type* $\theta 3$'s strategy, which implies that he will play **a** and **non-a** according to the (0.25, 0.75) probability distribution.

---

[18] Exactly this is required by Fudenberg and Levine's theorem.

3. GAMES OF REPUTATION AND COMPLIANCE

Then, after an initial sequence of N stage games (at least two stage games are needed where for chance he will play **non-a** and **a** respectively), the beliefs of the short-run players will evolve until they assign probability 1 to *type* θ3. Given these beliefs no short-run players will ever enter. Thus the long-run player's best reply will be to choose always **a** with at most the overall *payoff* $3\delta^{N+1}$. This is of course the lower bound equilibrium payoff predicted by Fudenberg and Levine's result. Moreover, assume that the only mixed strategy *type* possible is not the one we have hypothesised until now, but a different one, which uses the stage game strategies **non-a** with probability 0.33 and **a** with probability 0.66 and assume also that for some reason the long-run player planned to simulate this peculiar *type* from the beginning of the repeated game. Then after at least two periods in which the long-run player played the stage game strategies **a** and **non-a** once each, the conditional probability of the two pure strategy *types* becomes nil (because the conditional probability of a *type*, given evidences that have zero likelihood under that *type*, is zero) and the probability mass results completely concentrated on the sole mixed stage-game-strategy *type:* [(0.33), **non-a**; (0.66), **a**]. From this point on the short-run players will not learn anymore and, whatever the evidence they gain, they will not change their beliefs about the occurring *type* of long-run player. Each of them will face the same expected payoff both for entering and not entering, that is $0.33 \times 2 + 0.66 \times (-1) = 0$, which implies that they best reply is to enter with probability ½. The expected payoff of the long-run player can be computed accordingly for any repetition thereafter. If he will play **non-a** in each stage game he can expect no more that (½)2 in each repetition (discounted appropriately), but if he will play **a** the expected payoff is (½)3 (discounted appropriately) without any risk to endanger his reputation. Consequently the continuation equilibrium strategy of the long-run player simulating the mixed strategy type will be 'always **a**' with at most the total payoff $(\delta/1-\delta)(½)3 + (½)3\delta$ (under the hypothesis that, given the stated prior probabilities, he has played **non-a** at the first period and then has successfully abused for the first time at period two). This equilibrium *payoff* is strictly less than $(\delta/1-\delta)2$ for any value of the discount rate parameter $\delta \geq 0.65$ – that is for those values of the discount rate that imply the existence of the alternative 'Stackelberg-like' equilibrium point in the game.

Remarks It is important to remember the role of the assumption of simultaneity: if the players did not learn simultaneously of the result of each stage game, the long-run player would know before taking action that, if the short-run player had chosen **non-e** then the result is anyway (0,0), and thus his choice between **a** and **non-a** would lose significance (if in the game in fig. 3.2 player 1 chooses **non-e**, in effect player 2 is not even called into the game). Thus the short-run player, in cases when he does not come in, would have nothing to learn about the *type* of long-run player and thus the long-run player would have no way of signalling his *type*. But given that the long-run player's reputation is built up in N initial periods where the short-run player does not enter, it is clear that in the hypothesis that the game were played sequentially, the result would not follow. A weakening of the result that in any case guarantees reputation effects is discussed in Fudenberg and Levine (1989).

In conclusion, the result presented in this section depends basically on the fact that each short-run player can observe with certainty the outcome of each stage game and in particular that he can see the actions of the long-run player belonging to the history of the game before he is called to enter any particular stage game. Without that evidence, the basis for updating the conditional probability would also be missing, together with the dynamic of beliefs that enable us to identify the critical values p* for which the best reply of the short-run player is identical to the best reply to the "ethically constrained" *type*. However, it is possible to introduce the hypothesis of imperfect observability of the outcome of the stage game[19]. We admit the existence of a mechanism of communication of the outcomes of the game which may be subject to noise and error: every player could, with 1–r probability, receive at the end of every repetition a message containing the actual outcome, but with r probability, he could on the other hand receive a wrong message. Using the methods of Bayesian statistics it can be shown that, even where the players only have information on the probability of the outcomes rather than precise observations, a model of reputation effects can again be built up (on this see Fudenberg and Levine 1991 and Fudenberg, Kreps and Maskin 1990).

---

[19] This problem has been tackled in the literature as one of statistical uncertainty. It is to be noted that we will come back to *ex post* imperfect observability under a quite different approach, that is under the hypothesis of *ex ante* incomplete information that makes *ex post* vague the meaning of the observed action performed by the players. This aspect of *ex post* observability can not be tackled by standard statistical methods.

VI. Foundational Problems

We will now look at some foundational problems of this theory. The apparently paradoxical aspect of the theory is that cooperation becomes possible if there is a certain degree of uncertainty about the rationality level of the players. If a non-strategically rational and calculating player has on-zero initial probability, then cooperation can be supported by an equilibrium point of the game. Cooperation apparently advances together with the degree of uncertainty about the rationality of *types*, whereas it would seem more natural to hypothesise the opposite way round: a progression of cooperation together with a greater degree of rationality of the agents. Moreover it can be observed that we are dealing with the *apparent* irrationality of a player, while in fact he is a rational and calculating player. Thus, as the initial information about *types* increases, the probability of an irrational *type* decreases and so does the possibility of cooperation. Cooperation is thus in inverse proportion to the degree of information about *types* of players, whereas intuitively it would seem that the greater the knowledge shared by the players, the greater should be their capacity of reasoning and acting rationality and thus solving the problem of their strategic interaction[20].

On the contrary, it seems evident that if *types* are divided into the dichotomy 'rational' and 'irrational', then the notion of rationality becomes paradoxical: the more players are aware of interacting with rational oppo-

---

[20] On this topic see Yaari (1996). The most natural link suggested here (more rationality = more cooperation) has been discussed elsewhere (Sacconi 1993a), where the problem of compliance with the social contract was solved by defining the authority relations between two players, where one cedes to the other control over shares of his natural rights, in such a way that almost any authority relation satisfies the Nash equilibrium property. There, the equilibrium solution was made possible thanks to a progressive relaxation of the limits of rationality, rather than because of these limits themselves. By learning more and more alternatives, individuals, who are cognitively limited but able to improve their deductive capacity, discover the existence of more and more equilibrium solutions that were hidden by natural interaction. Then a solution is given (see Sacconi 1993b) by applying to the set of possible equilibrium authority relations the 'tracing procedure' meant as an equilibrium selection process which models the rational reasonings performed by players involved in a hypothetical "original" social contract.

nents, the worse their expected outcome of the game. The greater the expected number of rational individuals in any society (firm), the worse-off they must expect to fare.

A better interpretation of the model may be given in terms of commitment to predetermined rules of behaviour. In this case the *types* will alternately be either self-interested *types* following the best reply rule, or *types* who tend to follow arbitrary rules of conduct and, finally, or *types* who unfailingly keep to a predetermined ethical code. Here we are dealing with *schemes of behaviour* that must be seen as neutral with respect to the notion of strategic rationality. In characterising behavioural schemes we are not elaborating a normative theory, but rather focusing on to the description of *standard modes of behaviour* present in a population and associating them to *types* of players. None of these behavioural standards has to be described as rational in itself. Rationality is something that we look for at a second level, i.e. in relation to the reputation it is rational for a long-run player – who is able to think strategically about the interaction amongst uncertain short-run players and his possible *types* – to maintain with regard to these *types*. It is not irrationality but an ethical code, understood as an indefectible rule of conduct, that is included in the *types* of players. Explanation is in terms of *as if* reasoning: to act *as if* the player were a *follower* of the indefectible ethical code, given the hypothesis that the other believes him to be so. Given that there are various possible *types*, the player acts in such a way as to *simulate* the *type committed* to keep to the ethical code (the content of which is unconditional cooperation) in order to develop the appropriate belief on the part of the short-run players that allows the long-run player to get his higher payoff.

It is nevertheless clear that in this way the standards of behaviour are seen as exogenous to the theory of rational behaviour: a type can be described in as much as a certain number of the population has adopted a certain standard of behaviour. In particular we must suppose that the existing standards of behaviour of the population include also a rule of indefectible compliance with an ethical code. If, however, the ethical code is an exogenous entity, as we suppose, then we simply show the rationality of simulating the behaviour of one compliant with the code, but we do not give a fundamental explanation of why it appears *among the types* and why it is at least *probable* that some people are characterised by such a type. In fact it is just because there are, at least potentially, individuals who comply with the ethical code and thus the probability of a player complying with the ethical code is non-zero, that then it is rational to act *as if* the player were that *type* of player, i.e. to comply rationally with ethical code. It seems that we are able to demonstrate the rationality of compliance (or to stick to one's commitments), but unable to deal in terms of intentionally planned rational deliberation with the setting up of the code itself. It is true that it is possible for a player to plan a behaviour to 'simulate' behaviour according to the ethical code, but the ethical code must exist before and it must be at least probable that this ethical code is respected in order for the strategic reasoning that leads to compliance with the code to have a basis. Moreover, the problem remains that if the initial probability, associated with the hypothesis that the player does in fact follow the ethical code, disappears, then the possibility of cooperation disappears too. The question thus is: why should there be an initial positive probability of behaviour not conforming to the hypothesis of strategic rationality of the agents? Why should such things as indefectible ethical codes exist and be probable in a world populated with rational players?

We are, fortunately, able to suggest an endogenous explanation for the ethical code, but this involves 'bounded rationality' (Simon 1972a). Planning and setting up an ethical code is the rational mode of acting in the face of the agent's limited ability to predict future contingencies, admitted that he is aware of his limited cognitive abilities. It is a way of establishing contingent commitments not on a complete description of the possible states of the world, but only on an incomplete description given a vague and undetailed knowledge of the possible future states. We adopt an ethical code to generate reciprocal expectations in relation to the behaviour that can be undertaken when such contingencies occur. If we accept this hypothesis - which will be developed more in full in the following chapters - then we can explain endogenously the setting up of the ethical code as the solution to a problem of rational individual and collective decision making. When we do not know how to calculate the optimum strategy in terms of expected utility, given our awareness of the incompleteness of the set of 'possible' events we have in mind, then an intuitively rational behaviour is to establish general rules or norms of behaviour that compel us to behave according to certain *standards* in the future. We set these standards by generalisation out of the rules that behaved sufficiently well in the past in general. Without being able to see if this will be true in every detail with respect to the future events, we do that in such a way to create standards of behaviour that can be taken as the basis for sufficiently definite expectations on the reciprocal behaviour in the future, which allow reasonable reciprocal adaptation of individual choices. A requirement must be set however: standards must be maximally general and adaptable to a multiplicity of future contingencies, which we can be aware the existence of, even if we cannot describe them in detail as the *set of possible events*. This is why they must take the form of general ethical principles.

Summing up, giving a rationale for reputation effect models requires the following sequence: ethical codes help to solve a problem of limited rationality, i.e. a problem of rational decision-making in the presence of limited cognitive capacity; thus it is logical to assume that at least some rational individual adopts an ethical code. We can thus associate a non-zero prior probability with the *type* of agent acting as one compliant with the ethical code. But this prior probability creates an incentive for the agent himself to support his reputation of being exactly that *type* who sets up and comply with the ethical code.

Chapter 4

How Far Does Reputation Extend?
Abuse of Authority and Corporate Culture

I. Contexts of Transaction and the Scope of 'Reputation'

We did not concern ourselves in the previous chapter with the problems that arise when one tries to apply the theory of reputation effects to economic environments that are more precisely delineated as regards the structure of the information available to the players. That is the task of the present chapter.

What economic situations does the theory of the reputation effects apply to? In what cases does it succeed in guaranteeing the compliance with contracts or promises that are not in themselves binding? The usual view is to regard as appropriate those contexts in which an implicit contractual relationship arises between two or more parties, or where between the parties there is a contract that is explicit but not verifiable by an outside authority. Take, for example, the retail sale of a consumer commodity, in which the purchaser pays for the goods before they are supplied by the seller. This type of situation typically has the structure of a DP (the seller has no reason to supply after having been paid and of course the buyer has no reason to trust the seller). Nevertheless the parties do not resort to a written or explicit contract to ensure that the transaction will be completed. This naturally implies that compliance with the unwritten contract cannot easily be ascertained and enforced by a third party or by an external authority (for example, a judge). The parties allow the provisos of the contract to remain implicit because the structure of interaction is clear enough for the players' obligations to be enforced thanks to the endogenous mechanism of the repeated game.

We are in any case dealing here with implicit contracts of a relatively simple nature. The purchaser buys the goods (for example, the weekly order of fruit and vegetables) from the seller on the implicit undertaking that, come what may, the goods will be supplied the same day. The purchaser can easily observe whether the implicit undertaking has been respected, and he can derive from this the distribution of probabilities on the 'types' of the vendor, even in the absence of any external evidence observable by a third party (typically it is only we ourselves who know whether the greengrocer has 'pulled a fast one' on us, but this is enough to discipline the transaction, if the greengrocer sees us as a regular customer whose good opinion he wishes to retain).

As long as the reputation effects are seen as the rational explanation for simple implicit contracts, the theory seems to work rather well, but at the same time it seems not to have a very wide application. The applicability of the theory of reputation effects would be hugely extended if it were capable of explaining the stability of the authority relationships which form the basis of formal organisations. In fact, according to Kreps (1990c), what characterises firms is not the formal structure of property relationships but rather the substratum of fiduciary relationships (based on reputation) that make it possible for those legal relationships to survive.[1] To put it more correctly, the legal-formal structure of property rights offers an incomplete and inadequate explanation for the institution of authority relationships between the firm and the 'stakeholders', who accept that those who hold positions of authority in the firm are delegated the power to take decisions which are binding on all the others, who then have to carry out those decisions or suffer their consequences. A more complete explanation requires an analysis of how these stakeholders come to believe that those who occupy such positions of authority, settled by the allocation of property rights and control, will not abuse this power.

A hierarchical transaction is defined as a transaction that is regulated by a contract which *ex ante* (before the parties undertake specific investments and before a range of events has taken place) delegates to one of the two parties to the contract the right of making decisions, which will influence *ex post* the value of the transaction for all the participants. Typically, hierarchical transactions take place within firms and formal organisations, according to the definition of Williamson and the theory of Grossman, Hart and Moore

---

[1] The bulk of this chapter consists of a discussion of a single contribution by David Kreps, *Corporate Culture and Economic Theory* (Kreps 1990c) which can be considered a heuristic inquiry into the limits of game theory, limits beyond which microeconomic theory cannot go without undertaking not trivial conceptual innovations. Analogous heuristic indications can also be found in Kreps (1990a), chap 20. I remain of the same opinion even after the attempt made in Kreps (1990d) to reformulate the extent of the problems raised, and thus bring them back into the 'orthodox' context.

(Williamson 1975, 1986, Grossman and Hart 1986, Hart and Moore 1990). Such theories start from the analysis of employment contracts as instituting an authority relationship (Simon 1951), that is as a contract by means of which party A agrees to place under the control of deliberations by party B the decision as to which action, out of a predetermined set, A must carry out. The set of decisions under A's physical control is thus partially under B's formal control, so that it depends on B's decision which action, chosen from the range of options open to A, will be carried out. The problem is how such a relationship arises, that is, why A agrees to carry out any order given by B within the range of choices open to A under B's authority. Besides the case of the employer-employee relationship, other hierarchical transactions include those between an agent who holds the ownership and control of the organisation and the clients or investors who delegate to him or her the task of providing them with services that have a wide margin of discretion. And where they are also willing to accept a certain discipline in their behaviour in order to enable the counterpart to carry out his or her services. (Typically, this is the position of the student in educational institutions or of the patient in hospital, and in some ways of the small shareholder towards the management of a public company).

Neo-institutionalist theories of the firm respond by looking at the legal structure of the firm: they identify the position and exercise of authority with the availability of property rights over the firm's physical assets and the possibility of exclusion that ownership affords the owner with respect to all the other agents. Thus, authority is respected because it is protected by property rights. But all this does is to push the fundamental question back a step: why do the agents agree to enter into a contractual relationship with the holder of property rights? And more correctly, why do they cede control over their own actions to the person who holds the property rights over the physical assets? In general terms, why do agents, who co-operate by means of the firm, agree to cede their property rights to one agent amongst them, who will then exercise the authority associated with property rights over all the others?

The obvious answer – which says that the arrangement of rights that is chosen is the mutually advantageous one – is also clearly insufficient, since it is well known that the exercise of property rights is not exempt from the possibility of abuse. The person who is protected by property rights will simply defend the value of his or her investments, but this says nothing about protecting the value of the investments of the other stakeholders. On the contrary, as we know, the theory of Grossman and Hart predicts second-best (that is less than optimum) levels of investment by the stakeholders as a result of the exercise *ex post* of opportunism by the agent who controls those decisions which are not *ex ante* contractible, that is, those which come under his or her authority. Nor is the question resolved by recourse to the complete contract *ex ante* according to which the various exercises of discretionary authority are predicted, and an initial value established in relation to which the parties are prepared to agree to cede control over decisions that are not *ex ante* contractible. In fact, (a) if there are significant unforeseen contingencies, the cost of opportunism cannot be established *ex ante*; (b) even if the contract were not radically incomplete, the party in a position of authority could only undertake to remunerate the other parties 'in the course of time' on the basis of the value associated with the rights that they give up. That is, the compensation cannot in practice be made *ex ante*, but only over the course of the relationship. It is deferred in relation to the cession of rights and the institution of the authority relationship. Thus the party in authority can fail to honour the initial obligations if the contract is not self-binding (and all the more so if it is to a significant degree incomplete). Such problems can be ignored only if it is admitted that the contract is *ex ante* complete (that is, if it is possible to predict from the beginning the governance costs associated with every type of exercise of authority) and if it is verifiable, or enforced by some kind of external mechanism. It therefore suffers from the same paradox as the contractarian programme.

II. Reputation and Hierarchical Transactions

The explanation of the stability of authority relationships in the context of hierarchical transactions proposed by Kreps (1990c) promises to be much more general and fundamental, since it typically supposes a non-cooperative context of interaction, in which the possibility is explicitly expressed that once the power relationship is established, there may be an abuse of power by the agent in a position of authority in relation to control over decisions that were not contracted for *ex ante*. Thus, even if a contract is initially established, compliance with it cannot be taken for granted *ex ante*, but depends on the structure of the strategic interaction *ex post*. Or rather, it depends on whether resorting to an act which constitutes an abuse is, or is not, the optimal response of the agent holding authority to the decision of the agent who decides to accept a subordinate position. Kreps' is a non-cooperative explanation, which typically refers to the theory of the reputation effects in repeated games. It is because the agent with authority has an interest in keeping his or her reputation high with a view to future hierarchical transactions that he or she does not abuse, and this induces the agent, who has to decide whether to accept a subordinate position, to believe that the former will not abuse and therefore to accept his or her authority.

Let us assume that once he has entered into an authority relationship, the subordinate agent must obey the instructions of the agent entitled with authority, and let us assume that the latter is able both to choose actions whose outcome is mutually advantageous both for the subordinate party and the party in authority, and to choose actions whose outcome is advantageous only for the latter. The decision to enter into a subordinate position can be considered as a specific investment, which ties the party entering into a subordinate position to the organisation and which prevents him or her from leaving it, without incurring an unrecoverable cost. The lock-in effect is equivalent to the hypothesis that if the authority is accepted, it is respected *ex post*. The problem is why the party who enters into the subordinate position should do it rationally.

The model expressing this situation in abstract is the one illustrated by figs 3.1 and 3.2 in chapter 3, which we shall refer to from now on. Player 1 in this case is a stakeholder who enters or does not enter into a subordinate relation with a firm or organisation. Player 2 is the person in the organisation who holds formal authority. This basic game can be seen as the component game of an infinitely repeated game between a succession of short-term stakeholders (staying the game for single periods), and an organisation or institution that lasts for the whole of the infinite duration of the game[2]. In

---

[2]   It is obviously a simplification to assume that it is possible to identify the player who personally holds authority in the organisation, for a limited period, with the organisation itself, which can effectively be regarded as an entity that lasts for several generations, and in the case of a family firm passes 'from father to son', or has an administrative continuity that lasts beyond the period for which individual administrators hold office. The assumption is that we can treat a firm as a single player, identifying it with the individuals who hold positions of authority, and hypothesising that such individuals act as a single player over a long period. This is clearly a limitation of the model. one can observe that the more painless the passage from one administrator to another, and the more it preserves the continuity and identity of the firm and the or-

the role of player 1 we can therefore see an infinite succession of users of hospital services, or students in schools or universities. Or, in general, the customers of complex services who sign up to an explicit or implicit – but very general - contract regarding the terms of the service which player 2 must offer them, but who at the same time recognise player 2's authority to decide *ex post* at his own discretion some characteristics of the services which are not contractible *ex ante*. When it is the turn of player 2, therefore, the administration of the hospital or school decides whether to offer a high or low quality service, whether to set a price that is barely sufficient to cover the marginal costs of the productive factors involved, or whether to charge a higher price, which enables player 2 to obtain an income and wipes out the consumer's surplus. Alternatively, we can imagine a succession of workers in the part of player 1 who do or do not enter into the employ of a firm at a predetermined salary, with the firm then deciding at discretion on the position held or the tasks to be carried out. This decision has to be taken by the firm at the second move of the game and may mean that the salary initially agreed will cover the *cost* of the effort required of the worker, or it may be such that it leaves the worker with a negative utility. Or, analogously to the preceding case, the exact level of the salary of the worker, player 1, is a variable that in part depends on the decision of player 2, who is able *ex post* to fix the level of pay conditionally on the firm's results, which is not contractible *ex ante*, and the worker's remuneration may thus be such as to distribute part of the surplus to the worker or to retain the whole of the surplus for the management or the proprietor.

Let us suppose that *ex post* the information received by the clients of the organisation or by the employees of the firm at the end of each component game can not be verified by an external observer, or that it is difficult for them to go to a tribunal to show that the quality of the service was low, or the price too high, or that the amount of work required was too great in relation to the salary agreed. Nevertheless, in many cases they will be in a position to observe personally whether or not this is the case and will be in a position to communicate this information to other individuals who might subsequently enter into relations with the organisation or firm in the same subordinate position. This is enough to ensure that reputation effects disci-

---

ganisation, the more powerful are the reputation effects associated with the character of long term player which belongs to the firm or organisation.

92

pline the behaviour of player 2 and avoid the possibility of abusive behaviour on his part towards players who take the role of player 1.

Kreps stresses that the basic assumption is *observability*: it must be observable that *what should have been done has been done*. Expressed in terms of the abstract model, at the end of each component of the game player 1 must be able to observe whether player 2 has chosen action *a* or action *non-a*. Let us suppose that in the background there is a contract which allows player 2 to take a decision with a certain margin of discretion and that this decision can be made conditionally with respect to the occurrence of various states of the world. In the case of the patient, for example, the implicit agreement is to carry out the treatments that are most appropriate to their state of health as shown by specialised tests whose results are not yet known at the time of entering hospital. In the case of the student, it is the opportunity to follow complementary courses appropriate to his or her inclinations or the demands of the job market. In the case of the worker, it is the undertaking to guarantee the distribution of conditional rewards or salary increases on the basis of the productivity of work and the success of the firm. The condition of observability requires that when the relevant states of the world occur, the user of hospital services, the student or the worker can observe the state of the world that is occurring, and recognise whether, under these circumstances, the agreement that was originally reached, although general and not specific, has been complied with. If, on the occurrence of the relevant state of the world, player 2 does not carry out the action requested (the treatment of the patient is no longer appropriate, or the surgical operation is more expensive than it might have been under the circumstances, or the courses made available to the student do not correspond to academic standards, or the variable salary is not paid in the proportions originally agreed with regard to the firm's results), even though this cannot be established from outside, it can be observed ex post by the players participating in the component game in the role of player 1. It can therefore be communicated without difficulty to the players who will participate in successive games in the same role. If, conditionally on the occurrence of various states of the world, player 1 observes that the undertaking has not been respected, this information is sufficient to invalidate the hypothesis that player 2 can be of the 'committed' type, and player 2 thus reveals himself to be an opportunist. As the game continues, therefore, no other individual in the role of player 1 will enter into a subordinate position in an authority relationship with him. But, by the logic of strategic interaction, it is to player 2's advantage to maintain intact and even increase the probability associated with the hypothesis that he is a 'committed' type. Therefore, he does not abuse his discretionary power of decision making. Hierarchical transactions thus rest on a trust relationship based on the reputation accumulated by the player who holds the position of authority.

III. Unforeseen Contingencies

Let unforeseen contingencies now enter the picture: these are events that are not predicted *ex ante* – which occur in states of the world not adequately specified – with respect to which the original contract could not be complete. It should be noted that a contract can delegate to player 2 the authority to take certain decisions not contractible *ex ante,* since it would typically be too expensive to provide in the contract for all the decisions which player 2 must take in all conceivable circumstances, or because to write down these conditional provisos would in any case be superfluous, given that no external observer would be in a position to verify whether they have been respected. However, the decision to leave a margin of discretion to player 2 with regard to which decision he or she should pick out at a later date, is mainly due to the fact that the participants know that some states of the world or events will occur which they are not able to foresee at present, and they believe that player 2's decision may for some reason be the most efficient at the moment when these contingencies materialise. There exists, therefore, a set of decisions whose appropriateness cannot be established *ex ante*, in the absence of information about the state of the world which will occur in the future. We may also suppose that such decisions involve some kind of action on the part of player 1. Player 1 and player 2 agree, therefore, that it will be player 2 who will select a decision out of the above-mentioned set at a later date, that is, when he knows the state of the world which has come about. Since this decision will involve action on the part of player 1, this agreement assumes player 1's acceptance of player 2's authority. A hierarchical transaction takes place between them. Thus, the case in which the power to make discretionary decisions *ex post* is due to the existence of unforeseen contingencies is essential to the theory of hierarchical transactions. This new ingredient makes it necessary to verify the applicability of the model of reputation effects as a mechanism which is capable of regulating player 2's power to make discretionary decisions *ex post*.

4. HOW FAR DOES REPUTATION EXTEND?

At first glance, we could state that just as player 2 observes the state of the world *ex post* and deliberates on the decision that is to be carried out, so player 1 also observes the state of the world *ex post* and can therefore judge the action ordered by player 2. In fact, both the state of the world and the decision chosen by player 2 out of a set that is not contractible *ex ante*, are observable *ex post* even if *ex ante* at least part of the states were not foreseen. Therefore it seems that the introduction of unforeseen events does not modify the basic requirement for the application of the reputation effect mechanism.

However, closer examination reveals that the unforeseen events introduce an added difficulty, and one that is potentially destructive. The problem is that in the presence of unforeseen contingencies, we cannot say *whether what should have been done has been done*, because the explicit or implicit rules established by the initial contract have nothing to say about unforeseen events, upon which they cannot be conditional. The starting point is that players 1 and 2 are aware that *ex ante* it is not possible to establish which, among the decisions included in a given set, will be the most appropriate in the terms of some criterion to be implicitly or explicitly agreed between them in the contract. The criterion of appropriateness of the decision may be implicitly clear only for states of the world which are foreseen, but not for those which are unforeseen. Thus the delegation of authority to player 2, on the basis of the explicit or implicit contract, does not place any limits on the exercise of discretion by him or her. Whatever happens – as long as it is an unforeseen event – there is no action that player 2 is obliged to carry out and in the light of which player 1 can judge player 2's behaviour was the appropriate one *ex post*.

In brief, not knowing *ex ante* which action will be most appropriate, the other players delegate the job of deciding on it *ex post* to one party alone. Thus the decision as to which act is appropriate *ex post* depends solely on the discretionary and unilateral judgement of player 2. It is therefore likely that player 2 will *ex post* take the decision that is most favourable for him and least favourable for player 1, nevertheless, this does not mean that they are able to recognise that the appropriate *ex post* decision has not been taken, that is 'that what should have been done has not been done'. Rather, these appropriateness criteria – with reference to explicit or implicit agreements established between the players *ex ante* – are simply *empty*. On the other hand, it is for just this reason that player 2 will always take the decision that is most favourable for him, in the certainty that he will not be accused of not living up to his commitments to the other party. But this is a good reason for the other party not to agree to delegate authority to player 2, at least on those occasions when the power of discretionary decision-making, given unforeseen events, can not previously be considered as influencing the well-being of player 2 alone (obviously this does not happen in hierarchical organisations, in which it is clear that the exercise of authority by the ruling party affects the well-being of all the stakeholders).

If we try to state the problem in the abstract terms of the game model, the point is that actions **a** and **non-a** in figures 3.3 and 3.4 (chapter 3), whose meaning is 'abuse' and 'non-abuse', are not clearly distinguishable *ex post*, or rather are not capable of being exactly specified. We could obviously say that such a distinction is always possible, not on the basis of which action signifies 'abuse' in a given situation, but on the basis of the outcome associated with it, that is, on the basis of the pair of payoffs that appear at the ends of the game tree. But this is the same as saying that everything that is relevant in the description of the state of the world is already summed up in the final payoffs. Thus, effectively there are no unforeseen contingencies, given that the states of the world are divided into only two classes: those which contain a given pair of payoffs for the players, and those which contain the alternative pair[3].

In order to demonstrate the inadequacy of this reply, it is not necessary to recall that, if truly unforeseen events exist, pairs of payoffs that are different from those predicted *ex ante* should also occur. Even if we admit that all the payoffs which are observed at the end of the game can be traced back to the above pair, it should be clear that to admit the possibility of unforeseen events implies that the states of the world, in relation to which the acts of player 2 can produce approximately the two types of outcomes described above, must be able to be quite different one from the other. Thus an act, which determines a given pair of payoffs, can in one case be interpreted as an 'abuse', while in a different case, predicated on a different and unforeseen state, it may not be regarded as an 'abuse' of player 2's discretionary powers.

Let us suppose that given our usual understanding of the world, actions on the part of player 2 that give rise to outcomes (2,2) are not abusive while actions that lead to outcomes (−1,3) are abusive. In fact, the model in chapter 2 is constructed in the light of this understanding of the world. Let us suppose now that we become aware of the crudeness and incompleteness of our

---

3   See fig 3.2, chapter 3.

representation of the possible states of the world, although we are unable to give a more precise description of the alternative states. Now we can imagine that *ex post* a state of the world arises in which player 1's contribution to the firm not only is not useful, but is in fact damaging. For example, if player 2 could exclude player 1, the value of the productive coalition constituted by the firm could be such that player 2 could be in a position to hope for a pay-off 3. Let us suppose however that this cannot be done without a cost to 1. In this way, player 2's decision to select a pair of payoffs (−1,3) is a remuneration that reflects their contribution. It is clear that here the action that generates (2,2) would not be the one to which *ex post* we would intuitively assign the meaning of 'non-abuse'. On the other hand it might happen that to assign equal payments to the two players, in a state of the world in which it was revealed that player 2 occupies completely irrationally a position of governance in the firm, would also be an abuse with regard to player 1's expectations; while in the standard case we are impelled to believe that such an outcome is equivalent to a non-abusive behaviour on the part of player 2. The point is that each representation of the situation by the model is based on a certain *pre-understanding* of the meaning of actions **a** and **non-a**, with reference to the possible states of the world of which we are already aware. But we cannot exclude the possibility that, if completely unexpected states of the world were to occur, those same actions and those payoffs might *change their meaning*.

The situation that we are trying to analyse is that in which it is not clear whether the order given, in the presence of the new situation, is admissible or not in the terms of stated *ex ante* commitments, since the original agreement did not foresee an occurrence of that nature. Therefore the judgement of the act, contingent on the new state of the world, becomes indeterminate. If the events that occur are unforeseen, it is impossible to establish whether the agreement has been respected, simply because there was no agreement concerning that type of situation. If the events that occur are not only unforeseen, but significantly different from those which were seen as possible and predictable, it is likely that the same contractual criterion by which we would previously have identified an abusive and a non-abusive act will no longer be usable since it was devised for events too different from those which were seen *ex post* to have occurred. This also gives rise to a difficulty with regard to the carrying out of the theory of the reputation effects: it is certainly true that *ex post* we observe the state of the world and the action of player 2, but it has not been established what player 2's behaviour should be. In the new situation the type of player 2 is not specified, since we cannot say what action his characteristic strategy should prescribe for him. Thus the parameter or standard of behaviour on which player 2's reputation should depend is not established. Therefore the observability *ex post* of contingencies not foreseen *ex ante* and of the action of player 2 do not ensure the applicability of the solution based on reputation effects.

IV. Corporate Culture as a Basis for Reputation Effects

Having posed the problem discussed in the previous paragraph in far-reaching terms, Kreps (1990c) suggests a heuristic approach that is essential in order to extend the theory of reputation effects to the case of contractual incompleteness. It is a sketch of a theory of rational behaviour in the face of unforeseen contingencies, whose key concept is the role of general principles as a substitute for the contingent provisos in the contract that may be implicit or explicit, but are in any case concretely determined. Kreps' argument is in three stages:

(a) 'unforeseen contingencies follow patterns', that is, we may not have a complete description of them but nevertheless be able to predict on the basis of past experience that they will take a certain pattern or a particular recognisable silhouette. Consequently we are disposed to face unforeseen contingencies on the basis that they will present an analogous profile to those which have surprised us in the past:
"While the exact circumstances of future contingencies may be unimaginable (or too costly to think through), aspects of those contingencies can be anticipated. I contend that unforeseen contingencies follow patterns. At least, I, and I suspect others, act as if this is so. Accordingly. My provisions for unforeseen are somewhat evolutionary. I examine what has happened that was surprising in the recent and sometime distant past, and I provide for roughly similar contingencies"[4].

(b) Given this hypothesis, agreement is established between subordinates and their superiors *not* as to what should be done in the case of single contingencies concretely described, but as to *general rights and principles,*

---

[4]   Kreps (1990c) p.117.

which establish the abstract modality according to which such unforeseen contingencies should generally be faced. In fact, Kreps states that:

"The workers and students have certain rights that cannot be violated by the firm or the university (...) but usually agree at the outset that, in the face of unforeseen contingencies adaptation to those contingencies will be at the discretion of a boss or dean. (...) Why will workers and students enter into suc arrangement? What protection do they get? It is that the firm or university develops and maintains a reputation for how it meets unforeseen contingencies by the way in which it actually meets those contingencies. How the contingencies will be met is not verifiable, at least not in the sense that workers or students could take a firm or university to court and enforce a violated implicit contract. But the meeting of the contingencies is observable ex post, others can see what the firm or university did and decide whether to enter into similar transaction with either. (...) Most crucially, the meeting of unforeseen contingencies must conform to some pattern or rule that is observable – that is the organisation's reputation must be for something"[5].

(c) However, the extent to which the concrete action taken in a given contingency satisfies a principle is a matter of judgement or interpretation from which it is impossible to eliminate a certain degree of vagueness. The difficulty of the approach is that the adaptation of the behaviour to the contingencies on the basis of the general principle is ambiguous:

"This is especially problematic in the case of unforeseen contingencies. Once they arise, we may know what they are, but how do we know that they have been met as they are supposed to be met? Because the contingencies are unforeseen., we cannot specify in advance how to meet all possible contingencies and then observe that advance specification have been fulfilled. We are in a situation somewhat more analogous to that where the meeting of the future contingencies is not perfectly observable (...) At best, participants will have a rough sense as to general principles with which unforeseen contingencies will be met, and they will have to gauge the extent to which those principles have to be honestly applied"[6].

Summing up, what Kreps suggests is that the response to the problem of unforeseen contingencies is supplied by the use of norms or principles so

---

[5]   Ibid. p.119.
[6]   Ibid. p.120.

general that they can be adapted to multiple contingencies, including unforeseen ones, and that the price for this solution is a certain degree of
vagueness in the norms themselves. Thus we are led to recognise the merit
of vague general rules with comparison to contractual provisos that are concrete and fixed, but inevitably silent in the face of unforeseen events. What
conditions must these principles satisfy in order to render effective the
mechanism of the reputation effects? Kreps suggests that the principles must
satisfy two conditions[7]:

(i) A principle should be capable of establishing 'what should be done'
once a particular contingency has been observed, even if this contingency was
ex ante unforeseen; that is, it should be capable of eliminating a large part of
the ambiguity regarding the required behaviour also in relation to those
things that cannot be foreseen exactly. This means that the same principle
enunciated *ex ante* must be capable of being applied to contexts that are *ex
ante* unforeseen.

(ii) Furthermore the principle must be such that its application in various
contingencies will offer the party who has to enter into the hierarchical relationship in a subordinate position terms of co-operation that are sufficiently
good to make it advantageous for them to enter into the transaction with this
ex ante prospect.

How should the principles be defined in order to satisfy these criteria? The
first hypothesis to consider is that of rules so general that they pertain universally in every contingency, independently of the fact of whether these contingencies were foreseen *ex ante* or not. Rules that are universal and unambiguous may exist but, according to Kreps, they would not be relevant. If a rule is
truly universal, able to be applied in any case, even in the presence of unforeseen events, it must of necessity be subject to a certain ambiguity. In the opposite case, if the rule is formulated in terms which are precise and determined and we ask for its universal and irreversible application, it runs the
risk of imposing case by case on the unforeseen contingencies conduct that is
blatantly absurd. Knowing this, the party who has to enter into the transaction
will be led to doubt whether the principle has in effect been applied; or
whether, *ex post,* it can be clear what it means to apply it; or whether, if it
were to be applied, it would constitute an effective guarantee against the risk
of abuse. What is needed, therefore, according to Kreps, is something less
than complete generality and non-ambiguity: rules are needed whose flexible

---

[7]   Cf. Ibid. p.124.

application to the various cases shows itself to be sufficiently unambiguous and advantageous for the subordinates.

Having arrived at this point it would be possible to investigate the logical structure of rules formulated in universal terms but conditioned by [the fact that they have] certain characteristics (or in terms such as "for all x's, if x is a p, then ...") which are sufficiently general to be adaptable to many unforeseen contingencies (this is the approach that we shall take in the following chapters). Kreps, on the other hand, prefers to take a different approach: *de facto* - he says - these rules exist and are enclosed in the identifying culture of each organisation. Corporate cultures, in the contexts in which they are established, show that they have the properties required of "principles". Indeed one can say that the economic explanation of the corporate culture consists precisely in the attribution to it of the function of "principle", whose purpose is to give the subordinates in a hierarchical relationship the assurance that, when faced with unforeseen events, they will be able to say in a sufficiently unambiguous manner "what is to be done". Kreps states that: "My (limited) understanding of corporate culture of corporate culture is that it accomplishes just what the principle should - it gives hierarchical inferiors an idea ex ante how the organisation will react to circumstances as they arise; in a strong sense it gives an identity to the organization"[8].

In fact

"corporate culture also provides a means of measuring the performance of hierarchical superior. In many organisations individual have not fully internalised the common good – they are concerned with the their own welfare. Thus an organisation must monitor and control individual performance. If individuals within an organisation who exercise hierarchical authority are supposed to exercise that authority according to some clear principle, then it becomes easier ex post to monitor their performance (...) Hence in the usual fashion, efficiency can be increased by monitoring adherence to the principle (culture). Violation of the culture generates direct negative externalities insofar as it weakens the organisation's overall reputation"[9].

What does Kreps's theory suggest for our purposes, that is, for the purposes of the proposition that an ethical code is an indispensable pre-condition for the stability of an organisation? An ethical code that incorporates essen-

---

[8]   Ibid. p.125.
[9]   Ibid. p.126.

tially the condition of efficiency and fairness (see chap. 3) seems typically to respect the condition (ii) established by Kreps for principles. We could say, therefore, that the ethical codes of firms and organisations are the means of rendering explicit and communicating the corporate culture of a firm. However, there is a fundamental difference between our position and that held by Kreps: for he explains corporate culture by means of the functions it has in making possible the mechanism of reputation effects, but tells us nothing from the normative point of view about how we should set about constructing a corporate culture. He confines himself to the observation that such cultures do exist and, if they exist and need to be rationally explained, then this must be because they perform the function of principles, which make possible the reputation effects in the context that we are examining as well. In the normative perspective that we have adopted, on the other hand, it should be possible to identify the ethical code, or at least its general characteristics, in some sense *a priori*, that is, in a way that is not dependent on an *a posteriori* or empirical investigation into the cultures that happen *de facto* to satisfy the requirements.

V. Corporate Culture and 'Focal Points' A Critical Examination

The point at which Kreps' theory diverges from the position stated here is where he attempts to characterise the principles established by a given corporate culture in terms of *focal points* that we find in any game of co-ordination. Or in other words, corporate culture is summed up in the contextual elements that for every game, with a given structure, turn one of their points of equilibrium into a focal point. A 'focal point' is defined as a centre of attention of the players that is created in a situation of strategic interaction and generates a focus of reciprocal expectations among the players such that, thanks to the existence of the focal point, the players are able to resolve the problem of co-ordination. For example, let us consider the usual game of division: given a stake of 100 dollars , two players are asked to state a number between 0 and 100 such that if the pair of numbers is compatible (that is, if they add up to the same as or less than 100), then they receive a portion of the 100 equal to the number they said, otherwise they receive nothing. Obviously, all the combinations of pairs of numbers whose sum is 100 are Nash equilibria of the game. The problem the players have is to

102

agree on at least one pair among the many that are possible. The theory of *focal points* states that this problem of of equilibrium selection would be simply resolved if one of the pairs had the property of attracting the attention of the players and of generating the mutual expectation that the players' attention will be attracted by this pair. We would say that the pair is *salient*, in the sense that it attracts the players' attention. If we then assume *common knowledge* of salience, the consequence is that the *focal point* generates a system of reciprocal expectations which agree on the fact that that pair is able to attract the players' attention, on the fact that the one knows that the other is attracted by that pair, and that the other knows that the first is attracted by the pair, and that both know that each other knows that they are attracted by the pair and so on. Given a system of expectations of this type, a solution to the game is provided only by the salient equilibrium, since if one player thinks that the other is attracted by the pair, then it is rational to be attracted by the same pair (since to use one's strategy component of a given equilibrium pair is the best reply given the expectation that the other will play his strategy which is a component of he same equilibrium pair). If, on the other hand, one player thinks that the other expects him to be attracted, then he will believe that the other is even more disposed to use the above-mentioned pair, and therefore the former will have another reason to be attracted to the pair in question (this being the best reply given the expectation on the expectation of the other player) and so on. In sum, salience generates that state of *common knowledge* of the solution or, in other words, means that system of mutually consistent expectations about one another's behaviour, which is the basis for justifying the choice of a particular equilibrium as the rational solution for the game (Lewis 1969)[10].

---

[10]   An axiomatic formulation of the necessary and sufficient conditions regarding the players' beliefs in order to obtain various concepts of solution including Nash's equilibrium can be found in Bernheim (1984) and Tan and Werlang (1988). Bacharach (1987) argues that equilibrium requires common knowledge of the theory. The formulation according to which equilibrium is consistent with knowledge of the solution theory goes back to Luce and Raiffa (1957) while Lewis (1969) was the first to introduce the 'common knowledge' of the solution as the logical implication of an equilibrium being selected as the solution of a co-ordination game On this point see Sacconi (1993b). For the formulation of the logic of 'common knowledge' see Fagin, Halpern, Moses and Vardi (1995).

4.5 CORPORATE CULTURE AND FOCAL POINTS

The point is that frequently in the purely abstract description of the game there is no element which renders one equilibrium *salient* in comparison with all the others: according to the formal description, all equilibria are simply equilibria, that is, they share the same formal characteristic. *Salience* of a particular equilibrium, that is, the fact that it constitutes a focal point, will instead depend on some characteristic of the context or the situation of which the game is simply an abstract representation. Indeed, we will not normally be able to obtain from the formal representation of the game, in terms of normal or extended form, any salience for any equilibrium (apart from some mathematical-type symmetries), in such a way that the selection of an equilibrium depends on the abandonment of the purely abstract representation of the game and on the fact that the calculation of the theory is embedded in a concrete situation or interpreted in empirical terms (Shelling 1960, Kreps 1990b).

For example, let us suppose that we learn from the description of the context in which the game takes place that the first player belongs to a culture in which there exists historically an egalitarian social philosophy, such that it is reasonable to believe that he is particularly attracted to the solution to the problem of division into equal parts. Then, if the salience of the egalitarian solution in the view of the first player is common knowledge, the second player will predict that the first is attracted by the solution in equal parts and consequently will have a reason for choosing the pair that distributes the sum in equal parts. But then the first player will predict that the second player is also attracted by the solution in equal parts and will therefore be even more keen to choose the distribution in equal parts, and so on. On the other hand the same game could now be played by different individuals – that is, individuals who belong to different cultural contexts and socialised according to different norms, even if they are characterised by the same payment functions. Player 1 could, for example, be accustomed to a strictly hierarchical view of relations between individuals or to the solution of similar problems of division on the basis of seniority. Thus if player 2 is junior to player 1, he will expect player 1 to propose a pair of numbers for the division of the 100 dollars that is strongly biased in his own favour, so that player 2 has a strong incentive to use one of these pairs, but since 1 expects 2 to expect him to use one of these pairs, he has an additional reason to use one of these pairs and so on. In conclusion, a *focal point* within a game of co-ordination with multiple equilibria is a particular equilibrium which, in addition to the formal characteristics of being an equilibrium, also exhibits certain salient contextual characteristics, drawn, that is, from the empirical domain of interpretation in which the game exists, such as to generate a focus of reciprocal expectations.

This thesis – that the cultural context in which a game takes place is the basis for generating focal points which facilitate the identification of a solution – has a solid tradition in game theory (Shelling 1960, Lewis 1969, Kreps 1990b, Sugden 1986). On the other hand, a typical objection to this view is the fact that it resolves the problem of co-ordination in a circular fashion: the fact that social norms of a certain type hold sway in a population of players, that they generate the expectations of some solution to the problem of co-ordination, would not constitute a constructive way of resolving the problem of co-ordination, since the establishment of such social norms, and of the corresponding expectations, is precisely the problem that should be resolved by the analysis of the game of co-ordination[11]. Thus the solution to the problem of co-ordination by means of the social norms shared in a given culture would simply trivialise the problem of co-ordination. If the analysis of the strategic situations of co-ordination is to be of some use, it should explain *why* a given system of expectations develops, which renders a certain combination of equilibrium strategies salient; that is, it must explain why a given norm becomes accepted. The position of the theorist of salience, in conclusion, would be reduced to the thesis by which problems of co-ordination are not resolved endogenously by means of a theory of strategic rationality but rather exogenously: social norms – which for the game theorist are equilibria around which convergent expectations gather – would turn out to be external variables of the theory rather than outputs of it.

An additional problem arises, however, in relation to the hypothesis that the theory of focal points also constitutes a convincing reply to the problem of rationality in the face of unforeseen events, that is, in relation to the need to establish rules of behaviour or commitment that are valid to generate sufficiently stable expectations in relation to changes in the chosen environ-

---

[11] Harsanyi (1977) objects to 'salience' because it makes the solution of the game exogenous rather than making it depend on hypotheses of rationality over beliefs, while Harsanyi and Selten (1988) propose a theory of equilibrium selection that gives a rational choice theory of why systems of reciprocally consistent expectations develop. This is a model of the process of how beliefs are rationally and continually revised until they predict a particular equilibrium as the solution of the game, that is until that equilibrium comes out to be "salient". On this subject see also Sacconi (1993b).

ment generated by the occurrence of unforeseen events. According to this theory (Kreps 1990b) the focal point is the schema by means of which unforeseen contingencies are faced in a given culture. In fact a focal point has a (limited) normative force: given the evidence as to which is the salient equilibrium, it generates convergent reasons on the part of players to conform to that equilibrium.

This suggestion raises a fundamental objection. A 'focal point' is a means of creating a system of mutually consistent expectations that makes prominent one amongst various possible equilibria. It is a *generator* of converging beliefs among given alternatives. If many potential norms (that is equilibria) are possible in a particular context, and it is a case of co-ordinating on one of them, then the existence of a focal point will make it obvious which one should be chosen, that is, it will eliminate all uncertainty (or almost all uncertainty) about what should be done and about what the players should expect of one another. But the point here is that in the presence of contingencies unforeseen *ex post* it may be that there is no norm or combination of strategies that preserves the salience they had *ex ante*, in the sense that when the context changes the salient norm may also change. In this way the system of expectations, which leads to the selection of an equilibrium in the first context, will not be stable with regard to the move to the second context. Our problem is that the state of the world is unforeseen, and therefore we do not know *ex ante* which is the focal point on which we should concentrate and with respect to which we should check conformity of behaviour of the other party in the *ex post* perspective. The focal point *ex ante* is not a basis for forming an expectation regarding the behaviour *ex post* of the other party, nor is it a basis on which to judge their reputation.

Given a set of possible states of the world, a focal point concentrates attention on one of these: that is, it is selective. In fact, the focal point generates a distribution of probabilities within the space of possible alternatives that is perfectly determined: it makes the selection of one among the given alternatives more probable. We can expect our counterparts to act in a particular way, and we can expect them to expect a certain action of us, if we all share the *same* focal point, owing to the fact that we all belong to the *same* context. However, this has nothing to do with unforeseen contingencies, which change the basis for our probabilistic beliefs, introducing unexpected possibilities. Indeed, they can change the configuration of the problem and activate a *different* focal point. The point is that the focal point is a technique for resolving problems of co-ordination that is completely dependent

106

on *context*. The same games of co-ordination (identical in their mathematical structure) have different solutions depending on the context or on the domain of interpretation. But this is exactly the *opposite* of what is needed. If the parties regulate themselves by means of focal points that depend on the context, when the contexts change, the initial focal points are no longer a basis for judging behaviour. Rather, it is probable that ambiguity will be created, since a different focal point exists for each context, and it is necessary to be certain about the context in which one finds oneself. But it is precisely over the question of belonging to a context or to another that unforeseen events can create ambiguity or vagueness.

The reply of the supporter of the focal point theory is easy to imagine, but difficult to agree with. He will maintain that, even if the focal point changes with the change of context, nevertheless we know that a focal point always exists and therefore *ex post* we shall in any case have a focal point that we shall be able to use in order to resolve our problem of co-ordination. Thus, if we know all this, the problem of taking on a commitment can be resolved by saying that, given a game with a certain formal structure, the equilibrium on the basis of which we should co-ordinate our own behaviour and on the basis of which we can judge whether the other party has lived up to his promise to do what should be done, is simply whichever equilibrium can be identified, when the context changes, as the focal point of the situation that has been created. It is clear, however, that this response presupposes precisely that which the supporter of focal points tends to undervalue as a result of his contextualist position: which is that there have to be general principles, formulated in abstract and universal terms, and having a validity that crosses over the various contexts or is unchanged in relation to the contexts. The position of the supporter of focal points, as just stated, is in fact capable of generating stable expectations only insofar as the players share a general principle which does not depend on the particular contexts that arise as a result of unforeseen events. If they reason as the supporter of focal points requires, the players knowingly share the normative principle of a general theory of co-ordination: *in every game* of co-ordination the players must select one of the equilibria permitted by the formal structure of the game, and since for every interpretation of the game in a different empirical context (many of whose details are unpredictable), a focus of expectations exists, that is, some factor of the context – whatever it may be – that is salient, then it must be exploited to facilitate co-ordination. The principle is therefore that *for any context*, in which a focus of expectations exists that coincides with an equilibrium, this focus of expectations *must* be used to generate the forecast of the other player's expectations, and consequently *must* be used to establish how the players will behave.

The point is that the principle, 'use the contingent focal point to resolve the problem of co-ordination', is known *ex ante* and continues to be valid *ex post*, even if the particular content of this principle is learned only *ex post* with respect to the existence of a concrete context. In every context the principle gives us an independent criterion for identifying the required conduct, since it gives us a criterion – if only psychological – for identifying via focal point which social norms apply. Put a different way, the relativist adage, 'when in Rome, do as the Romans do' – that is, the principle always and everywhere to respect the social norms that apply in every context (even the most unpredictable), since they allow the players to co-ordinate their behaviour – this principle at least must be agreed by the players *a priori* and regardless of context[4].

VI. Explicit General Rules VS. Contextual Focal Points

The point under discussion can be clarified by means of the examples of a game of co-ordination: the game of the rules of the road (see fig. 4.1). The two players are car drivers who have to decide whether to keep to the right or the left when they meet coming from opposite directions on the same road. It is clear that keeping either to the right or the left is equally good for both players, so long as the other player does the same. What they must absolutely avoid is that when one decides to keep to the right the other decides to keep to the left, since that would cause them to crash (pair of payoffs 0,0).

This game shows that the rules of the road are conventions of co-ordination, whose rationality depends purely on what we expect other drivers to do, and have no intrinsic value in the absence of relevant expectations about the behaviour of others. This is emphasised by the fact that the game is one of identical interests: every player has the same motivation as every other player to undertake every joint course of action. The only important thing is to agree, while there is no distributive conflict regarding the various modalities of co-ordination (both equilibria give the payoff 2,2). As usual,

---

[4]   The idea that norms of morality may solve problems of co-ordination can be also find in Sugden (1996). See also Sugden (1995).

the problem of co-ordination consists of finding some factor that is able to justify the formation of a system of reciprocally consistent expectations, concentrated around one of the two equilibrium pairs: (*right, right*) or (*left, left*).

	right	left
right	**2,2**	**0,0**
left	**0,0**	**2,2**

Fig 4.1. *The game of rules of the road.*

Let us suppose that player 1 is driving along an English country road, far from major centres of habitation or the major tourist routes. She is Italian. Let us suppose a kind of 'state of nature' prevails in which the explicit highway codes backed by law do not exist, but that in every country there are tacit shared conventions that regulate the traffic and which the citizens of every country normally respect within their own territorial boundaries. Let us suppose also that there is no regulation providing that every citizen of the EU knows that they must obey the highway code of the country in which they find themselves, in the sense that no EC regulation exists stating that within each country the highway code imposed by the local authorities is the one that applies at all times.

Player 1, not being accustomed to drive according to British traffic conventions, which state that one should drive on the left, and given that the road is narrow and flanked by deep ditches, keeps to the centre of the road, ready to move as soon as another vehicle appears on the horizon. On several occasions in the past the problem of co-ordination has been resolved by *salience*: in the eyes of both drivers who happened to meet, moving to the left hand side of the road was the only salience, since in the British context the prevailing social conventions make precisely this move the focal point of the game and our Italian driver, supposing that the other drivers follow it, has the incentive to do as they do.

Let us suppose now that a vehicle comes round a corner, driving in the middle of the road just as the first driver is doing. Furthermore, he sees that the car has an Italian number plate. This is an unforeseen event. How should our player react? Up to now he has acted according to the rule that, since the British drive on the left, then it is rational to drive on the left, or rather that since in the context under examination cars keep to the left, it is rational to keep to the left in the current case. But now the oncoming driver, in the role of player 2, does not belong to the 'British context' so it is not clear that he will follow the social convention that applies in this context. Furthermore, in the context of Italian driving, player 2 is supposed to follow the conventions of Italian driving, which require drivers to keep to the right hand side of the road. The unforeseen event could be seen as generating a new context: two drivers normally accustomed to drive on the right must decide how to behave. If the two drivers recognise each other as belonging to the context of drivers who normally respect the Italian rules of the road, the rule of driving on the right is salient, and this makes the equilibrium (*right, right*) the focal one. Let us suppose that given the unforeseen event, at the actual observable moment, player 1 considers that the convention of driving on the right applies in the new context, while player 2, following the British rules of the road, moves to the left. The cars crash, even though not seriously enough to prevent the drivers from continuing on their way. Should player 1 regard player 2 as deserving a bad reputation? Should player 2 and any witnesses denounce 1 as a player who has the reputation of not conforming to the informal highway code? Player 2 will maintain that in the British context the salient solution for resolving the problem of co-ordination is to observe the local conventions. But player 1 will maintain that the event, unforeseen by both, of meeting a driver, on a remote country road (far from London and the main tourist routes), who is accustomed to follow the rule of driving on the right and clearly unsure of local rules creates a new context, that is, the context of an interaction between two players from countries accustomed to follow conventions that render (*right, right*) salient. The point illustrated by the example is that focal points resolve problems of co-ordination in a way that is relative to the context. Thus when unforeseen events occur, in order for co-ordination to have an obvious solution it is necessary that the unforeseen event should not introduce any ambiguity regarding the context in which the players are participating. But if the event is genuinely unforeseen,

110

it is improbable that the perception of the new context will be completely clear for each player, or rather that each will unequivocally recognise the current case as an example of a familiar or habitual context. And it is even more unlikely that this perception will be identical for both parties. There may be ambiguity regarding the attribution of the current occasion to one or the other context, so that there will be ambiguity about which convention is in force.

This ambiguity is precisely the phenomenon investigated by Kreps in relation to unforeseen events: when a new event occurs, what 'must be done' is ambiguous. The commitment, which characterises a *type* of player, is to adopt a given action, but only contingently on the known context, while in relation to the context in which the unforeseen event occurs 'what must be done' is neither specified nor obvious. For example, the *type* that 'respects the rules of the road' drives on the left, but only contingently upon an environment (Britain) in which other drivers are expected to follow the social convention which states that you should drive on the left. However, Kreps's suggestion is based on the assumption that a player can unexpectedly find himself in a different context, but that in every context he finds himself faced by cultures that are consolidated and shared by the members of the population under examination. Thus once these conventions have been learned, he always views as obvious the rule of behaviour which according to the current conventions is the salient one and permits problems of co-ordination to be resolved in the normal way. What Kreps does not consider is the occurrence of genuinely unforeseen events, since the unforeseen events could be understood properly as elements that generate non-habitual contexts, such as to render ambiguous existing social conventions or the judgement as to which convention applies.

There would be a natural solution to the problem if the two players could avail themselves (as happens in reality) of 'community norms' which stated, for example, (something that would be common knowledge) that within the frontiers of countries belonging to the EU, every EU or non-EU citizen must follow the local highway code of the state where he or she is. This would be the equivalent of a meta-norm that establishes which contextual norm is to be used in the various contingencies and which are the relevant characteristics (in this case territory) for establishing which is the current context and which convention is in force. A norm would therefore exist whose validity surpasses the various contexts and is more general than the single local conventions. It, would establish, in relation to any unforeseen event and any

111

context, independently of the description of the particular context, which should be considered the appropriate salient solution, and what should be taken as the focal point. In fact the meta-norm *is not contextual*, since it does not refer to particular countries, nor to particular contingencies (of the type 'Italian driver versus Italian driver on British territory'). It is a rule formulated in universal terms that prescribes differentiated behaviours on the basis of context.

VII. Moral Language

From these considerations we vindicate the approach based on *ethical codes* compared to that based on contextual *focal points*, belonging to the various corporate cultures. Ethical principles are principles that are *general* and *vague* but by definition, universalisable. They extend their application, at least tentatively, to any possible event, foreseen or unforeseen, which does not share all its descriptive characteristics with those that are known but rather just those characteristics that have moral value to a sufficient degree. This does not mean that every attempt to extend an ethical principle into a new and unforeseen context will be successful. It may happen that the principle, at least in its current formulation, reveals itself to be totally inadequate or counter-intuitive in the new context. What it does mean is that by its internal linguistic and logical formulation, the principle will be seen as universally valid or valid at least on all the occasions that some categories of very broadly defined and general characteristics apply. In this way, if on the occurrence of an unforeseen context the attempt to link the context to the principle fails, this will serve as a kind of 'falsification' of the principle, imposing on it some kind of reformulation or revision. That is, an ethical principle cannot *a priori* be understood as an *ad hoc* rule, contingently valid only for the context in which it was initially introduced.

An aspect of this is connected with the very notion of *universalisability* formulated by Hare (1963): an ethical judgement is a prescriptive judgement, that is, it contains a guiding criterion for action, which must however be *universalisable*. This requires that the judgement of what is good or just (or whatever) must be able to be extended into every other situation that is *analogous* or *similar* to the original one as regards the characteristic that is relevant to the judgement, and *independently* of every other descriptive characteristic. There exists therefore at least one descriptive characteristic of

112

the original context which, if found in other contexts, implies invariability of judgement. This descriptive characteristic assumes moral significance since it is clearly the characteristic of the original context to which the person who is judging attaches moral value. If it is found unchanged in other contexts, which are in other ways completely different, it nevertheless implies the same type of judgement. For example, the judgement 'it is right to give player x the larger portion of 100 dollars if his need for money is greater' identifies in the 'intensity of need' the characteristic that has moral value, with respect to which the judgement will be unchanging and extendable to other contexts. To the predicate 'having greater need' there corresponds some act of measuring or some description of the state of things. The fact however that this descriptive characteristic - 'having greater need' – is identified as the guiding criterion for action, with regard to which the judgement is unchanged in different contexts, has the result that it assumes a mainly moral meaning, that is, *prescriptive/universalisable*. How can we recognise whether the judgement in fact has moral significance? The answer is: by trying to apply them to contexts that are analogous through the similarity of the morally relevant characteristic. This means that, in carrying out the test of universalisability, we have no need of an *ex ante* complete description of the various situations or states of the world. For any description of the state of the world (including these about which we have no idea *ex ante*) we must verify the validity of the judgement 'it is right to give the greater proportion of X to the individual who has the greatest need', on condition that the only descriptive characteristic of 'need', abstracted from the other elements of the situation, is reasonably similar to the original case. This way of proceeding seems to have a natural application in the case of unforeseen events, since the extensibility of the moral judgement does not require that concreteness and specificity of description, which are needed if we want to apply a definite criterion contingently upon the description if a complete set of states of the world. It is sufficient to recognise the general shape of the case – for example, the fact that the decision concerns the distribution of some resource or good among individuals one of whom has greater need of that resource or good – to apply the ethical principle, even if the details of the situation are not completely known to us or cannot be related to previous experience.

113

Chapter 5

Information, Incomplete Contracts
and the Ethical Code

I. Default Rules and Contracts

This chapter deals with the system of (contractual, legal and moral) norms that must be postulated in order to guarantee stability of and compliance with incomplete contractual relationships in the context of hierarchical transactions within a system of governance such as the firm. In particular it shows why the system of norms regulating this type of transaction must contain an ethical code in the sense of a set of general norms and principles setting the 'constitution' of the firm that are not necessarily enforced by the law. It is the reference to these principles that can make reputation effects, seen as the driving force in the endogenous self-enforcement of the whole system of norms, a feasible proposition in this context. To this end it is essential that norms and principles create sufficiently determined *a priori* commitments and expectations about actions to be undertaken in the face of unforeseen states of the world, about which an incomplete contract is by definition silent.

The idea of a link between a corporate code of ethics and the constitutional social contract of the firm is very similar to that outlined by Jules Coleman (1992) describing the relationship between rational bargaining theory and default or gap-filling rules. The judge resorts to this type of rules when using his discretion in the absence of explicit contractual provisos that may express the will of the parties, and in the presence of contingencies giving rise to conflict between the parties themselves. Premise for this reasoning is that real world contracts are not complete contracts. Parties may not be in a position to provide conditional provisos for all possible contingencies or it may be deemed too costly to draw up *ex ante* a contract to allow for all possible events. Thus, for every contingency not provided for by the contract and that may give rise to a clash of interests - in the absence, that is, of an *ex post* agreement between the parties and an *ex ante* proviso that explicitly sets out the action to be taken - they can appeal to the court as last resort in solving the *dispute*. The rules used by the judge to fill the gap cre-

115

ated by the lack of explicitly agreed *ex ante* provisos are known as default or gap-filling rules.

Then we may ask:

a) what is the content of these rules?

b) what is the basis or justification for these rules?

Coleman answers both these questions by reference to an hypothetical *ex ante* contract model based on the theory of rational bargaining. A hypothetical *ex ante* contract is the contract the parties would have agreed before any appearance of gaps in the real contract, were they been able to anticipate unforeseen events and the related *disputes*. The model assumes the parties to be rational, equally and fully informed about any possible event (including the unforeseen), in a position to rationally bargain all details of the transaction starting from a status quo in which there is no violation of reciprocal rights, nor any exercise of force or fraud, parasitism or deception. On the basis of these hypotheses and in accordance with the theory of rational bargaining in co-operative games, we may construct a hypothetical bargaining game that will generate a rationally acceptable outcome and a unique allocation of payoffs amongst the parties[1]. In particular, in the *ex post* perspective, when the unforeseen *ex ante* events transpire. The rational bargaining model can be used to derive the rational contract that would have been drawn up between the parties, had they also been aware of the contingency that arose and had they not deferred definition of the agreement in relation to that possible contingency.

The theory of rational bargaining puts forward a single answer to this question and can thus be used to simulate the agreement the parties would have reached had they been able to consider the problem and were the negotiation between them been such to satisfy the conditions of rational bargaining. The result of this mental simulation process fills the contractual "gap" and enables the judge to dictate rights and liabilities of the contenders. In this way, according to Coleman, the theory of rational bargaining can account for the default rule adopted by judges in a better way that the other two competing theories - the consent theory and the theory of wealth maximisation[2].

---

[1]   An abstract model of rational bargaining is developed by Coleman (1992) ch.5, pp.105-121; for our bargaining model see chapter 2, *supra*.

[2]   Cf. Coleman (1992), p.166.

Moreover, the resorting to bargaining theory as a default rule perfectly matches the idea of rational agreement that could be undertaken *ex ante* by agents who are rational in the real (not idealised) sense, in other words who are aware of the limitations of available information. If they are both rational in the sense of rational bargaining but aware of their cognitive limits and of the costs to be borne in writing complete contracts, the parties will agree *ex ante* to a contract which is the outcome of rational bargaining, but limited to those contingencies they can predict without having to bear prohibitive negotiating costs. Being aware of the possible existence of unforeseen contingencies, about which conditional provisos have not been established, they will leave the remaining contract specifications to the judge agreeing between themselves merely on the abstract procedure by means of which the judge must simulate their rational bargaining in the case of conflict.

This procedure involves the reconstruction of the agreement that rational and well-informed individuals would have subscribed *ex ante* in ideal conditions of information and in the absence of coercion or fraud. In other words, the *ex ante* procedure – agreed and then delegated to the judge – amounts to the theory of rational bargaining[3]. The *ex ante* rational contract between non-idealised individuals is thus made up of two elements:

a) a concrete rational agreement stipulated according to the outcome of the rational bargaining model as applied to known or easily predictable possible contingencies;

b) a general scheme of agreement based on the abstract model of rational bargaining in relation to contingencies that are not known or are too costly to be included in the contract, whose application is delegated to the court in the case of unforeseen contingencies arising i.e. contingencies not accounted for in the explicit contract.

Then the parties allow that events not mentioned in the real contract may occur. They take just the prevention that at least the general scheme for adjudicating disputes that may arise in these contingencies be set out by common accord and coincide with what would have been agreed, had they not had to submit to the inevitable incompleteness of the real contract.

---

[3]   Cf. ibid. pp. 178-9.

II. Default Rules and Corporate Ethical Code

Coleman's theory adapts surprisingly well to our account of the ethical code as a condition for hierarchical corporate transactions taking place successfully in the face of incomplete contracts. Let's assume that the decision to leave the task of completing the contract to the court – by recourse to the bargaining model with ideally rational parties – is implicit, or that the court rationally reconstructs the decision as implicit in the intentions of the parties when they sign the real incomplete contract. In other words, the judge recognises that this hypothesis is a necessary logical prerequisite to explain why rational parties might have agreed the incomplete contract. In this case the judge is doing no more than reconstructing the implicit ethical code which is the premise for the contractual relationship between the parties. The implicit code explains the contract by giving a rational basis for expectations being brought to an agreement, the player being aware of the possibility of unforeseen contingencies[4].

Let us now suppose that the firm sets up the model by means of which, in the case of unforeseen or contractual gaps arising, disputes with the stakeholders must be judged. We suppose also that it states that the default rules to be used in completing the contract must be derived from the rational bargaining model between ideally rational and well-informed parties, uninfluenced by coercion or fraud. What more is this statement than the issuing of an ethical code, whose guiding principle is the idea of an efficient and fair social contract in terms of bargaining theory, understood as a pact underlying their concrete contractual relations? Seen as subjects involved in rational contracting, the firm's stakeholders should refer to the hypothetical model in rationally deciding whether to adhere to the real contract that submits them to an authority. It is because they believe that possible disputes can be resolved on the basis of what they would have ideally agreed, had the

---

[4]   In order not to suggest that the coincidence between my position and Coleman's is greater than it really is, it should be noted that according to Coleman resorting to the abstract model of rational bargaining to repair contract gaps does not necessarily imply that the final solution should be fair but only that it should be acceptable to rational players (cf. ibid. pp.49-59 and p.182). However I have defined fairness in terms of rational bargaining (see chapter 2 *supra*).

contract been fully explicit, that they agree to enter into this real contractual relationship.

Our thesis is that when a firm announces an ethical code it is to make explicit the criterion that lies behind the default rules that must be applied when contingencies arise that are not explicitly provided for in the contract between the firm and its stakeholders (patrons). In this way these rules can be acceptable *ex ante* to the stakeholders and become part of the explicit agreement on the basis of which they enter into the relationship with the firm. The ethical code is no more than the explicit, sometimes written, formulation of the model of the ideal social contract amongst stakeholders, to which recourse must be made to settle disputes where, in the case of unforeseen contingencies arising, the exercise of power by the stakeholder governing the firm may have consequences that the parties have not anticipated.

Reference to default rules appears particularly appropriate, in that both in the case of inferences to be made by the court when disputes are caused by incompleteness of contracts, and in the deductive structure of an ethical code, the prevailing logic is that of reasoning by default[5]. In short, in the absence of an actual proof of the fact that the parties have come to an agreement in one way or another in the presence of a given contingency, both the court and the ethical code admit that it is coherent to assume that the parties would have agreed on the basis of the criterion of rational bargaining that selects the efficient/fair solution in a cooperative game. A default inference, made in absence of an explicit proof indicating the contrary, is obviously fallible, in that it assumes the validity of a hypothesis with no demonstrative or empirical evidence (except for the evidence of the absence of the proof of the contrary). The conclusions based on these assumptions are thus fallible and the system of statements and beliefs derived can only be non monotonic: it will not necessarily grow as the theory is enriched with new inferences. In certain cases it may even *contract* or *reduce* due to the fact that some conclusions, inferred at an early stage, turn out to be false or based on hypotheses that cannot be defended (McDermott and Doyle 1980, Gärdenfors, 1988).

The idea of ethical code considerably extends, however, the sphere of default rules from the sphere of the court to the sphere of self-enforced rela-

---

[5]   For default logic see Reiter (1980), Geffner (1992) and Bacharach (1994).

tions between the parties. In fact an ethical code can be seen as the announcement on the part of the firm, or the person having major decisional power, of the scheme of default rules that must be followed when unforeseen events appear. This does not necessarily entail the intervention of the court. In these cases the parties themselves can settle their controversies by applying the relevant rules. In this way a fundamental incongruity in Coleman's analysis may be removed: the court intervenes in the case of incompleteness of contracts, but it is not necessarily true that it is in the best informative position *ex post* to judge the dispute. Its position in terms of information *ex post* may not be better than those of the parties.

III. Complete and Incomplete Contracts and Information

The reason why economic theory, including the neo-institutionalist, has so far paid insufficient attention to ethical codes is that it has never taken seriously the radical form of contract incompleteness that is a direct consequence of incomplete information (Kreps 1990b, 1990c are the obvious exceptions to this statement).

We can define *complete* information as the context in which an agent has access to an exhaustive *ex ante* description of the set of all logically possible alternatives (states of the world). This context does not exclude statistical uncertainty, in the sense of absence of knowledge of the real states of the world occurring and recourse to a degree of subjective belief, understood as the probability assigned to uncertain events or states. By incomplete information we mean a context of more radical ignorance: the absence of the description of at least part of the logically possible alternatives in the mind of the decision-maker, in other words the incapacity to foresee what, from an omniscient point of view, is logically possible given the agent's background information[6]. In this context a problem of decision is simply to establish the rational behaviour to follow when the agent is aware of not having access to a complete and exhaustive description of the relevant states of the world. When the decision-maker is not aware of this incompleteness, he simply believes he has a complete picture and consequently his decision-making

---

[6]   A similar description can to be found in Vercelli (1994). Attempts to investigate the logic of this epistemic situation in economics have been put forward by Modica and Rustichini (1994).

120

problem is similar to the case of complete information, with the obvious warning that he is likely to make mistake (but this observation is true for the observer but not for the decision-maker himself – if it were true for him, he would be aware of facing a problem of incomplete information)[7].

In the context of complete information we have two types of contracts.

a) *Complete contracts:* there are no costs of writing or verifying by a third party. Defection can be sanctioned and compliance enforced by the court by simply collecting evidence of a breach of the contract.

b) *Incomplete contracts in the weak sense:* there are costs of writing due to the size of the set of known possible events, or to non- verifiability (by third party) of compliance/non-compliance with the contract.

In this context we find sales contracts that are implicit and thus obviously incomplete as to the setting out of explicit provisos. With simple sales transactions, for example, it would be much too expensive to write a complete contract, given that fair trading provisos are implicit and the continua-

---

[7]   This point makes the main distinction between my own approach and the model put forward by Monica e Rustichini (1994). According to them the epistemic situation of incomplete information can be captured as unawareness, that is one is unaware about p if he is in the epistemic situation of 'not knowing that he doesn't know that p'. On the other hand awareness would be understood as 'knowing that one doesn't know that p', that is he doesn't know whether p or ¬p is true, but he knows that p is at least possible (which amounts to the 'negative introspection' axiom). Thus, either the knower doesn't even imagine to be possible p (and act as if p were not possible) or he knows that p is possible (even if he is not certain about its occurrence). This seems to exclude the cognitive situation which is really interesting for a theory of decision in the face of unforeseen contingencies. That is that the knower is to be aware that some generic p, different from the q which he knows to be possible, could be possible too (could come out in some state of the world), but he is not able to describe them in so much detail to enable him to say that he knows that a definite p is possible. We need to maintain some asymmetry between awareness of one's cognitive state (awareness of the set of states not being complete) and one's knowledge (knowledge that some statement is true in some but not all the possible states of the world). The knower has to be allowed to be aware that his system of knowledge, and the language that expresses it, may be incomplete – something may escape it – and at the same time not requiring that, given that he is aware that a generic p may transpire, because of saying that he knows of not knowing whether p is true, then in practice he must know the exact description of p.

tion of business is assured by the threat of endogenous sanctions involved in repeating the transaction. There is also a sub-class of hierarchical transactions falling into this case: when there are specific investments and one of the parties holds the risk of being expropriated, because of her idiosyncratic relationship to the firm, assigning discretionary decision-making power to the holders of these attributes is a protection against unilateral opportunism by the other members of the organisation. A complete contract *could* be written stipulating exactly how to protect the specific investment, but it would be costly and useless given its unverifiability by the Court. In this case we have an incomplete contract in the weak sense and it has the following structure:

i) a set of explicit provisos, contingent on the limited number of states of the world limiting the power of discretionary decision on the part of the party in authority;

ii) a weak default rule, stating that for the set of remaining contingencies the party delegated to decide shall be that in authority.

The rule is a 'default' since it states that in the case of an event for which the contract specifies no particular proviso – stating action to be taken by the parties and in particular what the party in authority can and can't ask the counterpart – recourse is made to the discretion of the party in a position of authority. It is a "weak" default since the absence of an explicit proviso does not constitute a real gap in the contract: the contract is purposely left unspecified with regard to a subset of states of the world that are foreseen but not explicitly regulated. In this context the behaviour of the parties will follow implicit norms. The party in authority will be allowed to make decisions that are the most advantageous for it without violating the limits set in relation to the particular states of the world that ask for specific regulation (i.e. the explicit part of the contract). Had the parties contracted explicitly on this set of states, they would have acted in the same way as the party in authority acted when left free to act according to his better judgement case by case. A weak default does not require the intervention of an outside authority nor the completion of the contract by an impersonal ethical or constitutional norm of reference. It refers to a concrete and contingent proviso, albeit implicit, simply delegating one party to put it into practice.

In the context examined so far all the explicit and implicit norms are concrete, specific and contingent on the various states known *ex ante*. Considering the two categories of provisos (implicit and explicit), the contract

122

may be said to be complete *sui generis* (while apparently incomplete, if by 'contract' we mean only the set of explicitly agreed provisos).

Thus, in a complete information context weakly incomplete contracts – in the sense of both sales contracts between autonomous parties and contracts where one party holds a hierarchically superordinate position, are imposed by the endogenous mechanism of reputation in repeated games. Complete information implies *ex post* observability of outcomes and thus the possibility of assessing behaviour in terms of reputation associated with the type of player who produces these outcomes. Observability goes from verifying compliance with explicitly stated provisos to tacitly understanding of compliance with implicit but concrete provisos that are contingent on events. For every *ex ante* foreseen state of the world, even if not externally verifiable and not necessarily governed by an explicit proviso, there is a contingent behaviour that is *ex ante* implicitly understood and expected by the parties. If this expected behaviour were not carried out, the implicit proviso would be violated and the information would be evident, if not to external observers at least to the parties directly concerned by the interaction The participants would therefore resort to endogenous sanctions against the agent responsible for a breach of the implicit contract, which may consists of a reduced level of investment or refusal to collaborate on future occasions.

As we know from Kreps (1990b), difficulties arise when we have a genuine context of incomplete information. It is a matter of fact that transaction-costs economics, seeing the firm as a form of unified governance of transactions, links *second best* efficiency with exactly this situation. Standard theory has, however, neglected the possibility of abuse in this case, erroneously assimilating this situation to that of contract incompleteness in the weak sense. On the contrary, the reputation mechanism cannot as such limit abuse of discretionary power within genuinely incomplete information situations. This does not mean that reputation does not have a role to play, but *not* in the simple form of a threat of endogenous sanctions against lack of compliance with implicit or explicit concrete provisos. If the firm is efficient in these contexts, it must be due to some other element that completes the governance structure. According to Arrow (1974), authority can be efficient if it allows important decisions to be delegated to the most interested parties and at the same time envisages an impartial responsibility mechanism in the case of abuse. Given that we are in a context where the court's intervention is by definition difficult, this responsibility cannot, however, coincide with civil or criminal responsibility. Rather it is a matter of subordination of personal authority to the impersonal authority of an ethical code seen as a set of general 'constitution-like' norms[8].

IV. The Logic of Incomplete Knowledge and Limited Reasoning

The context studied here is incomplete information. The agents will thus have a set of anticipated possible alternatives, called W, but will be aware that W is not an exhaustive account of all the possible states of the world (it does not satisfy the usual property of logical closure in the sense that the set of possible states is not constituted by the union of all the alternative states in which W is partitioned). There is an additional set of states Ω, the content of which is unknown *ex ante* and that, together with W, completes the set of logically possible states of the world. Specific, concrete and conditional provisos may be explicitly established, or implicitly present only about events that can be derived from the set of states known *ex ante*, W, but not with reference to the states of the world which make up the set Ω. In fact a proviso is explicitly established if the parties effectively examine a state of the world and, in the light of information contained therein and of general background information, subscribe to the admissibility or non-admissibility of a given behaviour in that state. On the other hand, implicit provisos are those that can be deductively derived from the explicit provisos of the contract and from general principles of the relevant law, so that for each state of the world it follows logically that a certain behaviour is admissible or not (according to whether it is true or false that the given proviso holds in the state) even if this state has not been effectively studied by the parties and the conditional proviso has not been stipulated by means of an explicit procedure (for example the writing of the contract). For an implicit proviso or norm to exist, however, the system must be deductively closed, i.e. there must be a chain of deductions, obtained by means of the usual rules of infer-

---

[8]   Cf. Arrow (1974) ch.4. To avoid misunderstanding it should be noted that Arrow emphasises the responsibility mechanism as a limit to discretionary authority in organisations, considering it a better solution and more flexible than recourse to legal and procedural codes, which are not detailed enough to provide for all the conditional provisos contingent on relevant events.

ence, by which it can be demonstrated, for every proposition formulated in the language of the normative system, whether it is true or not in each state.

This implies that the concept of implicit proviso or norm can be applied in an environment that behaves in a regular, *monotonic* way, where there are no surprises or real novelty. If some normative statement (proviso) holds in a state that presents certain features, it will also hold in any state having the same features, notwithstanding the fact that we have not studied that state explicitly.

The logic of explicit and implicit provisos is similar to the logic of *awareness* (Fagin and Halpern 1988)[9]. Take some formal language L able to formulate (by well formed formulas) propositions p, q ,r,..., whose content may be some proviso such as 'given X, behaviour C is right/wrong'. Leave out the analysis of the peculiar modal meaning of deontologic propositions and stick to the simpler question of whether these proposition are true in the sense that given the existing normative system, conditionally on some state where X holds, then "behaviour C is right/wrong" also holds. Consider then the application of the logic of implicit and explicit beliefs about these propositions. In other words we are dealing with the implicit/explicit belief about propositions stating the applicability of a proviso to various states of the world in such a way that the semantics of the possible worlds is used to establish the conditions of truth of propositions such as *in the state w, agent A believes (implicitly/explicitly) that 'given X, behaviour C is right/wrong'.*

This logic employs for every agent a Kripke structure, that is a n-tuple defined as follows: a set of states, including all the possible alternative descriptions of states of the world; for each agent an information partition or possibility relation defined on the set of states (each element of this partition indicates for each occurring state which other possible state is indistinguishable – i.e. mutually possible – from it given the agent's information); a basic function ascribing truth or falsehood to the atomic propositions of the language, and finally the operators of belief and awareness that we now are going to describe. An implicit belief in this context is set up in accordance with the definition of 'truth of a formula (belonging to the given language) in a state': the agent implicitly believes proposition p to be true in one state

---

[9]   Awareness in Fagin and Halpern's sense does not coincide however with our use of the term; by *awareness* they mean the cognitive situation in which we effectively go through the steps of a deduction so that the theorems are 'present in consciousness', that is awareness is knowledge in constructive sense.

if p is true in all the states included in the same element of the agent's information partition. Implicit belief is axiomatically characterised as the rational belief of a logically omniscient individual: (i) he believes all the propositional tautologies in the language; (ii) he doesn't believes falsehood, (iii) if he believes that p and that p implies q, than he implicitly believes also that p; (iv) if he believes p he also implicitly believes of believing p, (v) if he does not believes that p, then he also believes in not believing it; (vi) every logical consequence of p, if p is believed, is also believed; (vii) any theorem derivable from the knower's knowledge base, is implicitly believed[10].

Explicit belief is the belief of a non logically omniscient individual seen as a restriction on the set of implicit beliefs, construed by introducing an additional condition to those defining implicit belief: agent A in the state w believes explicitly that p if, as well as p being true in every state informatively indistinguishable from w (in the light of A' information partition), p is included in A's awareness set. In other words A must have proposition p 'present in consciousness' or must be in a condition of effectively proving in w that p is true. Thus what A believes explicitly is a *subset* of what he believes implicitly. There are implicitly believable propositions that A does not believe explicitly, since he has not actually carried out an operation by means of which he can ascertain the truth of the proposition in the states in question. As a matter of consequence, if q is an implication of p and p is believed implicitly, it doesn't follow that q must also be believed explicitly, since A might not be aware of q, i.e. he may not have an effective procedure for demonstrating the truth of q (or not be in a position to mentally represent q). This characterises explicit belief as a cognitive system that an agent could have if he were not able to follow all the logical consequences of his knowledge and existing beliefs. If, on the other hand, A increases his awareness, becoming aware of q, then he must necessarily believe q explicitly. A can only increase, and never decrease, the propositions he believes explicitly: it is not possible for A to explicitly believe q if q was not also implicitly believable. There can be neither revisions nor contractions of the set of propositions believed explicitly, as a function of the improvement in A's logical capacity. This characteristic defines what is called a monotonic logic of beliefs.

---

[10]   The last two conditions are the *modus ponens* and generalisation rules assumed as rules of inference of the rational reasoner.

5. INFORMATION, INCOMPLETE CONTRACTS AND ETHICAL CODE

It is an open question whether this property may be reasonably attached to the belief system of a non omniscient agent, who would perhaps be allowed to entertain mistaken beliefs due to imperfect inferential competence. This is not admitted in this logic because at the outset each agent is characterised by a Kripke structure within which he has an information partition defined on the 'true' state space W. It is precisely this property that cannot be retained when we go from the context of complete information to that of incomplete information. We admit that the set of states W does not include all the possible descriptions of states of the world, but only that subset which we are able to represent, and that another subset Ω exists, but we are unaware of its content. Although we are aware that W is not exhaustive (that is a further set of states Ω does exist), we are not aware however of the detailed contents of Ω. It is obvious that what is implicitly believable in W is not necessarily implicitly believable in Ω, for the simple reason that, even if p were true for all the states indistinguishable from the occurring w in W, A's information partition is not even defined on the set Ω, the elements of which are unknown to us. Consequently, if – as we assume – the agent is aware of the existence of Ω, although he cannot describe its contents, then the implicit believability of p must be delimited to the subset W of the descriptions of the state of the world. He implicitly believes p relative to W. Moreover, there is no reason to assume that a proposition that is 'logically valid' in W (i.e. which is true in all the possible states $w \in W$) must necessarily be so also with relation to Ω; an unforeseen state of the world may eventually display a feature that implies the negation of p. This would make p a truth that is contingent on some but not all of the logically possible states.

Obviously, if a proposition that is valid in W is implicitly believable relative to W, this has no implications with respect to its implicit believability in relation to Ω. If we claim to extend the validity of our propositions to the states in Ω, we can only do so *admitting the possibility of error*. Beliefs will consequently be provisional and conjectural. This leads to the logic of beliefs that can be built up in a context of reasoning by default. In the absence of a proof - even implicit - of the truth of a given proposition, it is assumed to be true in all the states whose *ex ante* description is vague and imprecise - i.e. does not allow for an exhaustive examination that can verify whether the proposition is true or false - as long as there is not proof of it being falsified. This leads us back to the logic of default reasoning (see note 5).

127

5.4 THE LOGIC OF INCOMPLETE KNOWLEDGE

Now, let's come to the analogy between the logic of implicit/explicit beliefs and explicit/implicit provisos. Let us say that in a state w we explicitly believe the proposition 'behaviour C is wrong' to be true, if in all the states that are indistinguishable from w, within the given normative system and given X, behaviour C is wrong and we are able to effectively imagine behaviour C in these various states and establish that it is illegitimate according to the normative system (that is 'wrong'). Then we say that there is an explicit proviso that prohibits behaviour C in the state w. Given that explicit belief asks for a decision procedure effectively carried out, we can say that an explicit proviso exists if the contract actually sets out that behaviour C is prohibited in the states indistinguishable from w – i.e. a contract exists in which there is an explicit prohibition of C contingent on w and on all the states indistinguishable from w.[11] [12]

If the source of the explicit proviso is the existence of a positive binding norm actually stipulated between the parties, what about the implicit pro-

---

[11]   The existence of the positive norm, resulting from an *ex ante* decision, has the same significance for the demonstration of the bindingness of the proviso as the existence of an effective procedure of demonstration or calculation for a theorem in the constructivist approach in mathematics.

[12]   For the semantics of possible worlds see Chellas (1981), Hughes and Cresswell (1968) and the more recent studies in Fagin, Halpern, Moses and Vardi (1995). Before going on some clarification is necessary. Our use of the notion of truth, and thus of the semantics of possible worlds, is limited to the question of whether it is true that a given norm holds, i.e. has normative validity, in some or every contingency (description of the world). Obviously here a predication of truth can be expressed that does not influence the judgement about the reasons for a given behaviour is required (a norm does apply). In fact the statement 'norm N holds (does apply) in situation S' is true simply if, given the existing or accepted normative system, norm N holds (does apply) in situation S. What is *true* is that the norm holds, *not* that the norm is *true*. Thus nothing is said about whether its terms of value may have also descriptive meaning beyond their prescriptive significance. The fact that a norm is binding would depend for example on the fact that the norm comes from general principles that all us intersubjectively and rationally do accept, so that form those principles, for all situations that display certain descriptive features, follows that a certain behaviour set out by the norm is required. Thus, if the state of the world under examination displays the given feature, then it is true (according to a judgement on a matter of fact) that in the state of the world the proviso does apply .

viso, about which nothing has been stipulated? According to the analogy with the logic of explicit/implicit belief, an implicit proviso q does exist if we have stipulated some positive norms that logically imply that (it is true that) a certain proviso q - inferable from p - is binding in the relevant situations, that is in all the situations in which (it is true that) p is binding. We may have not performed the deduction, but within the set of possible states considered in which (it is true that) p is binding, it will certainly be true that some logical implications of the propositions p are also true and these implications are all and solely the implicit provisos that are binding in the same states of the world. Logically they correspond to implicit beliefs. Thus, while the explicit provisos are actually stipulated, and their bindingness therefore effectively proven, the implicit provisos can only be derived by deductive inference from the explicit provisos and general knowledge and we cannot adopt the same operative procedure ('read the contract') to verify them.

It is now clear why we say that in the case of incomplete information we can speak neither of explicit contingent provisos nor of implicit (contingent and specific) provisos. In the same way as an implicit belief in W is not even specified with reference to the states in Ω, and a proposition that is valid with reference to W, i.e. true in all the states of W, is not necessarily valid in Ω, an implicit proviso existing in relation to the known states W is not defined with reference to unforeseen events, deriving from states in Ω.

In short: if there are genuinely new and unforeseen states of the world, it cannot be said that any concrete and contingent norm is implicit with respect to them; (it is equally clear, of course, that no contract can have been stipulated or a positive norm deliberated about them).

V. Explicit Contracts, Implicit Rules and Ethical Code

We will now look in greater detail at the system of norms governing an efficient and stable hierarchical transaction. For the sake of convenience we will look at a contract of employment. The system of norms governing this transaction consists of three types of rules:

a) *Explicit contingent contract.* An explicit contract sets out reciprocal obligations, for example the obligation on the part of the employee to carry out his job in the way described and for a certain number of hours per week, and constraints on the part of the employer regarding what he can ask and some prohibitions contingent on certain *ex ante* determined states of the

129

word; all this refers to *foreseen* contingencies, and as such refers to states in W.

b) *Delegation of authority*. In relation to all states about which there is no explicit proviso in the contract but which are known *ex ante*, a weak default rule is set up, by means of which, in all situations not described in the contract, the employer has the right to make requests he considers to be most appropriate concerning the job to be carried out by the employee. These requests are obviously constrained by the explicit part of the contract, i.e. by the type and length of job to be performed by the employee in each *ex ante* known situations and by the conditional prohibitions specified therein.

c) *Ethical code and (strong) default rule in relation to genuinely unforeseen events*. In relation to unforeseen events, about which the parties have neither explicitly nor implicitly agreed on the acceptable behaviour to be taken by the party in authority, an ethical code does apply, or in other words a set of general principles formulated in terms of non-contingent universal statements, or with reference to abstract categories and types of situations to which abstract and general principles are applied.

The rules in (b) would cover the whole set Ω if there were no limitations imposed by (c), so that this part of the system of rules governing the organisation can be seen as a constraint on the discretionary powers of the party in authority. This constraint is required in relation to the set of contingencies not covered by any implicit contract, such that the use of discretion in these contexts may be acceptable to both sides. Thus the ethical code serves as a (strong) default rule: it establishes what form of behaviour would be acceptable to the parties whenever no effective consensus has been revealed and there is no evidence of acceptance of a given conduct contingent on the occurrence of particular situations and contexts[13].

Let us take an example from the case of an employment contract. The ethical code could state (principle 1): 'the company, understood as a cooperative activity by means of which different stakeholders contribute to the

---

13 Traces of this can be seen in civil law when a party in the contract is given the right to make discretionary decisions constrained by general principles of 'good faith', 'due diligence', or 'according to the general spirit of the contract'. Our thesis is that these expressions refer back to a common understanding of the ethical values regulating contracts in general, that the ethical code simply makes explicit in as much as they are expressions of the social contract itself. For a similar interpretation of the norms of corporate law and the notion of 'good faith' in particular, cf. Preite (1992), pp. 178-200.

production of a surplus, must be fairly run by the manager. For this reason the investments of any sides, particularly those in a specific human assets are given incentive and protected, so that everyone can expect over the course of time to see his investment rewarded in proportion to his contribution to the wealth produced by the firm'. A further norm (principle 2) may be drawn from this general view 'in any event the firm undertakes to respect the value of human resources and of people and in particular to protect specific investments in human capital made by employees in contributing to the creation of wealth on the part of the firm'. These principles may give rise to a standard of conduct, according to which the firm undertakes to guarantee that an employee is not given inferior roles unless proved to be incompetent or he fails to behave diligently and that the professional skills of the employees are kept competitive by means of participation in training opportunities.

General and abstract norms of this type are set out in the hypothetical contract backing the firm. They have validity in general for every employment relationship, beyond considering specific aspects of the concrete agreements, and they are understood to hold *to a certain extent* even in the case of unforeseen events. It may in fact be supposed that the provisos of an explicit contract should include concrete guarantees for the employee in relation to the occurrence of some predictable states of the world. Beyond the guarantees stated with reference to these situations, however, *concrete* norms of protection are not specified. On the other hand, ethical principles set out protection of the employee in situations that are not foreseen. In order to do this a code of ethics employs general terms such as 'cooperative activity producing a surplus' or 'specific investment in human capital' to identify features of economic organisation that may come about in a wide category of contingencies, some of which are not foreseen at the time of signing the contract. Should these contingencies occur, the problem will be to decide whether they fall into the general category and whether the equity principle (principle 1) and the prescription of protection (principle 2) do apply to them. If the ethical norms have been well devised, features such as 'cooperative activity producing a surplus' or 'specific investment in human capital' will in fact be essential features of the firm's activity in unforeseen contingencies and will enable ethical criteria and appropriate standards of behaviour to be applied. Ethical principles thus identify certain general features and norms that have to be universally applied to all the situations displaying the given features.

From this example we can say that norms in (c) are not specific and contingent provisos but general rules formulated in universal and abstract terms, without making reference to specific concrete contingencies. Rather they are ethical principles that can be applied to situations in which a subject or agent has certain moral features (for example a 'need' or a 'moral right' etc.). Like universal moral principles, principles of an ethical code give rise to judgements that are valid in all similar case, where similarity is a property that is verified in terms of belonging to a certain abstract type, but cannot be ascertained by the personal identity of particular individuals or concrete things involved. Having a moral characteristic and being classified as a typical situation does not imply that the agent has any concrete knowledge of the specific case in point, but only t that he recognises that a situation belongs to a certain ethical abstract type or category or pattern, whose boundaries will normally be fuzzy.

VI. Vagueness VS. Precision

We must now look at the most significant aspect of ethical codes: *the importance of vagueness of ethical or constitutional norms* compared to the precision of provisos that are explicit or implicit in the contract. The problem is how to remedy the *ex post* gap in commitments based on provisos contingent on *ex ante* foreseeable events when of *ex post* events occur that were *ex ante* unpredictable or unpredicted. The *ex post* observability of the unforeseen event does not, as we have seen, mitigate the problem since, if the event derives solely from unforeseen states, the *ex ante* implicit or explicit provisions are not specified for this case, which means that their applicability to the observed event is indeterminate.

Ethical, like constitutional norms are thus expressed in abstract, general but vague terms, that can be adapted both to known and *not known* cases. If the norm 'do B if X occurs' is expressed in terms where the abstract premise X is general and vague, then in a number of cases we may have states displaying the precisely described event E1, or the precisely described event E2, but all of which may display the vague event X only to a certain degree. The *ex ante* known states will be 'X' to a certain extent because it is not possible to distinguish clearly between them on the basis of X. But the *ex post* observable unforeseen states will also be X to a certain extent and we will not be able to distinguish clearly between them either on the basis of X.

In short, we cannot by means of a vague term distinguish between known and unforeseen states. Unexpected states will share vague properties. Thus we can predicate a duty *ex ante* on the occurrence of vague properties. The effect is that this duty will be applied also in *ex ante* unknown states, at least as far as the *ex ante* unforeseen state comes *ex post* into the domain of application of the vague term.

Let us suppose for example that we have a contingent contract that sets out provisos for the supply of agricultural goods, considering price increases or reduced quantities, conditional on the number of days of bad weather foreseeable in the harvest season (let's assume summer). The possible states of the world are consequently partitioned on the basis of the degree of bad weather in the summer period. Let us suppose we have a precise but incomplete description of the list of states of bad weather. In fact on the basis of past experience we consider only 1 to 10 consecutive days of rain per month possible in the summer months. Given this description of the (meteorologically) possible alternative states of bad weather, we set out certain provisos asking for an increase in price or a reduction in quantity to be supplied in the case of bad weather.

Let us suppose now that an unforeseen event takes place that summer, such as 20 days of rain and 5 days of hail or snow in a month. No provisos are specified regarding this state, which differs in detail from the worst predicted one. One of the parties to the contract (the supplier) will therefore demand a greater reduction in quantity, but the other party (the buyer) may well call for the application of the greatest increase in price or reduction of quantity agreed *ex ante* and no more. There is here simply something missing, a gap in the contract. If, however, we had used vague terms such as 'average', 'extremely' or 'exceptionally' bad weather, all the bad weather states, those known *ex ante* as well as those not known *ex ante* but known *ex post*, would have been accounted for in one of the terms. Thus a commitment or proviso relating to the occurrence of 'exceptional bad weather' would be applied to the *ex ante* unforeseen but *ex post* observable event of 20 days of rain and 5 of hail in August, once we admit that this bad weather is understood as 'exceptional'.

We are thus in a position to recognise the *benefits of vagueness*. An abstract, general but vague term is likely to be able to capture a property that belongs also to not known states, in that unforeseen states are distinguished from known states not for their belonging in the vague general category but simply because they are quite different in terms of precise descriptions of concrete and specific features of each state, so that the unforeseen states add to the old descriptions new concrete features. In other words, the ever finer partitions lead to states about which it is, to say the least, doubtful as to whether the prescriptions established for components of rougher divisions apply. In fact what makes the description of possible alternative states of the world incomplete is exactly the never ending attempt to give more precise concrete description to each state, making a finer and finer distinction between them. For each fine partition made on the basis of a precise concrete description of features, nevertheless we will be able to go on to find a still more precise and finer partition. We must then admit that at every stage of our description of states of the world we must be ready to face the possibility of discovering the existence of other features (that is other descriptions) of the states of the world not yet considered.

The keystone lays in the relationship between the notion of states space, understood as the set of accurate, alternative and jointly exhaustive descriptions of the universe and the language used to express norms. If the language implied descriptions of the initial conditions for validity of norms in vague terms (such as 'high', 'medium', 'low'), we would not have a clear discrimination (or partition) of states as equivalence classes, clearly separate and mutually exclusive (some 'medium' states could also be to a certain extent 'high'). At the same time, however, we would not have totally unforeseen states, since any state - including those whose precise concrete description we cannot even imagine - could be 'high', at least to a certain degree. Consequently rules of conduct could be valid *ex post* for any state, including *ex ante* unforeseen ones.

In essence, there is a trade-off between vacuum or absence of norms and ambiguity and non-peremptoriness in application. If we wish to prescribe behaviour contingent on unforeseen events we have to use norms with vague terms but this will mean non-univocal application of norms to concrete situations. The alternative is between precise norms that are not binding and do not apply outside their context and vague norms that impose obligations whose application is ambivalent. Our problem is whether there is a way to deal with this vagueness and ambivalence of norms rationally, in order to establish behaviour in the face of unforeseen contingencies. Our thesis is that this is feasible and that it coincides with the definition *of a constitutional contract* and *ethical code*, as long as we admit the rationality of using 'vague' measures and reasoning by *default*.

Chapter 6

Dealing with Vagueness of Norms: the Theory of Fuzzy Sets

I. Introduction

In this chapter we introduce the basic theoretical concepts on 'fuzzy sets' and the lines along which fuzzy logic can be used to formally express the intuition that an ethical code essentially constitutes a response to the ambiguity created by the occurrence of unforeseen events in the context of economic decision making[1]. The theory of fuzzy sets was first formulated by Lotfi Zadeh in 1965 (Zadeh 1965) and since then has been theoretically developed and applied in various fields: mathematical analysis, logic, possibility theory, expert systems, pattern recognition, decision analysis, operation research (Kauffman 1975, Zimmerman 1991), robots, artificial intelligence and neural networks (Kosko 1993) and more recently in game theory (Billot 1991) and oligopoly theory (Mansur 1995). Although apparently developed independently, in fact fuzzy logic follows a path created by the non-bivalent logics proposed in the past by those (Russell, Lukasiewicz and many others) who were attempting to face a classical philosophical problem: the problem of vagueness (Williamson 1994).

Our normal everyday language contains a range of vague terms. The term 'heap' is normally used to set out the classic Sorites paradox: let us suppose that 1000 grains constitute a heap but that 10 grains do not; at what point do we pass from a heap to a non-heap? If we reduce the heap one grain at a time, is it logical to suppose that at a certain point we will pass from a heap to a non-heap by removing a single grain say from 250 (heap) to 249 (non-heap)? It seems obvious that if 250 is still a heap, 249 is too (try the following mental experiment: you see something that you regard as a heap and you are told that it contains 250 grains; if you take away a grain is it conceivable that you may not continue to regard it as a heap?). The same is

---

[1] A treatment of the ethical code in terms of a game in which reputation is associated with respect for ethical principles defined by fuzzy sets is developed in the following chapters 7 and 8.

true for every N, such that if N grains is a heap then N-1 grains is a heap. In short, the difference between a heap and a non-heap cannot consist of a single grain. But then we can go back to 11 grains which if you take away 1 becomes 10, which would still be a heap, in contradiction of the hypothesis. The answer is that 'heap' is intrinsically vague or that it is a term which denotes an insufficient or indeterminate state of knowledge regarding the state of the world. There must be at least a region, between n < 1000 and m > 10 in which a collection of x grains (for $n \geq x \geq m$) is an intermediate or vague entity between a heap and a non-heap, that it is at the same time 'heap' and 'non-heap' (or it is both things to a certain degree).

Similarly, terms such as 'young', 'close' and 'dark in colour' can be considered vague. They are all terms which indubitably have a meaning, but which refer to sets of objects at the edges of which there is a fuzzy area, which includes objects whose inclusion in the realm of 'young people', or 'close objects' or 'dark colours' is ambiguous. Moral expressions too such as 'equitable distribution' or 'deserving individual' can be seen as consisting of vague terms. For example, 'desert can be understood as the basis for a claim based on the exercise of effort or on the dedication of a given individual (and it certainly is understood in the way in many cases). But the capacity for effort and dedication to a particular task is in part a question of natural aptitude and in part due to the social environment in which one is born, something which happens without our having deserved it. Where personal capacity ceases to be based on accidental and chance factors and begins to be something for which we are in effect responsible is undoubtedly a vague boundary, similar to that which distinguishes a 'heap' from a 'non-heap'.

These concepts are clarified and made less ambiguous through the development of moral theories and sometimes through the insertion of moral theories into the context of the theory of rational choice. In this way the terms are defined and the margin of ambiguity is undoubtedly reduced. The need to give an unambiguous meaning to the normative judgement is furthermore evident from the fact that a normative criterion is a guide to action, so that the judgement 'X is rational', 'Y is right' etc mean above all that one should do X if one wants to achieve some goal or conform to some value, that one *must* do Y etc. In short they all contain the prescription 'do it'. If the judgements were vague, the prescription would be empty: the statement 'do and do not do X' is not a prescription of conduct and has a (normative) meaning that is certainly less plausible than the (descriptive) meaning of the affirmation that for certain numbers of grains it is vague as to whether they do or do not constitute a heap (we can accept that a vague term nevertheless has a descriptive meaning, but vagueness in a prescription simply destroys the prescription). If however with the development of normative theories we define the meaning of the terms so that the prescription is valid only for the cases in which the definition of the basic terms of the theory is satisfied, there nevertheless remains the problem of *which* concrete situations fall under the theory's domain of application, that is, which of them satisfy the definition of the basic terms. If, for example, the prescription 'give X more than Y', based on a criterion of equity, is applied where the individual X is more disadvantaged than the individual Y, or is in a condition of greater need, it still has to be established, situation by situation, who is the disadvantaged individual, or who is in a position of need. Even though we may have formal definitions of 'disadvantage' or of 'need', it may remain vague which individuals in the concrete situations come under these definitions. In a similar way, the normative models of economic theory identify the appropriate rational behaviour concept in various contexts where choices have to be made, which are defined by terms such as 'game of negotiation', 'cooperative game' 'context of mutually advantageous cooperation, mixed contexts' etc. But uncertainty remains regarding which empirical situations can be interpreted as examples of such definitions, for example whether a given situation is a cooperative game (do implicit social rules and explicit formal social rules define the context as cooperative or non-cooperative?)

None of this casts doubt on the coherence of the theory and the univocal nature of the deduction of prescribed rational behaviour (that is, the syntax of the theory) but it renders ambiguous its concrete applications and the identification of which concrete behaviour effectively corresponds to which requirement of the theory, that is, its meaning. In abstract we have clear formal definitions of the descriptive characteristics which must be satisfied in order for a context to come within a given definition of rational conduct, but in practice the judgement is vague regarding which situation exhibits one or the other descriptive characteristic such as to fall into the domain of a given definition.

II. Definition of Elementary Fuzzy Concepts[2]

The classic definition of a set is a collection of elements or objects. If we start from a collection X of elements (a set) and we want to define a subset of X, we must simply establish a relationship of membership of each element of X to the subset E. The relationship of membership is the key concept. It can be described by listing the elements of E, or by establishing a condition such that all x's with the property Y are elements of E, or by means of a characteristic function, which has value 0 for each element of the collection X if the element does not belong to the subset E and value 1 if the element belongs to the subset. These values can be interpreted as 'true' or 'false' values for the statement 'element x belongs to the set E'. If the relationship of membership is understood thus, the resulting subset E is a set whose limits are clear cut (classic set): for each element of X it can be clearly stated whether or not it belongs to E.

The definition of a fuzzy set follows naturally from the modification of that of a classic set. Let us consider a relationship of membership that is not univocal and not clear, but is such as to establish the degree to which an element of X belongs to the set $\underline{E}$. A degree of membership that is intermediate between clearly belonging and clearly not belonging is what is needed to express the fuzzy membership of an element $x \in X$ to $\underline{E}$. This gradation expresses a peculiar type of imperfection of knowledge , which we can more correctly call vagueness or ambiguity: it is not clear whether any $x \in X$ is a an $\underline{E}$ but – if we try to explain the relationship by any means – we can say that an x is an $\underline{E}$ only to the degree y (for $0 \leq y \leq 1$). We can state then that $\underline{E}$ is a fuzzy set. It is important to understand that this way of expressing things has nothing to do, their superficial similarity notwithstanding, with the probability of an event (or a casual variable) that can be referred back to a classic set: we do not want to know how likely it is that the event E will occur, that is the probability that at least one state $x \in X$ in which E happens will occur. Indeed, to proceed in this way, every x where E may happen must be an element strictly belonging to E, so that the probability of E would be the sum of the probabilities of the states that belong to E, and the grada-

---

[2]   The definitions given here are largely taken from Zimmerman (1991); see his book for further details. Cf. also Kaufmann (1975). The economic examples have been introduced *ex novo*, to underline the relevance of the theory to our purposes.

tion which we would have found would be the distribution of probabilities induced by E on the elements of X. The question about vagueness is completely different and in a certain sense preliminary: what we cannot state clearly is whether x belongs to $\underline{E}$ and therefore if, when the state x occurs, $\underline{E}$ would also occur, in the sense that together with x we would also observe an example (or an element) of $\underline{E}$. Thus the distribution induced by $\underline{E}$ on the elements of X captures a different notion of imperfect knowledge , which concerns the *ambiguity* or the *vagueness* of the description of each x *in terms* of E (or to put it another way the vagueness of the statement 'x is an E').

If therefore a classic set is a collection of objects, a fuzzy set is a set of ordered pairs

$$\underline{A} = \{x, \mu_{\underline{A}}(x) | x \in X\}$$

where the x's are elements of a classic set X and $\mu_{\underline{A}}(x)$ is the function of *membership* or *degree* of membership of the element x in the fuzzy set $\underline{A}$ that maps the set X to the space of membership M^3. The function of membership takes its values from a subset of real non-negative numbers whose upper limit is a finite real value and whose lower limit is 0. For the sake of convenience a *normalisation* of the set of real values from which a function of membership takes its values is normally assumed, so that - dividing every number assigned by the function of membership by the number corresponding to the value which constitutes the upper limit of the space of membership - the $\mu_{\underline{A}}(x)$ varies between 0 and 1.

As an example, let us suppose that the set $X = \{1,2,3, ...,10\}$ represents the ordered set of ten policies that the government can undertake in order to put public finances in order. We must express a judgement about the equity of the measure – or rather establish which subset of policies falls under the criterion of social equity. Taking account of the many dimensions of the measures and of the claims of many different groups, this is clearly a judgement which faces multiple interpretations of equity. The fuzzy set of equitable government economic measures in economic policy can be expressed as follows:

$$\underline{E} = \{(1, 0.2), (2, 0.5) (3, 0.8), ..., (9, 0.7), (10, 0.3)\}$$

---

[3]   Cf. Zimmerman (1991), p. 12.

Or for all $x \in X$

1	2	3,........ ....., 9	10
$\mu_{\underline{A}}(x)$ 0.2	0,5	0.8,.........., 0.7	0.3

As a second example, let us consider the set of firms X, and let us number these firms x_1, x_2, ... ,x_n. Let us suppose that the term firm is sufficiently clear to allow us to define a classic set and that furthermore the distinction between one firm and another is also sufficiently clear to permit us to count them and understand them as distinct elements in the classic set X. Now we are concerned to establish which among these firms have joint activity among their members, that realises a surplus with respect to the separate production which the members would be able to carry out if they acted as independent productive elements. Assume that the characteristic function of the coalition among all the members of a firm measures the coalition's value in terms of productivity. Then it is necessary to know whether the characteristic function is superadditive (that is, the value of the coalition among all the members is higher than the sum of the value of the sub-coalitions including the 'sole- coalitions' of a single player). This will depend partly on the nature of the investments. If the investments are specific and highly idiosyncratic it is best for them to be undertaken in a single productive unit, since their cooperation will produce a surplus with respect to the value which the agents could obtain by means of those investments if they were free to exchange with every other agent in the market. Thus investments that are highly specific and reciprocally functional to cooperation imply a superadditive characteristic function for the coalition between all members of the firm who undertake such investments. However, the judgement as to the specific or idiosyncratic nature of the investment can be vague, it depends on characteristics of the activity and of individuals the description of which is not clear. For example, a working 'atmosphere' may be a factor in the production of a surplus, if the individuals invest in human relationships based on trust and reciprocal respect. But although the judgement about the nature of such relationships is certainly possible, it must be vague. Let us suppose that the set of firms X is ordered on the basis of the number of members who participate in joint production. Analogously to the previous case, the fuzzy set of the firms which produce a cooperative surplus can be expressed

6. DEALING WITH VAGUENESS OF NORMS

$\underline{E} = \{(x_1, 0), (x_2, 0.8)\ (x_3, 0.9),\ ...,\ (x_9, 0.4), (x_{10}, 0.2)\}$

Now let us define the *support* of a fuzzy set $\underline{A}$, S(A), as the clear subset made up of all the elements x of a classic predefined set X for which the value of the function of membership in A is not nil. Having as a support a clear cut set of elements, which is a subset of a clear cut set of references (that is, X), it is evident that the fuzzy sets are subsets with fuzzy edges defined by elements of a clear cut set. In substance, we establish the degree to which clearly defined objects, as elements of the set X, belong to categories with fuzzy edges. In this way, however, we also say that any element of X was unclearly or ambiguously characterised as regards the characteristic with respect to which we define the set $\underline{E}$.

A general definition, and also a very useful one for our purposes, it that of a (clear cut) set of elements belonging to a fuzzy set $\underline{A}$ at least to the degree α, or to put it another way, the α-level set[4].

$A\alpha = \{x \in X \mid \mu_{\underline{A}}(x) \geq \alpha\}$

For example, in the case of the fuzzy set of firms that produce a cooperative surplus, the set of those which we consider to be at least at the level 0.8 as capable of producing a cooperative surplus can be made up of

$A_{0,8} = \{x_1,\ x_2,\ x_3,\ x_4\}$

It is clear that belonging to an α-level defines a clear cut set, which allows only degrees 0 or 1 (even if in the background there is a fuzzy set). The concept of α-level is an important one, because it permits us to derive a clear cut set, on which it is possible to predicate a clear action, as a set in which a vague property is *satisfied at least to a certain degree*, that is to treat the vague property 'as though' it were clearly satisfied, since we judge that it is 'sufficiently' satisfied.

In the case of the fuzzy sets, the traditional elementary operations of sets (union, intersection, complement) are defined by mathematical operations on the functions of membership, defining the basic fuzzy sets for which we

---

[4]   Cf. Ibid. p.14.

wish to calculate the intersection, the union and the complement[5]. In particular if we want to calculate the fuzzy set $\underline{C}$ derived from the intersection of two fuzzy sets $\underline{A} \cap \underline{E}$, we must find for each element x of X the minimum value of its functions of membership in $\underline{A}$ and $\underline{E}$ respectively

$$\mu_{\underline{C}}(x) = \text{MIN } \{\mu_{\underline{A}}(x), \mu_{\underline{E}}(x)\}, \quad \text{for all the } x \in X$$

To put it another way, the degree of membership of each x to the intersection set is given by the minimum value of membership in each of the two sets whose intersection is being defined. This seems intuitively correct: if an element x were not to any degree a member of one of the two fuzzy sets (for example $\underline{A}$), it would obviously not be a member of the intersection set either, which means that the value $\mu_{\underline{A}}(x) = 0$ must be reflected in $\mu_{\underline{C}}(x) = 0$, even if $\mu_{\underline{E}}(x) > 0$. In the same way it is reasonable to expect that if an element x is only to a small degree a member of the set $\underline{A}$, it can only belong to a small degree to the intersection set between $\underline{A}$ and every other fuzzy set. If on the other hand we want to calculate the fuzzy set $\underline{D}$ which derives from the union of two fuzzy sets $\underline{A} \cup \underline{E}$, we must find for every element x of X the maximum value of its function of membership respectively in each of the two original fuzzy sets

$$\mu_{\underline{D}}(x) = \text{MAX } \{\mu_{\underline{A}}(x), \mu_{\underline{E}}(x)\}, \quad \text{for all the } x \in X$$

To put it another way, the degree of membership of each x to the union set is given by the maximum value of the function of membership to the two sets whose union is being defined. The definition too seems intuitively correct. If an element belongs perfectly (that is at degree1) to one of the two sets from which we generate the union, then, even if it were not to any degree a member of the other set, it should nevertheless belong to the union set at a degree not lower than 1, since this set is nothing more than the sum of two sets in a single set, which combines all the elements which the two sets held separately. This intuition is equally valid, even if an element belongs to one of the two sets at a degree lower than unity, while it continues to be partially or completely absent from the other set in the union. In such a case we could choose between two degrees of membership, but to choose the lower degree of membership would contradict the intuition according to which the union

---

[5]   Cf. Ibid. pp.16-18.

preserves and unties all the elements (and degrees of membership) of the two separate sets. By the complement $\not\subset \underline{A}$ of the fuzzy set $\underline{A}$ on the other hand should be understood the fuzzy set which for every x has the function of membership

$$\mu_{\underline{A}}(x) = 1 - \mu_{\underline{A}}(x), \quad \text{for all the } x \in X$$

which is intuitively justified by the hypothesis of normalisation (if a statement 'X is an $\underline{E}$' is completely clear, it has the value 1, it's negation has the value 0, and the sum is 1; similarly if a statement is averagely vague, it has the value $0 < y < 1$, and its negation must have the value $1 - y$ if the parallel is to be maintained with the previous example). Let us consider, giving an example just for the first case, the intersection set between the equitable policies of the government and the efficient policies of the government . If we accept that the judgement as to whether each policy belongs to the two categories (equitable ones and efficient ones) can be represented by fuzzy functions of membership, then the set of the policies that are both equitable and efficient is given by the fuzzy set which to each policy associates the degree of membership that the policy has in the equitable set or in the efficient set, choosing always the *minimum* of the two.

III. Fuzzy Sets and Possibility

Up to now we have presented the theory of fuzzy sets by means of examples of vague economic terms. But the most interesting interpretation is one which takes the theory as a theory of possibility, opposed to the theory of probability (Zadeh 1978, Dubois and Prade 1988, Zimmerman 1991). In fact, up to now we have understood a fuzzy set as a way of expressing the statement 'x is an $\underline{E}$', where x's membership of the set $\underline{E}$ is ambiguous and the degree of membership therefore expresses the vagueness of the relationship of membership. What we now want is the *possibility* that each element in a universe of discourse will take place, that is that a variable, defined in a universe of discourse, can identify with each of the elements of the given universe. In classical terms, possibility is a strictly bivalent notion: a variable *may* or *may not* take on a given value, *tertium non datur*. If however a state of the world is characterised fuzzily (that is, it is an element in a fuzzy set) then the possibility that this state of the world will occur will be affected by its fuzzy character.

The basic concept needed to arrive at the notion of distribution of possibility is given by the definition of fuzzy constraint (Zadeh 1978): let U be a discourse universe, and let X be a variable defined in such a way as to permit the value of each element in such a universe to be taken. Now let us define a fuzzy set $\underline{F}$ such that each element $u_i \in U$ belongs to $\underline{F}$ to the degree $\mu_{\underline{F}}(u)$. $\underline{F}$ is called a fuzzy constraint on the variable X if the assigning to the variable X of each value u of the domain U is subject to the condition that it must have an identical form to that of the degree to which the particular element u of the domain belongs to $\underline{F}$: X is u to the degree $\mu_{\underline{F}}(u)$. In other words, $\mu_{\underline{F}}(u)$ is the degree to which the constraint $\underline{F}$ is satisfied when the value u is assigned to the variable X, or the degree to which the element of the domain U, which is selected when X assumes the value u, is compatible with the concept or the term $\underline{F}$ [6].

From here we can pass directly to the notion of *possibility*. The fuzzy constraint in fact associates a distribution of possibilities to the variable X. The possibility that X is a particular $u_i \in U$ is numerically equal to the degree to which X, when it is u_i satisfies the fuzzy constraint. Or in other words, the distribution of possibilities of X is

$$\pi_X = \mu_{\underline{F}}$$

while the possibility that X is each u_i is $\pi_X(u_i) = \mu_{\underline{F}}(u_i)$. In order to clarify this concept of possibility, let us look at the following example (Zadeh 1978): let us consider various ages, numerically determined (for example from one year to 90 years) and the fuzzy set 'young', which associates the value of membership to every age according to which, for example, a person of 28 is young (for example, 0.7). Let us now consider the variable 'one's age', which we assume varies in the universe of ages between 1 and 90 years (i.e. a clear cut set). Now, take the particular individual John. We want to know whether it is possible that John is each of the ages included in the universe of discourse, given that we have got the information that 'John is young'. Thus in assigning the possibility for John to be each age in the universe of discourse, we must take account of the fact that he is young.

---

[6]   Cf. Ibid. pp.111-112.

6. DEALING WITH VAGUENESS OF NORMS

Since 'young' is a fuzzy term, this piece of information does not allow us to exclude any possibilities or definitely allow others. On the contrary, it leads to a distribution of possibilities, where every age is weighted with a value between 0 and 1, which reflects the degree of membership according to which each age is an element in the set 'young'. In brief, the fuzzy constraint (the membership of every age to the set 'young') leads to the possibility that John is every age between 1 and 90 when we know that John is young. Therefore the proposition 'John is twenty-eight' has a possibility 0.7, that is, the same value which we used before to express the compatibility between John being 28 and being 'young'.

We should stress that, superficial similarities notwithstanding, the notion of possibility is not the same as probability. The distributions of probability and possibility for the same variable can in fact be completely different, since their meaning is completely different. For example, let us suppose that we want to know whether it is possible that firms with a varying number of components will produce positive cooperative surpluses in a given industry with given technologies. At the same time we want to express the subjective probability distribution that these firms will produce a positive level of cooperative surplus. Let us also suppose that we know that the technologies being used permit effective cooperation in a group of modest size of workers whose limits are however not clearly specified, that is, they depend partly on the subjective characteristics of the individuals:

u	1	2	3	4	5	6,......,28	29	30
$\pi_{\underline{X}}(u)$	0	1	1	1	0.8	0.5,....,0.2	0.1	0.08
$P_{\underline{X}}(u)$	0	0.2	0.3	0.4	0.1	0, ...,0	0	0

The possibility distribution π_X says that, given our information about technology, the net surplus can be produced precisely with groups of between 2 and 4 workers working cooperatively and then with decreasing possibility as the size of the group increases. The probability distribution P_X reflects our beliefs regarding the arrangement of the firm that is most likely to succeed in producing a positive surplus through the cooperation of its members. As can be seen, there is a considerable formal difference due to the fact that the measurement of possibility does not require that a pre-established mass should be distributed among various possibilities so that their probabilities sum to 1.

The formal characterisation of a fuzzy measure of possibility (Zadeh 1978) is in fact the following: given a set X and the power set P(X) which includes all the subsets of X, a measure of possibility definite on P(X) is a function Π from P(X) to the real line [0,1] which satisfies the conditions[7]:

1. The empty set has the possibility 0 ($\Pi\varnothing$) = 0),
the total set X has the possibility 1 ($\Pi(X) = 1$).
2. If a set is included in another set, then its possibility can not be lower than that
of the other set.
3. The possibility of the union of a series of sets, elements of P(X), is equal to that of the most possible element in the series, that is
$\Pi(U_{i \in I}A_i) = SUP \ \Pi_{i \in I}(A_i)$.

These conditions are notable for the absence of additivity, which is typical of probability (at least in standard definitions) and reflects onto probabilities the assumption of perfect knowledge of the space of possible states[8].

IV. Unforeseen Contingencies and Vagueness

The interpretation of fuzzy sets theory as a theory of possibility opens the doors to a discussion of the problem of unforeseen contingencies. In fact, the theory of fuzzy possibility focuses on the phenomenon of imprecision rather than on that of uncertainty. We have distributions of possibility, rather than clear distinctions between possible and impossible states, when some terms or statements that recur in the description of the states of the world are imprecise, such that we are unable to say whether, if a certain state should occur, it will bring with it an event which verifies the term or statement in

---

[7]   Cf. Ibid. p.46.

[8]   For the introduction of non-additivity into probability theory see Gilboa (1987), Schmeidler (1989), Gilboa and Schmeidler (1993). It is no coincidence that this is a way of seeking to capture a judgement of probability that expresses ambiguous beliefs and incomplete knowledge of the alternatives. The need for equipping a genuine subjectivist view of probability with a non logically omniscient theory of possibility was first pointed out by Hacking (1967).

cur, it will bring with it an event which verifies the term or statement in question. This throws a new light on the way in which the space of possibilities in decision theory is normally understood. Let $\Omega = \{\omega_1, \omega_2, \ldots, \omega_n\}$ be the set of states of the world, that is the set of the possible alternative 'complete' descriptions of the state of the world and let $P(\Omega)$ be the power set of the subsets of Ω, that is the events set. The set Ω is understood as a clear cut set whose elements clearly belong to it and are perfectly distinguishable from one another. In fact we may say that the set Ω is partitioned in equivalence classes, that is in all the alternative complete possible descriptions of the state of the world. Moreover, the subsets of Ω, which are elements of $P(\Omega)$, are also clear cut.

Now let us bring into play a new class of subsets of Ω, that is $\underline{P}(\Omega)$, which is made up of fuzzy sets. Each ω_i now also belongs to every fuzzy event to a given degree. If we know that the event which happens is indeed one of the fuzzy events, then that leads to a fuzzy distribution over the states of the world, which we can interpret as a distribution of possibilities over the alternative states of the world, given the information that the state of the world which occurs belongs to (to a certain degree) the relevant fuzzy set. In this way we represent the fact that in the description of the states, even though at first glance they are understood to be clear cut sets, there exists a level of imprecision regarding some characteristics, given that each state is member at a certain degree of each fuzzy event.

At first sight the fuzzy theory presents us with an approach linked to the old idea that the set of states Ω is univocally determined, by means of a partition into mutually exclusive and jointly exhaustive states: we have a reference set which is clear cut. We know univocally the states that belong to it and are able to distinguish them from one another. This would seem to leave no space for the idea of incomplete or imprecise knowledge of the basic possible alternatives. Nevertheless the fuzzy sets, insofar as they are subsets of Ω, introduce exactly this characterisation into the representation of the knowledge of the agents. A fuzzy set $\underline{E}$, to which a state ω_i 'imperfectly' belongs, means that that state is 'imperfectly' characterised as regards the property stated by the sentence corresponding to the event. Thus the description of the alternative states offered by Ω can certainly not be a complete, precise and exhaustive description of every characteristic that can be expressed using the resources of our natural language: we are not precise or univocal about the attribution of many characteristics to alternative states of the world (so that we cannot say that their description is devoid of ambiguity). Each ω_i represents a conjunction of the affirmation (or negation) of all the properties that can be expressed in language about any individual variables, but for many of these our 'state of the world' is not at all a precise and unambiguous description; in many ways it affirms that a given property is satisfied in that state *only to a certain degree*.

How can this imprecision or ambiguity exist in the description of the states ω_i? One possible reply is that there exist terms or concepts that are intrinsically imprecise, that they always have been so and always will be (for example the terms 'near', 'light' (applied to colours), 'young' etc.). It could also be suggested, however, that the ambiguity or imprecision involved in the description of states is introduced by the occurrence of unforeseen events. Fore example, whereas until recently we were sure about assigning certain substances to the category 'toxic', and excluding others, in the light of better information the boundaries between toxic (at a certain level) and non toxic have become less clear: certain substances previously regarded as innocuous now appear to be the cause of disorders, albeit at a low level, whilst others may be toxic but sometimes also beneficial[9]. All this depends

---

[9]   Other examples could be drawn from the history of theoretical terms of science, which change their meaning and become vague in the light of new scientific discoveries. The term *mass* seen through the eyes of classical physics or relativistic physics of, or the term 'Euler's polyhedron' in the light of the process of 'stretching concept' in mathematics, according to the definition given by Lakatos (1976), are good examples of how theoretical concept may become ambiguous after a new discovery. Then there are examples taken from legal language, under the impact of scientific and technological innovation. For example, what does 'asset' mean in the MO case, that is, in the case of cellular material removed from a cancer patient by a surgical operation, which benefited the patient, but whose specific genetic malformation was used to develop an innovative biotechnology technique for the treatment of a particular tumour which was then patented by the University where the operation was carried out? (cf. Erin 1994). Is the genetic information contained in body parts removed in the course of surgery an 'asset or surgical waste? If it is a necessary resource for the development of a new technique, insofar as the particular genetic malformation is the basis for the biotechnology technique that is developed, does the patient have intellectual property rights over the mutation that s/he has produced and which is indispensable for the new gene therapy technique? Apparently the case was resolved according to a different intuition. According to the judges, the University was legitimately entitled with the patent, but the patient was right in suing the University because the researchers failed in asking the

on the novelty and anomalousness of the new circumstances, and on the fact that the terms and concepts which previously appeared clear and distinct are revealed by the new experience to be confused, not able to be clearly distinguished, in a word 'fuzzy'. In this way it could be argued that one of the main sources of fuzzy events is the occurrence of unforeseen events, anomalies and surprises that partially subvert or render ambiguous and imprecise the terms in which we previously expressed our knowledge. On the other hand, since, when a state of the world occurs, I cannot say unambiguously whether the fuzzy event containing it also occurs, then the possibility of an event, traditionally regarded as clear, which also implies the description of the fuzzy characteristic itself becomes fuzzy.

In order to express all this in the terms of the space provided by the states of the world Ω, it could be stated that initially we have a set W of alternative descriptions of the world that are superficially complete and jointly

---

patient's informed consent to use his genetic material for the study. However the case itself proves the kind of ambiguity that an unforeseen event may create.

A further example is the discussion of bio-ethical committees on what has to be taken as a the basis for treating an embryo as a person or not: is it a person on the fourteenth day or, since it is vague, is it better to treat it 'as if' it were a person from conception, or, further, can 'personhood' be linked to the development of a nervous system that is capable of giving sensations of pleasure and pain – i.e. personhood intervene at a later time?

Finally let us consider ethical and economic terms in ordinary language: the expression 'abuse of the employee' may be vague in relation to the fact that unforeseen events occur: any request that the employee works extra hours without overtime is an 'abuse'. Let us suppose that there are extraordinary circumstances (a flood), so that the plant is flooded and the employer asks the employees to work all night to clean the mud out of the sheds. If some weeks later some of the workers ask for overtime and the employer refuses, is he guilty of abuse? Perhaps not, but the letter of the contract might say he is. If later on, however, the employer is faced with a crisis and sacks the employees who helped save the materials and machines which were threatened with damage, is he committing an abuse regarding the right which the employees acquired to use those materials? Perhaps he is, but it is hard to believe that this argument could be made to stick in front of a tribunal. There would in fact be intense discussion, more intense than normal trade union negotiation, which can justly be considered a *moral* discussion about the term 'abuse', which has become vague in relation to the occurrence of unforeseen events.

exhaustive. These descriptions of a state contain only properties that are clearly affirmed or denied. Subsequently, when unforeseen events occur, that is, events that are not included in the power set P(W), the set of states is extended, in the following way. The unforeseen events are sets to which the elements w ('clear-cut' states of the world) of W belong to a certain degree. Thus we add to the set of events P(W) the set of fuzzy events $\underline{P}$(W), defined on the reference set W (and as far as here it is the typical approach of the theory of the fuzzy sets). We can no longer be satisfied with the set of states W, however. In fact, what has been stated has important implications if we wish to speak not generically about the relationship between vague properties and a clear cut generic reference set X, but about the set of possible states of the world. In fact, in the case under examination the set of states Ω must include the description of all the properties which can be stated in a given discourse universe regarding the state of the world. If, therefore, a state must be a description (an affirmation or a negation) of all the properties that can be stated in the language, after the discovery of unforeseen events we should have states ω_i (extensions of the w_i) in which the affirmation of every vague property recurs, which have associated with them a degree of membership (and the negation of alternative degrees). These descriptions of a state which include vague statements are in fact the possible states of the world after the occurrence of unforeseen events has been discovered, that is, they constitute an extension of the states of the world that were initially understood as possible. Thus the effectively relevant set of states of the world is Ω, as an extension, by means of fuzzy properties, of W.

When we are dealing with unforeseen events, whose descriptions regularly include vague terms, what judgement should be made about their degree of possibility? *Ex ante*, before observing the event, the possibility of it happening, given that it is unforeseen, is nil. But when we have observed the occurrence of some unforeseen events, then we are in a position to establish their degree of possibility. From that moment on, such events come into the space of what is possible. However, they cannot be treated in the same way as events that are clearly possible (Poss = 1) or clearly impossible (Poss = 0). The occurrence of unforeseen circumstances generates fuzzy events, which happen in states of the world whose degree of membership in the events themselves is intermediate, expressing vagueness of the characteristic in question. The intermediate degree of membership is identical to the possibility that that state will occur, when the unforeseen event occurs.

V. Moral Code and Vagueness

The application of the logic of vagueness to moral codes could proceed in one of two ways. The first is to take the ethical terms themselves as vague terms. By that we mean that normative terms such as 'fair', 'good', 'equitable', 'X has the right to...' are vague. In this case it would be necessary to establish a fuzzy relationship between states of the world and sets corresponding to normative terms. That would mean that it is not clearly true or false whether a certain description of an action A carried out by an individual Y, which forms part of a state of the world, belongs to the set 'right' or 'good' etc. This would mean understanding normative terms as propositions corresponding to the description of certain characteristics of the world, in clear contrast with non-cognitivism in meta-ethics, according to which moral terms have mainly a prescriptive meaning. Furthermore, it would contradict subjectivism, according to which no ontological claim has to be made regarding the reality corresponding to moral judgements (that is, the values do not correspond to properties that belong to the objective constitution of the world out there, but are a result of our subjective judgement).

The second way of looking at the question, which is the one we shall adopt, does not imply any of the undesirable philosophical assumptions mentioned above. In particular, it is compatible with non-cognitivism in meta-ethics, according to which the main meaning of an ethical judgement is *prescriptive*, even if a moral judgement has to satisfy descriptive preconditions in order to be validly expressed (Hare 1963). In particular the judgement is associated with the presence of certain descriptive characteristics, to which a particular moral theory ascribes value, for example the presence of *pleasure* or *pain*, *preferences*, *claims*, instrumental *rational calculations*, *reasonableness* and so on. Moral theories treat the same characteristic invariably - always in the same way - in all situations that are similar as regards the occurrence of the relevant characteristic, and, this characteristic remaining equal, establish an invariable mode of behaviour with respect to changes in the other descriptive characteristics, which are regarded as morally irrelevant. In fact, moral judgement must be universalisable, as well as prescriptive, and this means that it can be extended to all situations which have similar *morally* significant characteristics (having descriptive content) while preserving its validity for the subject who is judging. In order to apply the theory of fuzzy sets to the notion of a moral code it is necessary concentrate on the notion of similarity.

Let us allow that the moral judgement that 'A's act X in situation Y with the characteristic Φ is *unfair*' is perfectly clear. First, the criterion of universalisability must be satisfied. Thus, let us suppose that, for every situation Q or Z that we substitute for Y and that for every name B, C that we substitute for A – provided the characteristic Φ remains constant – the judgement about the unfairness of action X will be equally clear. In other words, for whatever name is given to the agent, if Q resembles Y as regards the morally relevant descriptive characteristics Φ, and if the action X' – described in the new context – is effectively similar to the X of the original context, whenever the first judgement is prescriptive and universalisable then we maintain that the following judgement will also be valid: 'the act X' carried out by B in the situation Q, which has the characteristic Φ, is unfair'". Furthermore, the judgement about the action is not at all vague: X' is *clearly* unfair. The problem of vagueness arises when it is a question of attributing, on the basis of the relationship of similarity, the situations Q, Z to the set of situations that share the characteristic Φ with Y, or when it is a question of attributing B, C etc to the same set of individuals to which A belongs. These considerations concern the descriptive content of the terms: does Q describe the same characteristic Φ which is also described by Y? Does B belong to the same set of individuals as A? If the answer to this question is fuzzy, then the final judgement that 'B's act X' in the situation Q is unfair' is a vague judgement, not because the term "unfair' is vague, but because the attribution of the situation characterised by B and Q to the domain of the situations to which the criterion of unfairness is applied, as exemplified by the case of A and Y, is vague.

We can explore this point of view further. Intuitive ethical judgements are undoubtedly normally expressed by terms whose meaning cannot be specified exactly. But the ambivalence of these terms can be notably reduced by using moral theories. In particular, the use of moral theories which employ the formal language of the theory of rational choice can establish – on the basis of calculation of the rational solution to a problem of decision-making – which action is morally acceptable in every situation that satisfies the premises of the model.

Ethical judgement can be deduced from an axiomatic theory and have approximately the following structure:

6. DEALING WITH VAGUENESS OF NORMS

the space of payoff U, the concept of solution σ holds and the action (or vector of individual actions) which satisfies σ is called 'just'.

The theory is thus perfectly precise in calculating the 'just' action (choosing a vector of strategies and a vector of payoffs from the set of possibly outcomes). There may be vagueness, however, regarding which concrete situations satisfy the descriptive premises of the model (that is, if the ongoing social rules are R, if the relevant agents can be represented by N players, if they are sufficiently rational or have at their disposal actions and hold stakes that can be represented by Σ and U). This vagueness is *cognitive*, and *not* moral. It has to do with true/false judgements regarding whether a state of the world w_i satisfies the initial conditions of a certain theory, that is whether the state of the world is an interpretation or an empirical model of the theory, to which it is therefore appropriate to apply the concept of the solution σ. The solution may, for example, allow the exact calculation of the prescribed rational action, on condition that a game of negotiation exists between players 1 and 2, with an associated cooperative surplus and on the assumption that the agreed bargaining solution is then implemented in a cooperative game by means of a joint strategy, and with the additional condition that the status quo from which the surplus is calculated is free of force, fraud, parasitism etc. Vagueness may nevertheless reside in the identification of the situations that can be modelled in such as way as to satisfy the preceding conditions[10]. Do worker A and entrepreneur B cooperate effectively, in the sense that their partnership can give rise to a surplus over what they could produce as separate units? Is the entrepreneur's claim for recognition of the benefits deriving from his property rights over the firms' physical asset a just one, and not based on an original appropriation in which he exercised free riding over the worker or other agents? Judgement about these matters can be clear or vague according to how much information we have.

Allowing that vagueness relates to the descriptive premises for the application of a normative criterion, we may find situation S1 that satisfies completely the descriptive requirements to be regarded as a model of the game

---

[10]   The pioneeristic suggestion that the recognition of a game structure may be 'fuzzy' can be find in Ullman-Margalit (1977).

whose solution is σ, while another situation S2 does not fall so clearly into the domain of application of the same concept of solution [11].

As an illustration, let us suppose that we are faced by unforeseen events (see section 4) which take the form of clear cut sets or of sets that are themselves fuzzy. For example, we obtain an 'exceptionally high level of return' from the firm (higher than the most optimistic predictions). Or an entirely new technology appears, which will require a completely unknown kind of professional ability or level of education of the employee. These two events are in themselves fuzzy sets.

We could now point out that the unforeseen events (or states) are related to descriptive characteristics on the basis of which we establish whether the initial conditions of the game model are satisfied, to which the solution σ is applied. For example, it is not clear whether an exceptionally large surplus can be entirely attributed to the cooperative contribution of a group of people working together, or to an exogenous shock to the economic system in general. Or some of the capacities belonging to the abilities necessary to operate the technology are specific while others are not, and therefore overall it is vague whether the technology requires specific investments in human capital by the worker. In this way unforeseen events, or the states of the world that include their description, generate vagueness with regard to further terms: precisely those terms which we use to describe the conditions on the basis of which we establish whether it is appropriate to apply a given normative theory. That is, after we have learned of an unforeseen event (state) (preferably

---

[11]   Why should this happen? We have come up against the philosophical interpretations of the phenomenon of vagueness. One answer (typically that which is given by some fuzzy theorists, cf. Kosko 1993) is that the propositions regarding the descriptive properties are *intrinsically neither true nor false* i.e. vagueness is part of the ontological fabric of the world. However it is easy to decide relatively clearly on a case by case basis whether a situation of social interaction between two agents constitutes a mutually advantageous negotiation. Why in certain simple situations can this property be affirmed or denied by a true proposition, while in other difficult cases (those that are vague) I must accept that no proposition, either true or false, corresponds to this property? What remains therefore is the cognitive interpretation of vagueness (Williamson 1994). In this case, vagueness depends on the fact that our information is not sufficiently clear to enable us to establish definitively whether a situation of interaction belongs to the domain of application of a given theory or not. The theory addresses a property of our state of information or our knowledge, rather than the ontology of the thing itself.

vague itself), the descriptive terms which we use to identify the class of situations to which σ is applied, become a fuzzy set: now events (states) exist that belong to the domain of application σ *only to a certain degree*.

In substance, since when we define a normative theory in general and universal terms, we have in mind only a finite and limited number of possible models or empirical interpretations – that is, only a certain type of possible states of the world that can be formulated in a certain language – some situations that are in themselves possible escape us (for example, those which include characteristics that we can not imagine). When these appear, it may be that the applicability of the normative theory or moral principle remains doubtful. We cannot say whether it is true or false that the unforeseen situation falls into the domain of application of a given normative theory or moral principle: it falls into it *only to a certain degree*. The unforeseen events are therefore a source, perhaps the chief source, of the vagueness of the normative theories.

The existence of vagueness is however an inherent part of the normative theories based on universalisable theories and intended to have general validity. This does not render the univocal prescription of behaviour by the ethical code impossible. It establishes that, for the situations that satisfy particular descriptive requirements, a certain set of principles is valid. The admissibility or inadmissibility of a particular course of behaviour $a*$ follows deductively from the principles. Then the theory has to be applied to situations that are characterised by sufficiently general terms (cooperative surplus, specific investments, initial freedom from force or fraud etc) that they turn out to be vague in the face of unforeseen events. Such events (and the states that include their fuzzy description) will belong to the descriptive conditions of the models only to a certain degree, so that we shall have for unforeseen events (and states) fuzzy functions of membership in the set that defines the domain of application of the normative theory. This means that, rather than being mute in the face of unforeseen contingencies, the normative theory will find application in the new situations, *at least to a certain degree*.

How this happens may be suggested by returning to one of the fuzzy concepts introduced above. Let A_α be the set of unforeseen events which satisfy at level α the descriptive conditions of a model to which the theory of the solution σ is applied. Membership of an α-level is clear. The ethical code establishes that if an unforeseen events falls into the α-level, then this situation must be treated 'as if' it were in the domain of application of ethical principles. For example, an action $a*$ may be treated 'as if' it were right or wrong, since the act $a*$ occurs in a situation that falls into the α-level. But if the act $a*$ is right only until the contrary is proved, we can deduce albeit provisionally but unequivocally, that it is *admissible*. In the face of unforeseen events, the ethical code thus works as a system of principles, related to contexts of application that are wide and vague, and to norms and standards of behaviour, that are regarded as obligatory when an event involves the principle over a *certain level of significance*. It is obvious that the system of norms requires an *exercise of interpretation*. Every time we have to execute the exercise of measuring whether the current contingency falls into the domain of application of the principle to a sufficiently high degree, it is only by interpretation and judgement that we may be able to measure whether the α-level is satisfied or not.

VI. Limitations of this Way of Dealing with Vagueness

There are many objections to the way of dealing with vagueness suggested by the theory of fuzzy sets. Here we shall mention only those which most directly concern our application [12].

In the first place, the question whether a given context belongs to the domain of application of a principle *at least to a certain degree* is in itself the object of a judgement and this judgement may *itself* be vague. Thus the judgement as to whether a given α-level has been reached may be vague: is $\mu_A(x)$ at least α? Without needing to introduce *interpersonal* vagueness (different individuals could reach different judgements and disagree about whether α-level has been reached), at an *intrapersonal* level too a single individual might encounter vagueness regarding x's membership of $A\alpha$. In substance, given a fuzzy set $\underline{A}$, α is still always a clear number, but the function of membership, which establishes whether x's degree of membership of $\underline{A}$ reaches α-level, may in itself be fuzzy. Contrary to what was assumed in section 2 it would not therefore follow that

$$\mu_{A\alpha}(x) = 0 \text{ or } 1,$$

but that

---

[12]   For more general objections cf. Williamson (1994), pp.127-138.

6. DEALING WITH VAGUENESS OF NORMS

$\mu_A\alpha(w) = y$, with $0 \leq y \leq 1$.

To put it simply, the answer to the question 'does the state w have a degree of membership in $\underline{A}$ at least equal to the number α?' is 'to a certain degree'. If therefore we put α-level at $\alpha = 0.7$ and we consider the reference set of states of the world $W = \{w, w2, w3, w4, w5\}$ then

$$\mu_{0.7}(w) = \{(w_1, 0.1), (w_2, 0.8)\ (w_3, 0.3)\ (w_4, 1), (w_5, 0.1)\}.$$

Therefore $A_{0.7}$ (the set of states with the function of membership of at least level 0.7) is a fuzzy set: various states satisfy that clear soil level 'to a certain degree'. The vagueness in this case involves not only membership of $\underline{A}$ by the state w, but the *degree* of membership of the set $\underline{A}$, that is the value of the function $\mu_A(w)$. Therefore the question whether x is or is not a member of the set $A\alpha$ – that is, whether $\mu_A(w)$ reaches at least a certain level – also has a fuzzy value. In conclusion, this means that for every function of membership of w in $\underline{A}$ we can establish a distribution of possibilities, which expresses the possibility that the membership of a state in a fuzzy set $\underline{A}$ reaches a given level and at the same time reflects the vagueness that exists regarding the fact that that given level of membership has been reached.

In addition, the judgement regarding which α-level is appropriate may also be vague. Which α-level should we use? The α-level itself may be a fuzzy set. There may be not a single number corresponding to α, but a set of numbers, all of which satisfy α 'to a certain degree'. This is the case if by α we mean the (vague) *maximum level of vagueness* permitted in order to remain able to make a judgement. Different individuals may then have a different understanding of the appropriate α-level. This variety of opinions may be due to the inherent vagueness of the α-level understood as *level of maximum vagueness*: what level of vagueness cannot be exceeded in dealing with a property (satisfied to an intermediate degree) 'as if' it were perfectly satisfied?

In this case the value α itself is a fuzzy number (while in the previous case it was in any case a particular definite number that was satisfied to a certain degree). A distribution of degrees of membership is associated with a given set of clear cut values (for example those included in the range from 0 to 1). This is the fuzzy constraint which establishes the degree of compatibility between each of these clear cut values and the vague α. It can be used to establish the possibility distribution that assign the possibility that each number between 0 and 1 is α.

For example, hypothesise that the α-level must be the level of membership of the states of world to a certain fuzzy set, that identifies whether a norm has to be applied in the given state of the world. Therefore it must be a sufficiently high level in order to be able to treat a case 'as if' the requirements were perfectly satisfied. Then by making the reference set $X = [0,1]$ we could have the following fuzzy set:

$\alpha = \{(0.1, 0.01), (0.2, 0.05), (0.3, 0.15), (0.4, 0.2), (0.5, 0.4), (0.6, 0.5),$
$(0.7, 0.7), (0.8, 0.9), (0.9, 1), (1.1)\}.$

In short, being a level of acceptability is satisfied by various numbers between 0 and 1 to a certain degree. It is clearly so only for 0.9 and 1, but a significance level is reached for 0.7. Here α is a fuzzy number, while in the previous case the fuzzy set consisted of the set of degrees of membership that satisfied a given clearly determined α-level.

In general these observations lead to a single wider problem: assigning degrees of membership with clear cut numbers means trying to measure vagueness in terms which are not vague, and thus reducing the vagueness to clear terms. In this way, however, the problem of vagueness is simply shifted to a higher level: why should the judgement about the degree of membership ever be univocal? If we are in a domain of vagueness, it will itself be a vague matter. And if we try to fix a level in order to distinguish between high and low degrees of vagueness, why should that level be a clear term rather than a vague term, as indeed is intuitively suggested by the terms 'high' and 'low'? Finally, even if we succeeded in fixing levels of discrimination that were not vague, why should we be able to assign the degrees of membership to such sets univocally? In general the problem is one of a higher order vagueness. For every vague object, for which we attempt to express a fuzzy judgement by means of a clear cut degree of membership, in reality we generate a new vague object, which is the degree of membership itself.

This possibility is nevertheless taken account of by the theory, so that we cannot say that the higher order vagueness constitutes a counterexample to the theory. In the previous sections we considered fuzzy sets with clear cut functions of membership, but on the other hand we can define the notion of fuzzy sets whose function of membership or degree of membership is itself a fuzzy set (Zadeh 1975). In particular we can define as *type 1 fuzzy sets* those that were discussed in the first section of this chapter; that is, sets which associate a clear cut degree of membership to each of the elements of a given clear reference set, by means of a function from X to the real line [0,1]. A *type 2 fuzzy* set is a set which associates a fuzzy degree of membership to each element in the reference set X; that is, it associates a fuzzy set of degrees of membership to each element in such as way that for every $x \in X$ there is a set of clear membership values each of which has a function of membership associated with it which takes its value on the real line [0,1].

The definition of a *type 2* fuzzy set is therefore the following: a fuzzy set whose membership values are *type 1* fuzzy sets. In this way it is obvious how to define recursively fuzzy sets of any higher level. A *type m* fuzzy set is in fact a fuzzy set whose degrees of membership are *type m-1* fuzzy sets[13].

The problem with this type of fuzzy set is the difficulty of conceiving them constructively and even simply visualising them, when their level is higher than the third. Furthermore, conceptually all this constitutes a *regressus ad infinitum*. Nevertheless the theory of vagueness makes sense insofar as it is a possible characterisation of a limited reasoner, incapable of reaching precise knowledge on every subject, probably because s/he is incapable of following an unlimited train of reasoning. Thus there is no need for us to require of our reasoner that s/he carryout operations above the third level, that is beyond our habitual capacity to visualise fuzzy sets of a higher order. Simply, the agent cannot possibly be able to carry out the task. Thus the limit to the infinite regression can naturally be placed by the limits of our cognitive capacities.

---

[13]   Cf. Zimmerman (1991), p. 24.

Chapter 7

A Game Theoretic Model of Incomplete Contract and Ethical Code

I. The Hierarchical Transaction as a Game

In this chapter we set out a game theoretic model of a hierarchical transaction characterised by events that are not only uncertain but also unforeseen. We shall attempt to define operationally in this context two distinct normative mechanisms: the incomplete contract and the ethical code, both as expressions of a constitutional contract of the firm. The objective is to show how the ethical code constitutes a necessary complement for incomplete contracts, through more general norms, that succeed in dealing with unforeseen contingencies in the environment of hierarchical transactions involving the agent who runs the firm and the stakeholders of the firm

1.1   A Hierarchical Transaction

The situation under consideration is a hierarchical transaction in which player A (for example an employee) enters or not into a relationship of dependency with a second player B (for example, the owner or management of a firm), to whom he delegates the authority to tell him at a later date which action to perform. After A's move and before that of B, if 'enter' was chosen by A, a relationship of authority is established. By 'entering', A agrees to carry out the order which B will give, and for the sake of convenience we can assume that A, if he 'enters', not only by this act demonstrates his acceptance but in fact will carry out the task assigned to him. This makes the analysis considerably simpler, since it allows us to concentrate our attention on a simple game in which A – the employee – has to decide whether to 'enter' and therefore B, exercising his authority, must decide what order to give, that is, how to exercise this authority. Let us imagine that this situation is the base element (the stage game) of an interaction which is repeated, with the same form, between a potentially infinite succession of players in the positions of A and the single B. This allows us to hypothesise that B's reputation depends on the exercise of his authority and therefore suggests a

161

source of endogenous discipline of such an exercise of discretionary power, based on the fact that it is in B's interest to maintain his reputation in view of future transactions, which he will enter into with other agents in A's position. What makes such a situation interesting is obviously that in the course of the relationship between every A and the constant player B unforeseen events can arise. They render the explicit contract, on the basis of which A decides to enter into a dependent relationship with B, 'mute' and make ambiguous the information on the basis of which judgement is expressed as to whether a given exercise of authority should be regarded as corresponding to commitments undertaken explicitly or even implicitly. The problem is therefore – as in Kreps's discussion of the concept of corporate culture – why in any case A should 'trust' B and 'enter'. Against the background of the repeated game between the entrepreneur B and the succession of employees A_i (with i potentially growing ad *infinitum*) the problem on which we must focus is therefore already included in the single hierarchical transaction between a single A_i and B and in the signal that such a transaction transmits to a single succeeding player A_{i+1}.

1.2   The Game in Extended Form: the Moves of Player A

Let us now analyse the game played by A and B (see fig.7.1). At the first move of the game A has to choose out of 'entering' (*e*) or 'not entering' (*non-e*) into an authority relationship with B. 'Entering into a relationship of authority' means that A surrenders to B the right to decide at a later moment in the game some action within a set $a = \{a^*, a^c\}$, where *a* is a set of actions that must in effect be performed by player A, but the selection of which is under B's control. If A does not enter, the outcome of the game is immediately decided since, whatever B chooses to do, in reality B is not called upon to move in the game, and the outcome will give the payoffs (0,0), where the first and second number represents payoffs to player A and B respectively. If on the other hand A chooses to enter, immediately after taking this decision he incurs a sunk cost in terms of – for example - acquiring particular professional skills, learning the linguistic and cognitive codes typical of the internal environment of the firm, establishing fruitful human relationships with other members of the firm, which are specifically connected with the particular productive process carried out in the firm under B's direction etc. This is a cost that, on the occurrence of various states of the world and in varying measure according to them, turns out to be associated with a specific investment, one, that is, that can produce a benefit if A remains with the firm, but which would have no value if A leaves the firm. Let this investment be I_A and $c(I_A)$ its cost.

At the same time when A enters the firm, B also incurs a sunk cost, associated with reorganising the work in order to make use of A's abilities, which may include for example training A in relation to specific aspects of the productive activity. This cost, also contingent upon the occurrence of various states of the world, is associated with a specific investment I_B, whose cost shall be $c(I_B)$. It should be remembered that the specific nature of each player's investment is expressed in the form $V(e,a|I_i) - c(I_i) > r$, for $i =$ A,B where r is understood as the net benefit of the action a given the investment I_i outside the relationship between A and B, while $V(e,a|I_i)$ is the benefit of the action a ordered by B and carried out by A, given that A has entered (action e) and given the investments I_i within the relationship between A and B, so that both are essential for the production of a surplus. The symmetrically cooperative nature of the relationship between A and B, that is the additional benefit (a higher cooperative surplus) due to their joint specific investments, will therefore be expressed by $S = V(e,a|I_A, I_B) - c(I_A, I_B) > V(e,a| I_i) - c(I_i)$, where I_i is the investment of A or B but not both (assuming the cost of a to be constant in both contexts). It should be noted also that in our case the investments I_A and I_B are not considered as independent strategic moves within the game. They are simply a part of the description of A's decision to enter, i.e. they are directly determined consequences of A's choice e (in substance if A expects the interaction with B not to be advantageous, by not entering he saves the cost of the investment). On the other hand it is assumed that B's investment is implied by the fact that B occupies a position of authority.

Let us suppose that if A enters, then he receives a salary s such that $s - c(I_A) = p$, where the net payoff $p \geq 0$ is a constant. The assumption about s implies that A's initial salary is always able to cover the cost of A's specific investment, that is, that A's participation condition is satisfied. However it must be noted that, unless B decides otherwise, the p is intended to be the total payoff that A can employ to cover any other cost she may incur during the development of the interaction with B and it sets A's fixed level of participation in the surplus made possible by the two players joint action.

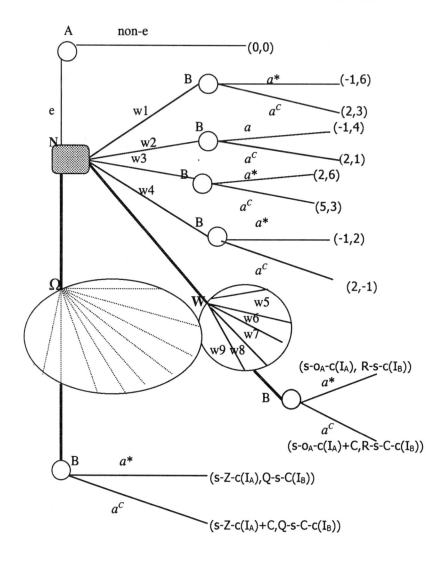

Fig 7.1. *Game of hierarchical transaction with incomplete information*

7. A GAME THEORETIC MODEL OF INCOMPLETE CONTRACT

1.3   The Moves of Nature

Once A's decision to enter has been made, a 'move of nature' occurs, that is, an event happens in the state of the world which is effective at that moment. For example the state of the economy or the environment are contingent events which occur before the start of the productive process. We can say therefore that nature selects a state of the world, which implies all the events that occur at that point in time. We say that the state of the world belongs to the set W (or $w_i \in W$) if the state of the world w_i is one of the alternative possible descriptions of the world, included in a set of descriptions which jointly are exhaustive, expressed by means of a given set of linguistic resources. A state of the world w_i is therefore understood to be one of the possible descriptions of a domain by means of a language. Let L be a formal language made up of a series of predicative letters $P_1, \ldots, P_n$, variables $x_1, \ldots, x_m$, individual constants $q_1, \ldots, q_n$, the usual logical connectives (conjunction, union, negation, implication) and by all the formulae that can be generated by operating with the connectives and the rules of inference on the base elements of the language.

Let us take therefore all the possible interpretations of L for a given empirical domain U (which is the universe of reference for our discourse), so that for every object belonging to U (whether an individual, a property or a relationship) there is a correspondence with an individual constant, a variable or a predicate of L. A possible world is a maximal set of (well formed) formulae of L (that is, one that cannot be increased by any formula without producing a contradiction), such that given a certain interpretation for this consistent maximal set there is a corresponding possible exhaustive description of the domain U.

Each state of the world w_i is made up of one of the possible maximal sets of terms of L that can be used to describe every object in the domain U (in effect a situation) and excludes the alternative states of the world, given that for at least one individual variable it contains a description in which a predicate is affirmed that is negated in the alternative states of the world. The set W is the set of all the alternative descriptions of the world, allowed by L, that is the union of all the alternative conjunctions of complete descriptions in L of all the objects belonging to our domain U. Given this definition of the state of the world w_i (or more properly the *description* of state of the world w_i) an event expressed with the linguistic resources of L occurs in a state w_i if the corresponding term is part of the terms affirmed by w_i. To put it another way, an event occurs in a state if its term is true for that description of the state of the world. In terms of set theory – as usual – an event will be the set of the states in which it occurs.

The alternative descriptions of the state of the world (or states of the world belonging to W) constitute a 'complete' set with regard to the language L used in describing W. Let us suppose however that we are aware that the set of possible states included in W may be incomplete, in the sense that the language L used to describe the universe U may not account for the description of some properties of U, although we may not be able *ex ante* to say which and nor even imagine them. Nevertheless sooner or later some unforeseen state will be revealed by an event selected by nature. In other words, we are aware that the language L is limited and that some properties (predicates) not included in L could eventually be exemplified by events which may occur as a result of the choice of nature. However we are simply not in a position even to imagine what properties these might be. Therefore let us suppose that the state of the world instead of being chosen by 'nature' within W can be selected also from a set Ω of unforeseen states of the world. The states $\omega_{ii} \in \Omega$ are other possible descriptions of our domain, expressed by means of predicates which *ex ante* we are not in a position to specify (beyond those included in L) and 'complete' with respect to the language as it will have been changed at a later stage of development. We can say therefore that W is an exhaustive set of all the possible descriptions of the world (or states of the world) only relative to the language L. It is however incomplete with reference to the language eventually used to describe the states in Ω, which nevertheless is literally unknown to us *ex ante*.

1.4　The Moves of Player B

Before starting to consider how the information delivered by a states of the world matters for the definition of the game, let us proceed to the move in which player B is called upon to decide. After a state of the world has been selected in W or in Ω, B must choose between ordering the action a^*, which is technically the most efficient way of running the firm and maximising the cooperative benefit $V(e, a | I_A, I_B) = R$, on the hypothesis that the return R net of the costs already sustained by B (that is $c(I_B)$ and s) is entirely taken by B, or action a^c, which is equally efficient, but also provides an additional compensation C for A. In this case B takes the return net of the costs for specific investments and the fixed quantity p, but in addition he rewards A with an additional constant C. The relevant costs for $a*$ on the other hand are the sum of the costs for the specific investments $c(I_A)$, $c(I_B)$, plus the cost of the additional fixed quantity p, included in the initial salary paid to A.

Let us regard actions included in $a = \{a*, a^c\}$ as constituting a variable cost for A as a function of the effort o_A spent on performing the action that B orders him to take. This cost however does not enter into the calculations at the basis of B's choice about $a*$: He assumes that the portion p of the salary, exceeding the cost of A's specific investment, should be sufficient for A to accept B's authority, even though in fact the cost, that A may have to bear in order to carry out B's orders, may perhaps exceed the additional constant p included in the salary. Intuitively the meaning of B's two actions is clear. In the case of $a*$ he runs the firm in a *capitalistic* way: he orders A to carry out the most efficient actions from the point of view of the maximisation of the cooperative surplus (made possible by the specific investments given) and he takes the residual net of the costs of the specific investments borne by him and the salary paid to A (which by assumption is never lower than the cost of A's specific investment), without bothering about the burdensomeness of the action that he orders with regard to the possible states of the world. In the case of a^c he runs the firm in a *participatory* way: he offers a reward (which for the sake of convenience we assume to be constant) which is capable of covering any additional costs incurred by A as a result of the burdensomeness of the action he is ordered to perform, and may also allow A to participate in the distribution of the net cooperative surplus.

1.5 Payoffs in the Case of Foreseeable States

The game in its extended form gives payoffs to the two players that are established according to the following expression, for A and B respectively:

$$u_A(e, a*|w_i) = s - c(I_A) - o_A; \quad u_A(e, a^c|w_i) = s + C - c(I_A) - o_A;$$

$$u_B(e, a*|w_i) = R - s - c(I_B); \quad u_B(e, a^c|w_i) = R - s - c(I_B) - C.$$

To find out their effective values it is necessary however to go back to the states of the world on which they depend. For the set of foreseeable states W this task is easily done, by considering the relevant information delivered by the descriptions of the states of the world, which are offered by every w_i and which are known *ex ante* (although it is uncertain which state will occur). For every w_i it is in fact known (that is, it happens and the players know that it happens) that:

• specific investments made by A and B are effectively and jointly indispensable for the production of a cooperative benefit (or surplus), that is, $V(e, a | I_A, I_B)$ is greater than the benefit brought by a in the absence of one or both of these investments, both in the context of this relationship or in relationship with others;

• assets that the parties engage in with their specific investments are something that they both have at their disposal independently of their mutual interaction and without one being a free rider or parasite of the other or being the object of the other's force, threat or fraud. Thus, in the perspective of a cooperative bargaining game each party can legitimately claim that if they participate in the production of the cooperative surplus R, by means of their own specific investment, then the level of utility that has to be paid can at least not be lower than the repayments of the cost of the specific investment itself.

If these are invariable characteristics for each of the states in W (that is, they are events that occur in every $w_i \in W$), the language used to describe the possible worlds in W on the other hand permits three different possible descriptions of the maximum level of return associated with the most efficient action in any state, that is $R = \{R_+, R_\approx, R_-\}$. Furthermore it allows three levels of effort $o_A = \{o_{A+}, o_{A\approx}, o_{A-}\}$, associated with the action which in each state maximises the marginal return given the specific investments. In other words these characteristics are variables which change their value from one state to another. Let us suppose however that, in accordance with our assumptions, the costs of the specific investments, the salary and the size of the final compensation are constant for every state of the world. On the basis of these limited resources of the language used to describe W, we can generate 9 states. Each of them associates a level of return to a level of effort of the most efficient action that A is ordered to take, keeping the remaining parameters constant. For each of these states the payments can therefore be defined given the action a^* or a^c.

As an illustration, let us choose the following values of the parameters for the variables

$$R_+ = 12, R_\approx = 10, R_- = 8, o_{A+} = 5, o_{A\approx} = 2, o_{A-} = 0,$$

while the constants are

$$c = 3, \; s = 5, \; c(I_A) = c(I_B) = 1.$$

The resulting payoffs have been recorded at the end of the branches of the game tree in fig. 1, relative to only four states $w_1 = (R_+, o_{A+})$, $w_2 = (R_\approx o_{A+})$, $w_3 = (R_+, o_{A\approx})$, $w_4 = (R_-, o_{A+})$ [1].

It is clear for this representation that if A 'enters', B's dominant action is always to choose a^* without more compensation. In all the situations in which the burden of the efficient action a^* is high, this implies that player A obtains a payoff (-1) lower than what she would obtain by not entering, and consequently in these cases (w_1, w_2, w_4) her best reply is *non-e*. This game (contingent upon the states now considered) seems therefore to be an extension of the traditional '*Prisoner's Dilemma*' (PD game) since the equilibrium profile in these cases implies a sub-optimal outcome (0,0). For an appropriate choice of the probabilities assigned to the states (such that the probability of the event o_{A+} is close to 1) this game would be reduced to the sequential PD, in which the only feasible equilibrium would be (*non-e*, a^*). However in the remaining cases A's best reply is in any case e, with the equilibrium outcome (e, a^*). What A's optimal action effectively is depends therefore on her probabilistic beliefs regarding the states of the world in W.

---

[1]   The remaining cases can easily be calculated: $w5 = (R_\approx, o_{A\approx})$, $w6 = (R_\approx o, {}_{A-})$, $w7 = (R_+, o_{A-})$, $w8 = (R_-, o_{A\approx})$, $w9 = (R_-, o_{A-})$. For i = A,B in fact

$u_i(e,a^*|w1) = (-1,6); \; u_i(e,a^C|w1) = (2, 3);$

$u_i(e,a^*|w2) = (-1,4); \; u_i(e,a^C|w2) = (2, 1);$

$u_i(e,a^*|w3) = (2,6); \; u_i(e,a^C|w3) = (5, 3);$

$u_i(e,a^*|w4) = (-1,2); \; u_i(a^C|w4) = (2, -1);$

$u_i(e,a^*|w5) = (4,6); \; u_i(e,a^C|w5) = (7, 3);$

$u_i(e,a^*|w6) = (2,4); \; u_i(e,a^C|w6) = (5, 1);$

$u_i(e,a^*|w7) = (4,4); \; u_i(e,a^C|w7) = (7, 1);$

$u_i(e,a^*|w8) = (2,2); \; u_i(e,a^C|w8) = (5, -1);$

$u_i(e,a^*|w9) = (4,2); \; u_i(e,a^C|w9) = (7, -1).$

Let us consider now what A would learn if she observed the choice $a*$ by B in the context of a repeated game (that will influence the probabilities that A can rationally assign to B's behaviour, and B's behaviour itself if he knows A's rule of learning). The possibility of associating the meaning 'defection' or 'abuse' to the action $a*$, typical of the PD, depends on the state that occurs: in $w1$, $w2$ and $w3$ this may seem obvious, while the meaning of action $a*$ is unclear in $w4$, since a^c would imply a symmetrical payoff to B's disadvantage. In essence the judgement about $a*$ is *dependent* on the state.

II. The Game in the Presence of Unforeseen Events and Vague Knowledge

The specification of the game is much less clear if nature chooses a state from the set Ω, that is, from the set of states of the world where unforeseen events may occur, that can not be described by means of the linguistic resources included in L. Since we do not know *ex ante* at least in part the characteristics contained in each state ω_i, we are unable to give a description of the outcomes of the game contingent on the occurrence of each of these state, respectively for the actions $a*$ and a^c. *Ex ante* we know that, whichever state ω_i may be selected, we will have a generic return Q, described in terms of monetary gains. Moreover we may give some description in physical terms of the characteristics of the most efficient action A can be ordered to carry out, for example in terms of the number Z of hours to be worked. We may also know that the possible returns in every state of Ω are contained between a minimum (0 for convenience) and a maximum N, and that the number Z also has some known upper and lower limits. We know however that every ω_i will imply events that we are not at present able to specify, since they come into the general category of unforeseen or unforeseeable events. For example, in each state there could be unexpected changes in the available technologies, which are unforeseeable in themselves and which generate completely unimaginable consequences; or unexpected human skills will be discovered in A or B; some external shock, whether environmental, natural or social may have a determining causal influence on the value of the cooperation between A and B or on the burden on A represented by a particular task in the changing environmental conditions. We cannot say *a priori* what unexpected events of this type may occur in each state ω_i. But we guess what the effect would be if we learned of them *ex post* once they had happened. In fact we know that for each of these states, even if the numerical value of Q and the value of Z were completely known, the economic meaning of the outcomes of the game would not be clear. In particular there would be ambiguity, that is neither clear truth nor clear falsehood, regarding the benefits and costs of the interaction between A and B:

(i) *The joint nature of the return*: there would be ambiguity about whether Q can still be considered as a output of the joint contributions to cooperation by means of specific investments of both players. In fact a sudden technological change could render the investment of one of the parties superfluous, or make its value within the relationship equal to the exit option (that is, make that party replaceable by any other outside the relationship). Or the discovery of particular human skills could show one party that he/she does not in fact need the other party in order to obtain the expected benefit from his/her investment;

(ii) *The size of the cooperative benefit:* even if we were to admit that at the basis of Q there are effectively specific investments by A and B, nevertheless the part of Q that could be attributed to such investments would be vague. For example, assuming that Q exceeds the cooperative surplus, it might happen that at least a considerable portion of Q may be due to unforeseen events which have no connection with such investments: a sudden improvement in the climate, the placing by a third party at the disposal of A and B of a technology which they are allowed to use, thus incurring the obligation of restitution at a future date. If Q is lower than the cooperative surplus, this could be due to a sudden unfavourable climatic event, or the manifestation of an unexpected genetic disorder in one or both of the parties;

(iii) *The existence of externality*: it would be doubtful whether the specific investments I_A and I_B are in effect independent decisions, that is whether their cost is a burden, which the parties bear independently in order to contribute to the cooperation, or whether there are externalities of one investment on another. For example, it could be discovered, with the occurrence of an unforeseen event, that B's investment in training is in fact parasitic upon A's investment in human capital, that is, as A's investment in learning increases, the need for B to invest in training decrease;

(iv) *The size of the burden of B's orders to A:* finally, for the same reasons listed above, for any numerical value of Z that value could have a completely different meaning in terms of effort of the most efficient service that B can ask of A. For example, in the presence of a technological revolution the same task (although the number of hours worked remains the same) could require greater effort, smaller effort, or no effort at all.

We can allow therefore that the players know that every outcome, in the presence of a state ω_i, will be characterised by numerical values for Q and Z that vary between a minimum and a maximum known *ex ante*. Thus, other parameters of the game being constant, we can specify various payoffs related to the admitted possible value of Q and Z. This nominal specification of the payoffs is however of little use in understanding *ex ante* the outcomes that will face the players when unforeseen events, implied in each state ω_i, occur – at least as long as we regard the characteristics of joint production as relevant to the judgement that a given A_i makes at the end of a stage game regarding B's behaviour and that is to be transmitted to the succeeding A_{i+1}. It would no longer be possible simply to make the equation $Q = V(e, a|I_A, I_B)$, nor would it make sense to concentrate on the distribution of the difference $Q - c(I_A) + c(I_B)$, nor could we univocally say how the value o_A comes into the payment function of A, even assuming the remaining parameters to be constant. In fact *ex ante* the players have at their disposal only an incomplete description of the possible outcomes of the game. In order to give a strategic evaluation of the consequences they require something more than the specification of monetary payoffs. But in the *ex ante* perspective everything that exceeds the possible numerical values of Q and Z is simply absent. On the other hand, in the *ex post* perspective the economic meaning of outcomes and payoffs is ambiguous and this makes judgement about B's behaviour vague.

Before leaving this point, we should be as precise as possible about the state of information of both players in relation to the occurrence of the states ω_i:

• *ex ante* they *know* that Q and Z can vary between an upper and a lower boundary and they *know* that *ex post* these values can be precisely known, but they also are *aware* that the state which will occur will imply events that are unforeseen *ex ante*, that is, that the state will exhibit additional characteristics, which they, from their current viewpoint, can *not* predict. In addition, they *know ex ante* that *ex post*, whatever the value that will be revealed by the state which has occurred as regards Z and Q, because of the occurrence also of unforeseen events, the meaning of these values will never be clear;

• *ex post* the state of information of the players will obviously change. They will be able not only to know the nominal value of Q and Z with precision, but they will also learn in detail of the events which were *ex ante* unforeseen and now are exemplified by the state ω_i: technological revolutions, discoveries relating to the psychology and skills of the parties, environmental, natural or social events, will all then be able to be described with the same care as the descriptions offered by W. However the general assumptions that were true *ex ante* will still be true *ex post*: in the presence of unforeseen or unexpected events, that is in the presence of genuine surprises, certain pieces of information will remain vague. Or rather, judgement about the exact economic meaning of the subjects listed under the four points above will still be vague.

III. Incomplete Contract and Ethical Code

Given the way we have presented the situation, *ex ante* the solution depends on the probability distribution over the states W, or it is indeterminate because of the inability to describe appropriately the outcomes contingent upon Ω. The information, which A can receive *ex post* about B's behaviour, is conditional upon the state that occurs in W, or it is simply badly specified on Ω. In the perspective of a repeated game of reputation the problem is that there is no univocal and absolute way in which B can take on a commitment to perform an action, by means of which he can persuade A to enter. In particular, B has not an unambiguous way to commit himself to perform an action in every case, in order that A, focusing on observing the execution of that action, can make B's reputation depend on it.

How can this situation be faced? How can player B take on a commitment regarding an action that he orders A to carry out in such a way that (i) even in the extreme hypothesis that A has a prior probability distribution concentrated on the states w_i with o_{A+}, the sub-optimal outcome (0,0) is avoided; (ii) the behaviour to be carried out is specified not only contingently upon the occurrence of the states in W, but is also such as to establish the course of action required on the occurrence of the states ω_i which implies unforeseen events?

Clearly, any solution to such a problem must take account of the two different informational contexts included in the same game. In fact, in the first case it is a question of specifying commitments that are conditional on states which are possible but foreseeable *ex ante*. In the second case, on the other hand, it is not possible to write provisos that are conditional on the occurrence of states, that we are able to describe completely, since these descriptions are simply absent. The solution consists in having recourse to the *constitutional contract* of the firm as expressed by two types of norm[2]:

(a)   *in relation to* W: an *incomplete contract* which establishes what must be done contingently upon a restricted set of variables or possible worlds belonging to W, and leaves B full discretion in relation to the remaining states in W (marked in *figure 7.1* with the symbol W+), presupposing that the remaining states and the individually rational conduct of B contingent upon them are implicitly known, even if the contract does not include explicit contingent provisos regarding such states. In this way the contract permits admissible behaviour to be distinguished from inadmissible behaviour contingent upon the states in W;

(b)   *in relation to* Ω: an ethical code i.e. (i) a set of explicitly stated constitutional, general moral principles, and (ii) a set of interpretative rules that establish in what conditions a concrete case falls under the domain of application of a principle and consequently establish the conditions under which each action $a*$ or a^C should be considered admissible or inadmissible, when one is faced by unforeseen contingencies.

It should be noted that both types of norm are based on the same general view, that is, on the idea of the constitutional contract of the organisation, according to which, in the presence of specific investments and joint production of a cooperative surplus by A and B, the distribution must satisfy the Nash bargaining solution (see ch.2). The difference is that in the case of the incomplete contract the constitutional principles can remain implicit, because it is *ex ante* known how they behave in every possible state, while in the case of the ethical code the general constitutional principles must be made explicit and utilised directly as the parameter of evaluation of unforeseen events.

Intuitively, Nash bargaining solution states that, given a *status quo*, the rational solution to negotiation is that point on the Pareto frontier, between the limits of concession established by the *status quo* itself, by which the distribution of the surplus is equal between the parties on condition that the payoff space is symmetrical. In the context of a constitutional contract, this solution must be calculated on the basis of a *fair status quo,* which establishes the maximum level of concession of the parties without recourse to the

---

[2]   In fact the solution requires the utilisation of such norms as the basis for the effects of reputation, as illustrated in ch. 6.

use of force or fraud, threat or parasitism, by one party on another. To put it another way, it must not reflect externalities of the actions of one individual on another. The Nash bargaining solution for cooperative bargaining games obviously performs the role of a regulatory principle with regard to the game under examination: it is the solution to which the parties would converge, under the hypothesis that joint production may be mutually advantageous for both of them, surplus, if they were able to agree that their interaction is to be structured as a cooperative game. In this case they can hypothesise that, before a joint plan of action is implemented, they take part in a bargaining session, through which they converge on a mutually acceptable plan of action. In essence, using Nash's model of cooperative bargaining amounts to hypothesising that the players accept the 'as if' reasoning that the game they are playing – in fact non-cooperative – is to be played as if it were a cooperative one, in which action a must be decided on as a part of a joint strategy.

In this section we specify the contract, contingent upon W but incomplete, in which the constitutional principles are not explicitly invoked, reserving for the following section the ethical code which is indispensable for establishing the conduct of B in the case of unforeseen contingencies. The Nash solution requires Pareto Optimality, which is guaranteed both by $a*$ and a^c since both by definition ensure maximum R in the conditions given. It further requires that the parties obtain payoffs at least equal to the fair *status quo*, which in our case, if linear utilities in monetary payments are assumed, implies

$$u_A(d) = c(I_A) + o_A$$

$$u_B(d) = c(I_B)$$

where the constant o_A figures in A's outside option since if it were not so A would leave the bargaining table in a worse condition than the one in which she joined it. The Nash solution requires that the players' payoffs are such that

$$Max_{u_i} \; \Pi_i \; (u_i(V(e,a|I_A,I_B) - u_i(d)) , \quad \text{for } i = \text{A and B}$$

7.3 INCOMPLETE CONTRACT AND ETHICAL CODE

In our case, participation in the cooperative return, still on the hypothesis of linear utilities, is expressed by:

$$u_A \left(V(e,a|I_A,I_B) \right) = s + C$$

$$u_B \left(V(e,a|I_A,I_B) \right) = R - s - C$$

The Nash' solution therefore asks one to choose an action $a \in a$ so that, for the selected value of C (which indeed is the variable under control by the choice between $a*$ and a^C) the following is valid:

$$max \; [(s + C) - (c(I_A) + o_A) \times (R - s - C) - c(I_B)]$$

In our case, the cooperative benefit is $R = V(e,a|I_A,I_B)$ and the surplus net of the *status quo* is given by

$$R - (c(I_A) + c(I_B) + o_A)$$

If we had taken C as a continuous variable, the solution to the problem would therefore be given by the following payoffs:

$$s + C = (c(I_A) + o_A) + \tfrac{1}{2} \, [R - (c(I_A) + c(I_B) + o_A)]$$

$$R - s - C = c(I_B) + \tfrac{1}{2} \, [R - (c(I_A) + c(I_B) + o_A)]$$

Since however C is a constant, for every state of the world we can only choose from the pair of alternatives $a*$ and a^c the action which most closely approximates to the above value, satisfying Nash's condition of maximum product.

Let us consider the payoffs associated to the pairs of actions $(e, a*)$ and (e, a^c) referred to in note 1 for both players. For all the states from $w5$ to $w9$ the Nash solution is satisfied by the action $a*$. On the contrary, for the states $w1$, $w2$, $w3$ Nash's condition requires that a^c be chosen. Let us assume that action $a*$ will be selected when Nash product is equivalent for both actions, then $a*$ will be the Nash solution for $w4$ also. In every case the interpretation is in terms of fairness. In fact, in the states $w1$-$w3$ either the cost of effort is very high (o_{A+}) or the surplus is in any case very high relative to a middle

176

level effort by A. In any case, the salary would not be a sufficient compensation and therefore some redistribution is would be needed to give A a share in the surplus that rewards her participation in the joint production. In the cases $w5$-$w9$ any additional redistribution would be superfluous, since the initial salary already contains a compensation element which is sufficient to approximate the Nash solution. In the case of $w4$ the compensation would be supererogatory for B.

The incomplete contract, with discretionary power being given to B, therefore consists of a simple function that permits action $a*$, provided that states of the world with respect to which it is explicitly prohibited do not occur:

$$f(a*|w_i) = \begin{cases} 0 \text{ if } wi = w1,\ w2,\ w3 \\ 1 \text{ otherwise (that is for every other } w_i \in W) \end{cases}$$

To put it in words, action $a*$ is explicitly forbidden in $w1$, $w2$, $w3$ and is left to B's discretion in all other states making up W. The contract does not specify the required behaviour of B except contingently upon the states $w1$, $w2$, $w3$. But it is implicit that in all other states B will choose $a*$ which, as well as being permitted by the contract, is also the action which maximises B's payoff. Leaving B free to act according to his best reply, the contract of delegation ensures that the solution is always in line with the Nash bargaining solution of negotiation[3].

In the case of the incomplete contract it is possible to establish the admissibility or inadmissibility of an action that is contingent on the occurrence of states of the world which are uncertain but clearly foreseeable. The contract is able to establish explicitly the actions forbidden, but it is not required to affirm explicitly the constitutional principle. This may remain in the background as an implicit premise of the will of the parties who adhere to such a contract, understood as the sole explanation of the reason why such a contract could have been adhered to. In this case therefore, a simple in-

---

[3]   It should be noted that in the single stage game which we are examining, A does not consider the result of $a*$ in $w4$ an abuse, even if it generates a lower payoff than the option not to enter the game. This is a consequence of the fact that "abuse" by B is signalled not by the payoff that A effectively gets but by compliance with the contract.

complete contract, without of the constitutional principles being made explicit, is enough to identify the actions and guarantee the working of a reputation effect mechanism.

IV. 'Mute' Contractual Rules VS. 'Vague' Moral Principles

Things are different with regard to the set of states Ω, about which the ethical code is required. The aim of the ethical code is to put B in a position where he can persuade A to accept his authority, secure in the fact that the code offers player A, and any other party entering the game in A's position, a method of keeping B's behaviour under control in the presence of unforeseen events, and the ability to subject it to endogenous sanctions in the case of abuse.

The ethical code can be characterised better by contrasting it with the contingent contract. To this end let us look at the definition of an *act* offered by Savage (1972): an *act* is a function that for every possible state selects a consequence. Thus we can redefine the generic action a as a function $f_a(w_i)$ whose argument is a state of the world w_i and whose value is a consequence c. Savage assumes that the decision maker has at her disposal a complete and exhaustive description of the possible states of the world set. Consequently the function, which represents an act, always has a definite value: it identifies a description of the outcome of the decision, on which the decision maker defines her own utility. The contingent contract can therefore be understood as a partition of the consequences set into two mutually exclusive subsets, each of them explicitly and directly characterised. In correspondence with consequences belonging to each subset, an evaluation of the act in terms of its admissibility or inadmissibility can be found.

$$\text{if } f_a(w_i) = c \in C+ \text{ then } f_a(w_i) \text{ is admissible;}$$

$$\text{if } f_a(w_i) = c \in C- \text{ then } f_a(w_i) \text{ is inadmissible}$$

where $C+$ and $C-$ are the subsets into which the set of consequences C is partitioned. In other words, from the examination of the consequences for each act we deduce if it falls into the set of consequences which imply the admissibility or inadmissibility of the act. What happens to this schema in the case of states of the world that are not clearly specified *ex ante* or that

178

implies unforeseen events? Given that the state ω_i is not known *ex ante*, its consequence, function of the act a, will also be unspecified ($f_a(\omega_i) = ?$). This is the first important difference, since in the hypothesis of a set of possible states that is completely known *ex ante*, the decision maker can anticipate every contingency that has not yet happened and imagine the consequence if such a contingency were to occur. This possibility of anticipation is clearly excluded in the case of unforeseen states of the world. But the most important difference is that, even if *ex post* the decision maker will be able to determine the consequence, its description will be such that it will not be possible to include it univocally in the sets of consequences defined *ex ante*, since the new state of the world will include some factors that were completely absent from what he was able *ex ante* to foresee. So that *ex post* may happen

$$f_a(\omega_i) = c \notin (C+ \cup C-)$$

This formula obviously expresses the fact that *ex post*, the set of consequences C cannot be perfectly partitioined into the two sets $C+$ and $C-$. Other characteristics have emerged meanwhile, which do not permit this partition. Evaluation in the light of the *ex ante* consequences does not apply, for the simple reason that the criterion established *ex ante* for admissibility or inadmissibility consists of determining whether the act generates a consequence that belongs to the sets $C+$ or $C-$. Since c does not belong to either of these two sets, the criterion is undetermined and the contract is mute. It should be noted that in the case of an incomplete contract, which specifies only the inadmissible acts on the basis of the relevant set of consequences – as in section 3 – being introduced to take over the contingent contract, then the muteness of contract upon the occurrence of unforeseen events would imply that B has complete discretion.

Why can an ethical code succeed where the contract fails? The underlying idea of the ethical code is that general principles, formulated in universal terms, although vague in their application, constitute a term of reference, both for events that are *foreseen ex ante* and for events that are *unforeseen ex ante* or simply 'new'. The type of reference is a relationship of membership: the state of the world belongs and does *not* belong to the domain of application of the constitutional norm *to a certain degree*. The membership relationship can therefore *always* be specified (although by expressing a sense of vagueness). Consequently the ethical code *is never mute* in relation to events, including events that were unforeseen *ex ante*.

The correlated trade-off is however that unforeseen events introduce vagueness in the membership relationship. Whilst in the light of previous experience, usually we are able to clearly assign a state of the world to the domain of application of a general norm, the same judgement is less clear in the case of states of the world that are completely new or unforeseen. As a matter of fact, general norms or principles are always vague, in the sense that they involve concepts in relation to which it is not always possible to establish univocally whether a particular case belongs or does not belong to them (there will be cases that are definitely included, cases that are certainly excluded, but also borderline cases about which judgement is vague). The hypothesis that we make is simply that there is a greater measure of vagueness associated with the discovery of unforeseen facts, so that we must resort to the use of terms not provided for by the *ex ante* language used to describe the *ex ante* possible states of the world. Assume that I describe a situation by means of a given language, in whose terms a system of general norms is also formulated. The vagueness of the reference of specific contingencies to the norms may be substantial, but nevertheless ambiguity and vagueness of the normative system will undoubtedly be lower than if I discover 'new' events, to describe which I must resort to linguistic resources not used in the traditional language, in which the system of norms is also formulated. This situation asks more acutely the question whether new situations, described in the enriched language, can be brought into the domain of application of the norm determined *ex ante* in the traditional language.

Although unforeseen events generate vagueness, however this situation is not structurally different from the case of the known situations or the states foreseen *ex ante*: it is *simply* a matter of *degree*. We can always refer concrete cases (*ex ante* foreseen or *ex ante* unforeseen) to the ethical principle, by means of a membership relationship with the domain of application of the principle. Membership will be satisfied to a greater or lesser degree, but nevertheless always capable of being explicitly defined. Instead of having an extremely precise normative system, but *mute* in relation to the consequences generated as a result of unforeseen states, we shall now have a normative system that is capable of classifying *every* contingency as regards its satisfaction of the ethical principle, according to the membership relationship with the domain of application of the constitutional principle, even if in *vague* terms.

7. A GAME THEORETIC MODEL OF INCOMPLETE CONTRACT

To this end we can draw from the distinction between $C+$ and $C-$ the implicit criterion for their separation. The consequences will in fact have been classified on the basis of certain abstract characteristics, beyond the simple measure of preferences. For example, descriptions of the action as joint or not, as a cooperative outcome (with an associated surplus) or not, as implying a certain distribution and a certain proportion between the payoffs of the players or not etc. In the light of these characteristics, we infer the general normative principle which holds under these large classes of circumstances, and leaves aside the concrete descriptions of the consequences. It holds for any consequence that may exhibit the relevant abstract characteristics, independently of whether it can be traced back to the 'concrete' sets of consequences $C+$ or $C-$. We call the abstract constitutional principle P and the event whereby 'the constitutional principle P is fulfilled' we call E. With regard to the event E, no state of the world foreseen *ex ante* or unforeseen *ex ante* is mute: every state can be referred in some degree to the event under examination. Simply, this relationship can be vague.

To deal explicitly with this relationship we will introduce some fuzzy sets modelling [4]. For now, we need only to remember that, when an ordinary set of objects X has been defined, a fuzzy set $\underline{E}$ is the subset of those objects belonging to X which are also elements of $\underline{E}$ *to a certain degree*. The degree of belonging is given by a membership function μ with domain the set X and co-domain the real line $[0,1]$. A fuzzy set $\underline{E}$ is the set of ordered pairs which associates to every element of I its degree of membership to $\underline{E}$. Now we have simply to understand the set of concrete cases, which are the domain of application of a norm, as the fuzzy set $\underline{E}$. What we must regard as belonging to $\underline{E}$ are alternative descriptions of the state of the world, some known *ex ante* and others unforeseen *ex ante*. Agreeing with Savage, we assume that the change of perspective between *ex ante* and *ex post* does not bring about any difference in the case of states foreseen *ex ante*. In the case of states unforeseen *ex ante*, on the other hand, the evaluation cannot be expressed except in the perspective *ex post* (*ex ante* the state is undetermined and therefore an evaluation cannot be expressed). Let us assume therefore that the passage to the *ex post* perspective implies a net gain in information – the possibility of describing a set of ordinary states Ω - but not the acquisition of complete clarity of knowledge: with regard to states that can be de-

---

[4]   See chapter 6 for the basic definitions and chapter 8 for the fuzzy model of a
        code of ethics.

scribed *ex post* the relationship to the principles, i.e. their belonging to the set $\underline{E}$, is not perfectly clear.

Finally, we have assumed that, although the agent is not *ex ante* in a position to describe the set Ω, he is nevertheless *aware* of its possible existence. The agent knows that *ex post* he will be able to verify the existence of some membership relationship between $\omega_i \in \Omega$ and $\underline{E}$. He can not therefore undertake commitments contingent upon the concrete descriptions of elements in Ω, for these are unforeseen. But he can undertake commitments regarding the occurrence *ex post* of a certain membership relationship between any generic element of Ω and the set $\underline{E}$. In keeping with the discussion up to now, we can summarise the distinction between conditional contract and ethical code as follows:

$$\forall c \in C+, \ f_a(w_i) = c \Rightarrow \mu_{\underline{E}}(w_i) = 1$$

$$\forall c \in C-, \ f_a(w_i) = c \Rightarrow \mu_{\underline{E}}(w_i) = 0$$

$$\forall c \notin (C+ \cup C-), \ f_a(\omega_i) = c \Rightarrow \mu_{\underline{E}}(\omega_i) = x, \ \text{for } 0 \leq x \leq 1$$

These formulas imply that if the consequences are generated from states that are known *ex ante*, then the assignation by the contract to the sets of consequences is perfect, and the adjudication of a state to the domain of application of the general norm is also clear. If on the other hand the consequence of the action cannot be assigned to any of the sets of consequences established *ex ante*, that depends on the fact that the state of the world is unforeseen *ex ante* and it follows that its belonging to the domain of application of the norm is vague also *ex post*. While the contract is in this case 'mute', however, the moral principle on the other hand constitutes a term of reference for measuring (in the interval between 0 and 1) the degree of conformity of the act to the principle itself.

Coming back to the game under examination, we must recall that *ex post* various aspects that we have to consider in order to decide whether a constitutional principle does matter in any particular situation will remain vague. But knowledge of this fact can be anticipated *ex ante*, before concrete knowledge is obtained about unforeseen events and the values of Q and Z. What B must simply do therefore is to undertake commitments on the basis of principles and criteria that are invariable with respect to the *constant state of vagueness*, so that the respect of these principles or criteria can be understood in the same way and verified *ex post* in exactly the same sense in which it was understood *ex ante*. To this end it is clear that the ethical code must settle explicitly the constitutional principle of fair/efficient distribution of the surplus shares due to cooperation between A and B..

Furthermore, we must notice that the constitutional principle of fair/efficient distribution of the surplus shares is not a vague principle. It is rather operationally univocal and calculable, once the values of the relevant parameters are given. What is vague, on the other hand, is the set of descriptive premises which have to be satisfied in order for the model of cooperative bargaining – which specifies the constitutional principle of cooperation – to be applied. The ethical code must therefore constitute the procedure we use in establishing which concrete contexts must be brought within the domain of application of the constitutional principle of efficient and fair cooperation and how that application must be made operable. It will have to establish *for what* level of vagueness we are justified in assuming that the principle has to be applied. The ethical code is therefore also a procedure for the interpretation and application of the constitutional principles, explicitly cited as the major premise of the ethical code itself[5]. Once it has

---

[5]   Bobbio (1979) points out various interpretative methods of the norms within the perspective of legal positivism, distinguishing *textual* interpretation from *extra-textual* interpretation. Among the forms of textual interpretation are the *lexical, teleological, systematic* and *historical*. Alongside these forms however there are extra-textual forms of interpretation, whose basis is the admission of the incompleteness of norms. These consist of *analogical* interpretation and interpretation based on *analogia juris*, that is, on recourse to the general principles of the legal system by means of the double procedure of *abstraction* for particular norms and their generalisation, or the *subsumption* of new cases, which are not disciplined by the usual norms of comparison, beneath general and abstract concepts. Undoubtedly the idea of ethical code as an expression of the constitutional contract, has a great resemblance to *analogia juris*. Furthermore Cass Sunstein (1990) says that *extratextual* norms – that is, grounding constitutional principles – play a crucial role in the interpretation of laws and indeed of contracts. Dworkin (1985) answers the problem of interpretation with an argument which typically goes back to reasoning by *default*: if we lack a factual or logical demonstration, we can have recourse to the criterion of *normative coherence* analogous to that of *narrative coherence*: just as in an unfinished story there is a conclusion that seems more consequential than others, because it is coherent with the general structure of narration up to that point, thus a difficult legal case has a logical adjudication, although not a demonstration,

been established that a situation comes into the domain of application of a principle if the membership relationship does not exceed a given level of admissible vagueness, this condition remains invariable both *ex ante* and *ex post*. Thus the respect for the condition can be verified *ex post* exactly in the sense in which it is understood *ex ante*. There is therefore no ambiguity regarding the way in which this procedure treats vagueness.

---

in that such an adjudication is more coherent with the political theory and its general principles which succeed in giving justification and ensuring consistency to the main parts of the legal system. Cf. Dworkin (1985), pp.175-177.

Chapter 8

Ethical Decision-making Procedure: Vagueness, Default Reasoning and Reputation

I. Vagueness and Application of the Constitutional Principle (the First Step in the Ethical Procedure)

This chapter will illustrate the ethical code as a decision-making procedure. The code resorts to fuzzy logic to assimilate unforeseen events. As they happen, they fall within the domain of known normative concepts at a certain degree. Thus at each moment it reaches definite conclusions (albeit ones that are only provisionally valid, according to the typical modality of default reasoning) about what is admissible or inadmissible in every context. On the basis of this procedure, the player running the firm will be able to take on commitments *vis-à-vis* the firm's stakeholders. Compliance with these commitments can be ascertained by the latter and the reputation of the player running the firm can be made to depend on this. In conclusion we will be able to come back to reputation effects as the driving force of compliance, in exactly the same sense as for the game of reputation introduced in chapter 3.

Elaborating on the microeconomic model outlined in chapter 7^1, we will set out an ethical procedure of rational deliberation able to say whether a given action (say $a*$) is permissible in the light of a constitutional principles. What we will be defining is an operational decision-making procedure. Thus we shall deal with it as it were to be carried out by a *moral automaton*, that is a *predictable* program for dealing with *unpredictable* events. In this sense what we are doing is outlining a first approach to linking strategic (game theoretic) interaction and procedural rationality, both of them seen in the face of unforeseen contingencies and limited predictability of possible events (Simon 1972a,b). Notice however that, though the deliberation is procedural, it asks nevertheless for genuine human judgement at least where the degree of relevance of a principle for any unforeseen event has to be es-

---

[1]   This chapter necessarily presupposes the reading of the previous two. See in particular ch.7 secs.1-2.

timated. Moreover a player decides to conform his practical conduct to what the ethical automaton prescribes depending on the calculation of the player's best reply in a repeated game, that is, if the procedure is effective in triggering a reputation effect mechanism.

The aim of the procedure is to establish, for every unforeseen state $\omega_i \in \Omega$, *first* whether it belongs to the set of situations to which the Nash's solution of cooperative bargaining games starting from a fair *status-quo* (fixed by the costs of the specific investments, as well as of the variable o_A) can be applied. *Second*, whether this state ω_i belongs to the set of situations in which, assuming that B chooses a^*, if nature selects a state ω_i then the outcome is *efficient/fair* (that is, it satisfies the Nash bargaining solution). *Third*, once these two conditions have been verified, the procedure prescribes a certain type of behaviour, in the sense that it syllogistically 'deduces' the permissible actions from the constitutional principles and from the satisfying of the conditions for their application. Therefore when actions that the procedure defines permissible are observed *ex post*, there is no basis for imputing 'abusive' behaviour to player B.

Let us define the two events that are required for the application of the constitutional principle. Call the first event *E1* and let it be constructed so that it corresponds to the first condition described above: let Γ be the name of the game that we described, and let Gc be the abbreviation for a cooperative bargaining game with fair *status-quo*. *E1* stands for 'Γ is a Gc'. This event is made up of the joint statement of two properties, or two *qualitative* judgements: the first is that the return Q has the *nature* (regardless of the *extent*) of a *cooperative benefit* which is fruit of A's and B's mutual specific investment. To say it formally, let us define $R(\omega_i) = V(a|I_A, I_B)$, where $V(e,a|I_A, I_B) > V(e,a|I_A) = V(e,a|I_B) > V(e,a|I_C)$ for every other individual C $\neq$ A, B and for each $a_i \in a$. Then we say that $R(\omega_i) = R^* \subseteq Q$. To put it in words, the return Q coincides wholly or in part with a cooperative benefit R^* which is the joint output of the specific investments made by A and B. Let us come now to the second property. If for R^* we define a cooperative bargaining game with fair *status-quo* by means of the usual ordered pair (R^*, D^*), where R^* is the payoff space of the cooperative game and D^* is its fair *status-quo*, then in our case it should be that $D^* = [c(I_A) + o_A, c(I_B)]$, that is, the cost of the specific investments corresponds to the fair *status-quo* of the game unless there is a positive variable equal to the cost of A's action to be added to his fair exit option. To keep things simple assume $[c(I_A), c(I_B)] = D^*$. Therefore, by means of a harmless abuse of notation, we say that *E1* =

(R* ∩ D*), that is the event 'Γ is a Gc' is the set theoretical intersection of the two vents (sets) 'the game outcomes contain a cooperative surplus' and 'the initial investments of the parties define a fair *status- quo* for Gc'.

Let now define the event corresponding to the second condition ('the outcome of the game is *efficient/fair*, given a^*'). This is the same as saying that, if B chooses a^*, i.e. even in the absence of the additional constant c in A's payoff, the intersection $(R_i^* \cap o_{Ai})$ of the values taken by the two variables R^* and o_A is such as to guarantee an *efficient/fair* outcome.

First let us remember that there is no vagueness about any of the states $w_i \in W$ and, on the basis of the assumptions made, we know that they fall into the domain of application of the theory of cooperative bargaining games[2]. Thus

$$\forall w_i \in W, \quad \mu_{E1}(w_i) = 1.$$

As regards the membership of the state $\omega_i \in \Omega$ in the event $E1$, we know that checking the conditions for applying the solution for cooperative bargaining games will be a matter of vagueness: we cannot expect that there will be a clear description of whether these conditions are satisfied (for each ω_i) in the presence of unforeseen and unexpected events such as technological changes, discovery of previously unknown and unimaginable characteristics in the players, or unusual natural, climatic or social events. However univocal the solution theory may be, in each case the question of which concrete situations it can be applied to remains a non-univocal question of judgement. On the other hand, the set Ω is an ordinary set of elements that, although unknown *ex ante*, *ex post* turn out to be univocally describable as regards the variables Q and Z and also as regards the unforeseen characteristics. The point is that all these characteristics, clearly described *ex post*, can be interpreted non univocally in terms of the membership of each ω_i to $E1$. Let us therefore describe the membership of the state ω_i in the sets corresponding to the characteristics R^* and D^* in terms of a fuzzy membership function. Take the fuzzy set of ordered pairs

$$\underline{R}^* = \{(\omega_i, \mu_{\underline{R}^*}(\omega_i)) | \omega_i \in \Omega\}$$

---

[2]   See ch. 7 section 1.5.

where the membership function $\mu_{\underline{R}^*}(\omega_i) = x$, for $1 \leq x \leq 0$, defines the usual degree of membership in $\underline{R}^*$ as any value between 0 and 1. This expresses the degree of vagueness which we attach to the judgement that in each given ω_i the return Q of the game is a cooperative return R^* (or the compatibility between ω_i and the cooperative nature of the returns). We understand the set of ordered pairs

$$\underline{D}^* = \{(\omega_i, \mu_{\underline{D}^*}(\omega_i))| \; \omega_i \in \Omega\}$$

in the same way, that is, as the fuzzy set defined by the function of membership $\mu_{\underline{D}^*}(\omega_i) = r$, for $1 \leq r \leq 0$, which, with any degree of membership between 0 and 1, expresses the vagueness that for every ω_i only the costs for specific investments are determining for the fair *status-quo* of a bargaining game. Now let us take the set of ordered pairs

$$\underline{R}^* \cap \underline{D}^* = \{(\omega_i, \mu_{\underline{R}^* \cap \underline{D}^*}(\omega_i))| \; \omega_i \in \Omega\}$$

which defines the fuzzy intersection set in terms of the function of membership $\mu_{\underline{R}^* \cap \underline{D}^*}(\omega_i)$[3]. We can now conclude that membership of every state of the world ω_i in the event $E1$ is measured by

$$\mu_{E1}(\omega_i) = MIN(\mu_{\underline{R}^*}(\omega_i), \mu_{\underline{D}^*}(\omega_i)).$$

Therefore $E1$ is a fuzzy event, that is, it is the vague statement that the game, when unforeseen events occurs, satisfies the initial conditions for the application of the cooperative bargaining games solution, and where this vagueness is expressed explicitly by means of the membership function $\mu_{E1}(\omega_i)$. Let us also say that $\mu_{E1}(\omega_i)$ measures the possibility (as distinct from the probability) that in every state ω_i the game Γ satisfies the initial conditions for being treated as a cooperative bargaining game Gc (that is, it answers the joint questions: 'Might it be the case that Q is a cooperative benefit which is the fruit of specific joint efforts?' and 'Might it be the case that the specific investments establish the fair *status-quo* of the game?') We can now intro-

---

[3]   It should remembered that the membership degree of an element of a ordinary set in the intersection of two fuzzy sets is obtained by the lowest of the values of the membership functions relative to the two sets under consideration,

$$\mu_{\underline{R}^* \cap \underline{D}^*}(\omega_i) = MIN(\mu_{\underline{R}^*}(\omega_i), \mu_{\underline{D}^*}(\omega_i)).$$

duce an α–*level* of vagueness in order to discriminate between the states in which the game satisfies the conditions for a Gc sufficiently to enable the application of Nash's *efficient/fair* solution and those in which the vagueness is too great to permit such an application. We therefore say that α establishes an *ethical threshold*. For $\alpha = 0.5$, we can separate the states ω_i that exceed the ethical threshold from those which remain below, by means of the function of ordinary membership

$$\mu_{E1}\alpha(\omega_i) = \begin{cases} 1 \text{ if } \mu_{E1}(\omega_i) \geq 0.5 \\ \\ 0 \text{ if } \mu_{E1}(\omega_i) < 0.5 \end{cases}$$

This condition can be stated *ex ante*, and its fulfilment can be checked *ex post*, so that *ex post* we will always be in a position to establish which of the states that were unforeseen *ex ante* exceed the ethical threshold of admissibility for the application of the *efficient/fair* solution, simply by calculating the ordinary set

$$El_\alpha = \{\omega_i \in \Omega \mid \mu_{E1}(\omega_i) \geq 0.5\}$$

where the set El_α does not reveal any vagueness about the states that can be treated 'as if in them the game were a fair and cooperative bargaining game. If, for example, the players find out a description *ex post* of the states $\omega_i \in \Omega$ and establish the following fuzzy set

	$\omega 1$	$\omega 2$	$\omega 3$	$\omega 4$	$\omega 5$
$\mu_{E1}(\omega_i) =$	0.1	0.6	0.8	0.4	0.9

on the basis of the admissibility threshold established *ex ante*, they know that only some states can be treated 'as if' in them the game were a cooperative bargaining game, to be solved according to the Nash bargaining solution calculated from a fair *status-quo*. That is

	$\omega 1$	$\omega 2$	$\omega 3$	$\omega 4$	$\omega 5$
$\mu_{E1}\alpha(\omega_i) =$	0	1	1	0	1

189

Thus the admissible set $El_\alpha = \{\omega2, \omega3, \omega5\}$ is the set of states which exceed the threshold of admissibility, so that the Nash bargaining solution is applicable to them. Its range is what we agree can be treated as the domain of application of the solution. Obviously this is not the set of situations in which we know clearly that the conditions of application for the theory are perfectly or precisely fulfilled, but only the set of situations in which we regard it as permissible to act 'as if' they were fulfilled (since the admissible vagueness threshold is exceeded). It should be noted that *ex ante* we undertake the commitment to treat the game as the domain of application of the cooperative bargaining theory if a state of the world ω_i, although *ex ante* indeterminate in many essential ways, falls *ex post* into the admissible set El_α. Then *ex post*, when we have come to know the extent of the vagueness relative to the membership of each state ω_i in the set El_α – which does not mean that they are no longer vague – we shall be able to determine without any ambiguity whether, in appropriate cases, the cooperative bargaining theory has effectively to be applied to obtain the solution of the game.

II. The Second Step in the Ethical Procedure: Fuzzy Measures of Surplus and Effort

Focusing now on the elements of the set El_α we can ask whether the event $E2$ is true and whether given the choice a^*, the occurrence of various possible and admissible states of the world, that is $(\omega_i|a^*)$, implies an *efficient/fair* outcome in the sense of a Nash solution. The condition to be verified in this case is the following:

$$\forall \omega_i \in El_a$$
$$u_i(e,\omega_i, a^*) = MAX_{a\in a}\Pi_i[u_i(R^*) - u_i(D^*)], \quad (for\ i = A,B)$$

Since the salary s is a constant, and the action a^* is the most advantageous to B for it avoids the additional compensation c for A, it is clear that the possibility that $(\omega_i|a^*)$ for $\omega_i \in El_\alpha$ has an *efficient/fair* outcome depends on some proportion between the size of the cooperative return R^*, that is to say the *extent* of R^*, and the size of effort o_A of the task a^* which B orders A to do. We know that, after every ω_i has occurred, the players learn a particular value of the return Q (a natural number equal or superior to 0) and a particular physical description Z of the task a^* (also a natural number that is probably positive.). What remains vague *ex post* is the meaning of these figures – perfectly precise in themselves – in terms of the size of the cooperative return R^*, which must be distributed on the basis of the constitutional principle of *efficient/fair* cooperation, and in terms of effort o_A for player A.

As regards the component Q of the event *E2*, the source of the vagueness is the indeterminacy of the causal relationship that a particular external shock may have influenced the size of the return, apart from the effects on it of the specific investments made by A and B. A new technology introduced from outside, or an unforeseen and unaccustomed change in environmental, natural or social conditions, renders ambiguous the judgement about the *extent* to which the 'merit' of a particular output should be ascribed to the cooperation between A and B, even when the presence of this cooperation (the existence of specific reciprocal investments) has been allowed. In essence, it is the indeterminacy of the causal relationship between the physical amount of the return and the external shocks that makes it hard to distinguish between the two quantities making up the *ex post* observed value of Q: the cooperative component R^* and the non-cooperative component $Q - R^*$. Thus, whatever the numerical level of the cooperative benefit R^* considered, the set of the observable returns Q (exhibited by the states $\omega_i \in \Omega$) that satisfy – contain – the given level of cooperative benefit, is a fuzzy set.

Since we have already defined a fuzzy set of a different nature in relation to R^*, it should be recalled that, while in the previous discussion we have taken R^* to be generically the property of a return Q of containing any cooperative benefit, now we refer to the *size* of R^* in relation to the particular observed value of Q. Previously we were interested in the judgement that Q, having been observed, could contain (in whole or in part) the fruit of reciprocal and specific investments – i.e. a cooperative surplus. Therefore the fuzzy set then defined concerned the qualitative evaluation of the nature of the contributions made by the parties. Now, however, we are concerned with a more delicate evaluation about *which portion* of the observed Q is effectively an R^* and we discover that this evaluation too is vague – because of vagueness of the causal relationship between external shocks and Q.

Let us suppose for the sake of convenience that Q can vary between 0 and 20, that is that there are at least 20 states ω_i which can be ordered on the basis of the numerical value of the return observed in them. We want to know which of these returns belong to the following five classes of cooperative benefit, which we put as being equal to $R^*_{--} = 0 \leq R^* \leq 6$; R^*_-

$= 7 \leq R^* \leq 9; R^* \approx = 10 \leq R^* \leq 12; R^*_+ = 13 \leq R^* \leq 16; R^*_{++} = 17 \leq R^* \leq 20$. It should be noted that in this way we eliminate the inherent vagueness in the qualitative expressions 'very high', 'low' etc., but not the vagueness that we are interested in, which is that, even in the presence of classes of benefit understood as the intervals of a variable, the causal relationship between unforeseen events and the size of the return nevertheless remains vague, so that the attribution of each return to a class of benefit is still always vague. Each class of benefit is therefore a fuzzy set of states. For example the class of benefit R^*_{++} will be the set of ordered pairs

$$\{(\omega_i, \mu_{\underline{R}^*_{++}}(\omega_i))| \ \forall \omega_i \in EI \ \}$$

For every state ω_i characterised by a given numerical value of Q, the function of membership $\mu_{\underline{R}^*_{++}}(\omega_i)$ will express the degree of possibility that such a return will contain a certain level of cooperative benefit, or in other words will express the possibility that in that state the event of a given cooperative benefit will occur.

The second component of the judgement that leads us to conclude that a given state ω_i belongs to the situation in which the choice of a^* generates an *efficient/fair* outcome is given by the variable Z. Z is a description of a^* in physical terms, for example in terms of the number of hours required to carry out the task required. But to express a judgement about the fairness of the outcome under a^* it is necessary to translate the value of Z into a measure of the effort cost o_A for A, for example in terms of the tiredness or conversely the enjoyment experienced by A in carrying out a^*. This evaluation is inevitably vague, because of the novelty and unpredictability *ex ante* of the events which occur in ω_i. Let us define three classes of effort of a^*, that is o_{A-} = 'low', $o_{A\approx}$ = 'medium' and o_{A+} = 'high', to which, for each value of Z, every state of the world can belong to a certain degree, according to the unforeseen events which occur. In this case too the fuzzy function of membership can be understood as expressing the possibility that, given a value Z, in each of the states of the world it happens that A must face a low, medium or high level of effort.

III. Vagueness of Efficient/Fair Outcomes: the Third Step in the Ethical Procedure

Having established a method for dealing with the vagueness of the two components of the judgement that, in every state of the world, we have to express about the efficiency/fairness of the outcomes of $a*$, we can now ask how the two components must be combined in order to express an overall – albeit vague – judgement. First we must consider the conjunction of the two events $(R*_j \cap o_{Aj})$ where $R*_j$ and o_{Aj} represent the jth levels of cooperative benefit and effort which are part of those considered in the previous section. Clearly every event $(R*_j \cap o_{Aj})$ is a fuzzy set

$$(R*_j \cap o_{Aj}) = \{(\omega_i, \mu_{(R*_j \cap o_{Aj})}(\omega_i)| \; \omega_i \in El_a\}$$

Furthermore we know that in the case of the intersection of two fuzzy sets, the function of membership assigns to every state ω_i a degree of membership in the intersection set which is the lowest of the membership degrees of the same state to the two sets taken separately, and that this value can be regarded as the possibility that the combined event occurs in the state ω_i. Thus if·we want to establish what is the generic possibility of the jth intersection event $(R*_j \cap o_{Aj})$, that is, the possibility that any state ω_i occurs among those in which (to a certain degree) $(R*_j \cap o_{Aj})$ also occurs, we must find the state for which the function of membership in the intersection event is at the minimum amongst those established for the states under consideration, and take that value as expressing the general possibility that $(R*_j \cap o_{Aj})$ occurs in Ω.

We are thus in a position to establish the possibility of each of the intersection events that can be generated by the various levels of $R*$ and o_A. Given the five classes of possible cooperative return and the three classes of effort, there are 15 such events since each is the combination of one class of cooperative benefit out of five with one level of effort out of three.

It should be noted that vagueness applies for statements of the type 'in ω_i the cooperative return $R*$ is in the class $R*_+$ and the effort associated with the action $a*$ is at the level o_{A+}' since we are not in a position to establish unambiguously whether the true state of things is such as to satisfy the combination of the two properties. The vagueness lies in the relationship of compatibility between the description of states of world ω_i and the combined statement of the two properties mentioned above. To say 'ω_i is a $R*_+$ and a o_{A+}' is to make a vague statement. However, on the syntactic level, regardless of the conditions of truth of the statements, we are perfectly entitled to infer that '$if \omega_i$ is an example of $R*_+$ and an example of o_{A+} *then* $\neg p$', where p is some formal property of the payoffs. This statement could be true even if $\neg p$ were false, if the premises were false, or even if $\neg p$ were vague, if the premises themselves were vague. Let p be the property of maximum Nash product:

$$(s - c(I_A) - o_{Aj}, R*_j - s - c(I_B)) = MAX_{a \in a} \Pi_i(u_i(R*_j) - u_i(D*))$$
$$(for \ i = A,B)$$

Since s, $c(I_A)$, $c(I_B)$ and the possible payment C are constant, while o_{Aj}, $R*_j$ are sizes that can be specified at least in terms of numerical intervals, the validity of this statement can always be established. For every class of cooperative benefit and every level of effort we can therefore calculate whether p or $\neg p$. Independently of the vagueness that characterises the premises for the deduction, for every state ω_i given each of the classes of cooperative benefit and of effort levels in which ω_i can be included, we can therefore calculate whether the payments associated with $a*$ maximise the product of the payoffs of the players (net of specific investments and costs) or whether this product is maximised by the alternative action a^c. For every ω_i hat satisfies a category $R*$ and o_A we can therefore say whether p is valid. Let us suppose for the sake of simplicity that o_{A-} is 'nearly' 0, $o_{A\approx}$ 'is nearly' 2, o_{A+} is 'nearly' 5. Calculation of the combinations $(R*_j \cap o_{Aj})$ such that it is true that, given $a*$, the Nash product is maximised, is summarised in table 1.

	$0 < R*_- < 6$,	$7 < R*_{--} < 9$,	$10 < R*_\approx < 11$,	$12 < R*_+ < 16$,	$17 < R*_{++} < 20$
$o_{A-} = 0$	p	p	p	$\neg p$	$\neg p$
$o_{A\approx} = 2$	p	p	$\neg p$	$\neg p$	$\neg p$
$o_{A+} = 5$	p	$\neg p$	$\neg p$	$\neg p$	$\neg p$

Table 1 (p *means tha, for that couple of parameters o_A and $R*$, Nash product is maximised*).

8. ETHICAL DECISION-MAKING PROCEDURE

We now know that for some events with the form $(R^*_j \cap o_{Aj})$ it necessarily occurs that under a^* the outcome is *efficient/fair*, while for other events with this form this is certainly excluded. Let us now take only the events with the form $(R^*_j \cap o_{Aj})$ for which the efficiency/fairness of the outcome is implied. Each of these events is a fuzzy set which establishes the fuzzy membership to it of any state ω_i. We can therefore use these fuzzy sets to establish, for each combined event with the form $(R^*_j \cap o_{Aj})$ - having the property of implying an *efficient/fair* outcome under a^* - its degree of possibility.

Let us now consider the peculiar event that the action a^*, given any combination of cooperative benefit and effort, implies an *efficient/fair* outcome. To this end all we have to do is to take the union of all the events that have the above property

$$U_{[(R^*_j \cap o_{Aj})^*]} = \{(R^*_- \cap o_{A-}) \cup (R^*_- \cap o_{A-}) \cup (R^*_\approx \cap o_{Aj}) \cup$$
$$\cup (R^*_- \cap o_{A\approx}) \cup (R^*_- \cap o_{A\approx})\}.$$

This is the union set of all the fuzzy sets for which it is true that the choice a^* generates an *efficient/fair* outcome. We call this set event *E2*. Clearly the overall possibility of such an event can be derived from the appropriate operation on the fuzzy membership functions of the various states in the sets under examination.

What we in effect want to know, for each state, is to what degree – considering the vagueness of this knowledge – choosing a^* is *efficient/fair* or – to put it another way – to what degree, if a^* is chosen, the occurrence of every given state implies that the outcome will be *efficient/fair*. This is the same as asking, for every state ω_i to what degree it is a member of the union set of all the sets $(R^*_j \cap o_{Aj})^*$ for which the *efficient/fair* outcome is implied. Therefore it amounts to asking about the function of membership of any ω_i in the event *E2*. As usual, the function of membership of an ordinary set, with respect to the union set generated by two or more fuzzy sets, is the maximum value that the membership function for that element takes with respect to each fuzzy set allowed in the union[4].

We therefore have a method which the parties will adopt when, as events occur described by the set Ω (but which were unknown *ex ante*), they will attempt to express the vagueness of their knowledge about the efficiency

---

[4]   See ch.6 sec. 2, *supra*.

and fairness of the outcome given choice $a*$. This method can be perfectly known *ex ante* and be included in the procedures of application of the ethical code. What can not be known *ex ante* are the specific values which the function of membership will take *ex post*, that is, after the unforeseen events have occurred. Since *ex ante* only the spaces of variation of the possible non-vague variables Q and Z are known, whereas the unforeseen events associated with each ω_i, are completely unexpressed, the vague relationship between Q and $R*$ and between Z and o_A is also unexpressed. And therefore the membership of each state in the events for which it can be concluded that $a*$ is efficient and fair or not also remains completely unexpressed. Nevertheless what really matters is that the *method* for dealing with vagueness can be left unchanged whenever the perspective is *ex ante* or *ex post*.

Within the limits of the states (unknown *ex ante*) for which $E1_\alpha$ holds, that is that are admissible as the domain of application of the constitutional principle, a second criterion of admissibility is established: the level of membership above which it is admissible to consider such states as situations in which the choice $a*$ generates an *efficient/fair* outcome. The set $E2_\beta$ is therefore defined as the set of those states (unknown *ex ante*) whose degree of membership to the event $E2$ is not lower than level β, that is

$$E2_\beta = \{\omega_i \in E1_\alpha | \mu_{E2}(\omega_i|a*) \geq 0.5\}$$

Membership in this set is defined by the non-fuzzy membership function

$$\mu_{E2\beta}(\omega_i) = \begin{cases} 1 \text{ if } \mu_{E2}(\omega_i|a*) \geq 0.5 \\ 0 \text{ if } \mu_{E2}(\omega_i|a*) < 0.5 \end{cases}$$

so that for each state that belongs to $E1_\alpha$ (i.e. satisfies the first level of admissibility) we can establish univocally its admissibility to the second level. We therefore have at our disposal a criterion for saying in which states the action $a*$ must be considered admissible, or be treated 'as if' it were *efficient/fair*. This does not mean, again, that we are able to demonstrate that it is effectively *efficient/fair*, but only that the level of vagueness under which we decide to treat it 'as if' it were *efficient/fair* is satisfied.

196

8. ETHICAL DECISION-MAKING PROCEDURE

Taking for granted the above construction, B can take on the commitment that, only if the state of the world which will come about belongs to the set of conditions of admissibility for which the outcome given $a*$ is *efficient/fair*, will action $a*$ be considered admissible and will therefore be carried out. If B's behaviour in such a situation is not consistent with these conditions, then B could unambiguously be regarded as carrying out an abuse[5].

IV. Default Deduction of Admissible Actions (the Fourth Step in the Ethical Procedure)

We can now present the rule of inference adopted by the ethical procedure to draw conclusions about the admissibility or inadmissibility of B's actions, in the light of the vague relationships between ethical principles and unexpected events. Let π be an evaluation function of actions, with a domain consisting of the two values set {*admissible, inadmissible*} and co-domain B's conditional choice set. The rule is thus simply

$$\forall \omega_i \in \Omega, \quad If \, \mu_{E2\beta}\,(\omega_i|a*) \neq 0 \, then \, \pi(a*|\omega_i) = \{admissible\}$$

---

[5] It is obvious – and we shall return to the point in section 7 – that to this end there must be a certain level of commonness or agreement between A and B in their judgements about the membership of each state in the sets characterising the conditions of application of the principles, which are vague by definition. This point serves to underline, if it were necessary, the difference between the notion of *vague knowledge* and the notion of *subjective probability*. Vagueness is not concerned with subjective beliefs, but rather is inherent in states of affairs that are objectively vague, or in a vague knowledge residing in the inability to assign facts, events or states of affairs (unforeseen *ex ante* and whose description *ex post* is incomplete in the terms of the language known *ex ante*) to classes or categories or concepts (known in the language adopted *ex ante*). Absence of specification and precision is different from uncertainty regarding which out of a set of perfectly specified and precisely described possible events will actually occur. One relevant aspect of vague or imprecise knowledge could be – at least we assume that it is – the fact that it does not present that personal and subjective variability which is typical of degrees of belief expressed by subjective probabilities.

197

8.4 THE FOURTH STEP IN THE ETHICAL PROCEDURE

To put it in words, if – supposing that B chooses $a*$ – the state of the world that occurs falls within the conditions in which choosing $a*$ produces an *efficient/fair* outcome, then for B to choose $a*$ in the occurring state of the world is admissible.

The purpose of this section is to show that the above scheme of inference belongs to the inferences allowed by systems of *default logic* (Reiter 1980). In these systems, a statement is allowed among the deductive consequences of a theory, that is among its theorems – for a given extension of its assumptions – when, in a check of the consequences of the theory, the negation of the given statement does not occur. In such cases it is regarded as consistent with the basis of knowledge to extend the premises of the theory by the assumptions that allow inference of the non-refuted statement. The resulting statement is therefore valid 'until proved otherwise' (i.e. by default) – where a 'contrary proof' would obviously lead to elimination of the additional and provisional assumption which allows the statement to be numbered among the 'theorems' of the theory. Default logic tries to express the way in which we reason when we infer conclusions reasonably, but fallibly, on the basis of incomplete information. Typically, the following is a default inference that a child might make when hearing for the first time of a bird called 'Tweety the penguin' (so that the penguin is for him an 'unforeseen event'):

Tweety is a bird: M (Tweety flies)

.: Tweety flies.

M stands for 'it is consistent to assume that...'. The inference (clearly false) is based on the fact that, not having encountered a bird that cannot fly, the child extends to all birds the property of flight (that is, she regards it as a reasonable assumption on the basis of her knowledge that also Tweety, which is a bird, flies), so that, together with the postulate that the penguin Tweety is a bird (which is the postulate of the 'theory') and the "consistency default assumption" that also Tweety flies, it follows by default that Tweety flies. Although it is false, this inference is not unreasonable if up to now the child has encountered only birds that fly, that is, if she is not able to prove any statement that contains the negation of the statement 'penguins fly'. Furthermore the resulting system of logic is clearly *non monotonic* since its theorems can change (and typically the default theorems of a theory can be

198

eliminated) after an increase in the available information (for example the observation of some penguins that do not fly). Default reasoning proceeds as follows: if, for all the examples of a given set of objects, that have been effectively examined, no counterexamples to a given property has been found, then it is consistent with the available information to assume that this property is valid for all the elements of this set even if we have not been able to search through all the elements of the set. If, however, we discover that the property in question is not true for a given subset (penguins are a subset of the set of birds, and Tweety in an element of it), then we revise the assumption about the larger set, in order to safeguard the more specific information about the given subset.

In order to appreciate the similarity between default reasoning and our rule of inference, consider the typical asymmetry in default reasoning between having a positive demonstration of a statement and not encountering its negation: default logic assumes the consistency of the premise for p, and therefore deduces p, when ¬p is *not* encountered by means of an effective decision procedure, even if p has not been effectively demonstrated. On the other hand the ethical procedure concludes $\pi(a*|\omega_i) = \{admissible\}$ if it simply discovers that the degree of membership of $(\omega_i|a*)$ in $E2_\beta$ is not zero. It should be recalled that we can state $\mu_{E2\beta}(\omega_i|a*) = 0$ not only if the *efficient/fair* outcome is clearly false in ω_i but also if the membership degree of ω_i to the set of conditions which give an efficient/fair outcome is such as to exclude it from the admissible set. In other words, the condition requires us to infer the admissibility of $a*$ only if the degree of compatibility between the state ω_i (under $a*$) and the efficiency/fairness of the outcome exceeds the stated level.

The analogy between the two schemes of inference resides in the fact that, as in default logic we acknowledge the validity of a statement when we do not have proof of the contrary, similarly the inference based on fuzzy logic establishes the admissibility of an act in a state even if we *do not* have proof of the exclusion of the state from the conditions of compatibility between the state and an event. If the event, which affirms the efficiency and fairness of the act, is *not incompatible* with the occurrence of the state over a certain level, the act is admissible. It must be recalled that the fuzzy structure underlying the notion of admissibility requires that the level of membership of the state in the fuzzy set, identifying the event, exceeds a certain threshold. Thus it only asks that we do not have a definite proof that the event in the state is false and that any proof of falsehood remains vague over a certain level.

According to a well-known interpretation (Reiter 1980, McDermott and Doyle 1980) a default inference has a precise operational interpretation: if our finite decision procedure for statements or for testing hypotheses does not have a negative outcome then, provisionally, we assume the statement to be true. The idea of a threshold ensures the same: when unforeseen events occur, it happens that you have not univocal judgements, but you are anyway able to express them quantitatively regarding the compatibility between the occurrence of a state of the world and an event. If the threshold is exceeded, even in the absence of proof that in the state the event does occur, we assume provisionally the validity of the statement regarding the occurrence of the event.

There follows the schema for a default inference applicable to our case:

(1) $\forall\ \Gamma$, where Γ is a non-cooperative game, if for Γ it is possible todefine a hypothetical cooperative bargaining game Gc, construed out of a pair (R^*, D^*), then the Nash bargaining solution to Gc is also the *efficient/fair* solution of Γ,

(2) M (for the game Γ in the state ω_i, $Q \supseteq R^*$ and $[c(I_A) + o_A, c(I_B)]=D^*$),

(3) M $((\omega_i|a^*) =$ an *efficient/fair* outcome),

(4) If $(\omega_i|a^*) =$ an *efficient/fair* outcome, then $\pi(a^*|\omega_i) = \{admissible\}$

$\therefore (a^*|\omega_i) = \{admissible\}$

Premise 1 is our normative base theory (the social contract theory of the firm), while premise 4 is a consequence of our normative base theory. According to it the admissibility of an action depends on the efficiency/fairness of the outcome. Premises 2 and 3 in which the operator M appears ('it is consistent to assume that...') are typical default reasoning assumptions, based on consistency. We make them in so far as they do not contradict the information at our disposal. The relevant information is given here by the membership of the state under examination in the sets $E1\alpha$ and $E2$ (if a state belongs to the two sets, then it is consistent to assume the corresponding statement, because we do not clearly know that it is false, nor are there sufficient proofs of this –relative to that state). These assumptions are added to the base theory and generate a new theory which is an extension of the initial one, whose 'theorems', being in the mode of default inference, are not guaranteed once and for all. Among these theorems are the deductive conclusions regarding the admissibility of actions contingent upon states which were *ex ante* unforeseen. It should be noted that the schema of inference explained above includes all the elements for showing how the ethical code operates: the statement of the constitutional principle and of the prescriptive role of such a general principle, then the assumptions regarding the applicability of the principle in the presence of unforeseen circumstances, the rule for inferring admissibility from efficiency and fairness and finally the conclusion about the admissibility of an action in such circumstances.

Like every system based on default inferences, the ethical code is 'non monotonic' (McDermott and Doyle 1980). Non-monotonicity is evident from the following consideration: if the value of the function of membership changes, and the degree of membership of a state in the set $E2$ for example falls below 0.5, then assumption (3) is no longer valid and the conclusion cannot be drawn. Further information may eliminate a 'deductive' conclusion that had previously been drawn. This of course does not concern the base theory built up around the constitutional principle (the solution for cooperative situations) or the criterion of admissibility for actions (the connection between efficiency/equity and admissibility) – that is, premises (1) and (4) of the inference schema. Rather the default extensions (2) and (3) can undergo revisions. The relevant pieces of *ex post* information on states of the world which were unforeseen *ex ante* may change over time. How they come about, we can derive new default inferences *ex post,* which might be incompatible with the older ones, since they are based on different extensions of the base theory (Reiter 1980). This reflects the fact that the ethical code includes an interpretation procedure for the constitutional principles with respect to circumstances which were unforeseen *ex ante*. Consequently it requires the typical flexibility of constitutional interpretation, that is a precondition for the possibility that a system of fundamental principles may be extended to cover contexts which were not known at the moment of its stipulation. Thus, when contexts vary, interpretations may also vary *ex post*.

However, what is really important is that the ethical code contains rules or procedures for the interpretation of the constitutional norms which are themselves *invariable* in the passage from the *ex ante* to the *ex post* perspective: *ex ante* each player knows that an action will be judged admissible *ex post* if the unforeseen state of the world, which will occur, is adjudged *ex post* to belong to the admissible set of vagueness. *Ex post* the fulfilment of this condition, with respect to every state which has occurred, can be ascertained and can justify the inference about the admissibility of every action contingent upon the state of the world. The rules for interpreting the constitutional norm are always the same, even when the pieces of information vary *ex post*: if the information about the states *ex post* varies, the judgement about applicability of the norm may also vary in consequence, but always following the same interpretative rules which permit us to deal with the vagueness of the relationship between unforeseen events and fundamental norms.

V. Back to Reputation Effects

We now have an appropriate basis for player A to calculate the reputation of player B and for B to return to taking account of the reputation effects his own behaviour has on the behaviour maintained by the succession of players who will successively occupy A's position. In this case the theory of games of reputation, as described in chapter 3, section 5, does apply (Fudenberg and Levine 1989, 1991). A game between a constant player (B in our case) and an infinite succession of players who play for a single period (the succession of players, who take part in the stage game, which from now on we shall refer to on the basis of the index of entry i, as player A_i). The game defined in the previous chapter (see figure 7.1) now simply becomes the stage game (called a *play*) of the repeated game, so that the strategies of player B for the repeated game will become rules which establish his choice between $a*$ and a^c for each play, contingently on the previous history of the game up to the present play. At the same time each A_i will decide, solely from the standpoint of the stage game in which he is taking part, whether to enter or not (*e, non-e*) contingently on the previous history.

In order for reputation effects to regain their effectiveness, it is necessary that there should be no ambiguity *ex post* regarding B's compliance or non-compliance with the obligations undertaken *ex ante*. *Ex post*, A_i must be able to check whether B fulfilled the obligation, which implies that the obligation is sufficiently univocal regarding the behaviour that B must maintain when states or events, that were not known *ex ante*, occur. This condition is satisfied by the model illustrated so far. B's commitment is taken not as the maintenance of a specific action but with reference to an ethical code. It establishes a constitutional principle and the conditions to which this applies, with the consequent derivation of permitted or prohibited acts conditional upon the fulfilment of the conditions of application: with respect to each ω_i, which can not be specified *ex ante*, the code asserts that, whatever the specification of ω_i, if this state satisfies the level of membership 1 in $E1_\alpha$ and level 0 in $E2_\beta$, then the action $a*$ (*ex ante* perfectly known) is *prohibited*. To put it briefly, *ex ante* the code states that any use of $a*$ conditional on the occurrence of any state ω_i (although not specifiable *ex ante*) which belongs to $E1_\alpha$ and not to $E2_\beta$ must be considered an abuse. *Ex post*, when the state ω_i has been observed and the unforeseen events have occurred, it can be ascertained whether the state ω_i which actually occurred satisfies the pre-established conditions. The *types* of player B can be associated not so much to the use of particular actions as to the fulfilment or nonfulfilment of the conditions laid down by the code. If *ex post* A learns of $a*$, when the conditions established *ex ante* for inadmissibility are satisfied by the state ω_i, which has occurred in the meantime, the probability associated with the *type* who respects the code becomes zero. This signal is transmitted to the player who immediately follows A_i in the same position: there is zero probability that B will be the *type* who respects the code in the following interaction and therefore A_i's successor will certainly not enter. B therefore has reason to be concerned about his reputation and to decide on the most appropriate strategy for maintaining reputation.

Analogously with what was established in chapter 3, there are three *types* of player B – labelled $\theta1$, $\theta2$, $\theta3$ – that is, three *types* of possible commitment which player B can take on with regard to how he will play in the course of the repeated game. It is not essential for B to *actually* take on these commitments. It is sufficient to hypothesise that every A_i believes that the *types* are possible and *a priori* assigns to each not zero probability . Let these be:

$$\theta1 = \begin{cases} (a^c|\omega_i), \ \forall \omega_i \ such \ that \ (a*|\omega_i) \ is \ inadmissible \\ \\ (a*|\omega_i) \ otherwise \end{cases}$$

$$\theta2 = \forall \omega_i, \ (a*|\omega_i)$$

$$\theta 3 \; = \; \begin{cases} (a^c|\omega_i) \; \textit{with probability 0.25,} \; \forall \omega_i \; \textit{such that} \; (a^*|\omega_i) \; \textit{is inadmissible} \\ \\ (a^*|\omega_i) \; \textit{otherwise} \end{cases}$$

It is clear that the *types* establish a rule of conduct which is conditional on the state of the world which occurs (in the definition we cite the states ω_i to emphasise the fact that the *types* establish a way of behaving that is valid for the vague situations generated by the occurrence of unforeseen events). *Type* $\theta 1$ is a *type* of player B who takes on the commitment to follow the ethical code as a guide for his behaviour in each play. *Type* $\theta 2$ on the other hand always adopts a^* since it is the individually dominant action in each state of the world (after A_i has entered it is always the optimal response in the current game to 'reward' him at the lower level). *Type* $\theta 3$ tries to make his behaviour 'unpredictable'.

The interesting case is obviously *type* $\theta 1$. The code signals the possibility of the *type*, but the fact that an ethical code has been established or agreed between the parties *ex ante,* does not in itself imply that player B in fact follows the behaviour of that *type*, nor that this is the most probable *type*. This reflects the non-cooperative nature of the game which we are studying. The ethical code establishes a set of constitutional rules *ex ante*, which could have been agreed by means of hypothetical rational bargaining (on the hypothesis that the state of the world admits cooperative bargaining). However, it does not automatically bind the behaviour of the players at the moment in which they have to carry out their actions. Compliance with the code depends instead on reputation effects.

To begin with, all that is required is that the prior probability assigned to the *type* $\theta 1$ who respects the code should not be zero (plus the hypothesis that player B is not short-sighted). We therefore write the *a priori* probabilities of the *types* as follows:

$$p(\theta 1) = p, \; p(\theta 2) = q, \; p(\theta 3) = r$$

and for the sake of the argument, let us say that $p = 0.2$, $q = 0.6$, $r = 0.2$.

8. ETHICAL DECISION-MAKING PROCEDURE

The rule for updating the probabilities of the *types* is Bayesian. Since the actions of the players are conditional on the states as well as on the *types*, in order to express the dynamics of beliefs in the light of the observed player B's behaviour in previous plays, it is necessary to express both the probability *a priori* of the states and the likelihood of the actions, *for each state* of the world, given each *type*. Let us start from the case of an environment of possible known states W. The likelihood of actions $a*$ and a^c must be defined conditionally on each state given a *type*. The expression $(a^c |w_i \cap \theta1)$ should be read as 'the occurrence of the action a^c in the state w_i given that player B is the *type* $\theta1$'.

In the case of the *type* $\theta1$:

$$p(a^c |w_i \cap \theta1) = \begin{cases} 1 \text{ if } (a*|w_i) = inadmissible \\ \\ 0 \text{ if } (a*|w_i) = admissible \end{cases}$$

$$p(a* |w_i \cap \theta1) = \begin{cases} 0 \text{ if } (a*|w_i) = inadmissible \\ \\ 1 \text{ if } (a*|w_i) = admissible \end{cases}$$

In the case of the *type* $\theta2$:

$$p(a^c |w_i \cap \theta2) = \begin{cases} 0 \text{ if } (a*|w_i) = inadmissible \\ \\ 0 \text{ if } (a*|w_i) = admissible \end{cases}$$

$$p(a* |w_i \cap \theta2) = \begin{cases} 1 \text{ if } (a*|w_i) = inadmissible \\ \\ 1 \text{ if } (a*|w_i) = admissible \end{cases}$$

In the case of the *type* $\theta3$:

205

$$p(a^c|w_i \cap \theta 3) = \begin{cases} 0.25 \text{ if } (a^*|w_i) = \text{inadmissible} \\ \\ 0 \text{ if } (a^*|w_i) = \text{admissible} \end{cases}$$

$$p(a^*|w_i \cap \theta 3) = \begin{cases} 0.75 \text{ if } (a^*|w_i) = \text{inadmissible} \\ \\ 1 \text{ if } (a^*|w_i) = \text{admissible} \end{cases}$$

It is clear from the above likelihood functions that learning is allowed only in the case in which the code establishes that $(a^*|w_i) = inadmissible$ – which happens only in some states $w_i \in W$ – since only in this case do the *types* require behaviour which is substantially different from one case to the other. Thus players A_i derive relevant information about B's *type* from the observation of a^c in this case. Let us posit the cardinality of W, $|W| = m$ and assume that in k out of m states in W the evaluation $(a^*|w_i) = inadmissible$ follows, while in the remaining $m-k$ $(a^*|w_i) = admissible$ follws. The conditional probability of *type* $\theta 1$, given the observation of the act undertaken in the preceding stage game, must be calculated, with reference to each state of the world w_i by means of *Bayes rule*[6].

It is clear that if in a state in which the code establishes the inadmissibility of a^* player B nevertheless chooses a^*, then the conditional probability of *type* $\theta 1$ is nil, since the likelihood of this observation is zero under the hypothesis of $\theta 1$. The reputation of being a $\theta 1$ *type* may then be lost on a single occasion if the ethical code is breached. Furthermore, some observation of a^c, in the states in which the code requires it, is sufficient to increase the conditional probability of *type* $\theta 1$ to the extent that from a certain period on (say n) the decision to enter (*e*) becomes appealing in terms of the expected utility for each A_{n+1}.

---

6   Bayes rule in this respect, where θj stands for $\theta 1, \theta 2, \theta 3$, is

$$p(\theta 1|w_i \cap a^c) = \frac{p(a^c|w_i \cap \theta 1)\, p(w_i)\, p(\theta 1)}{\sum_j \sum_{i=1}^{k} p(a^c|w_i \cap \theta j)\, p(w_i)p\theta j) + \sum_{i=k+1}^{m} p(a^c|w_i \cap \theta j)\, p(w_i)\, p(\theta j)}$$

206

VI. Reputation in Unforeseen States of the World

The extension of the analysis to cases where there are unforeseen states of the world presents additional difficulties. The states $\omega_i \in \Omega$ are unforeseen, so that the description of what and how many they are is completely unknown *ex ante* – we assume only that the players suspect that unforeseen states may exist[7]. In principle the prior probability of unforeseen states is nil, since they are not part of the support of the probability distribution over the state space (and therefore over foreseen states). It is reasonable to think that the likelihood functions of the action a^c in each state ω_i, given the *type*, are completely analogous to those described relative to the states w_i, depending at least for $\theta 1$ and $\theta 3$ on what is admissible according to the code in the various states which *ex ante* are unforeseen but *ex post* are evaluated according to the ethical procedure. However, if the probability *a priori* of the unforeseen states is zero, *Bayes rule* always gives the result zero for each conditional probability.

The problem can be resolved if we consider the cognitive situation of the agents more accurately: let us suppose that they have in their minds a representation of the possible alternative states of the world W, which is exhaustive in terms of the language used, but that at the same time they are aware that this representation could be incomplete owing to the fact that they might have omitted to consider some characteristics which the language is not sufficiently rich to express. Thus the agents suspect that an additional set of states Ω is possible, whose elements however lack any clear definition. This cognitive situation should be reflected in some way by the prior distribution of probability over the states. In particular we can express the 'doubt' of the agents with the hypothesis that the probability of the total set of states W rather than the usual $P(W) = 1$ is $P(W) = 1 - \varepsilon$, such that the small at will

---

[7]   In terms of recent models of epistemic logic for the foundation of game theory it could be said that we are defining matters in such a way that the player are aware of Ω, but not of the elements contained in Ω. If we equate awareness to a sort of knowledge, given how epistemic logic defines knowledge, it would be as if the players knew that some states Ω are possible but not which of them is true. But this would amount to say that they know *ex ante* the set of possible states of the world, exactly the opposite that we maintain. We must remember again that some asymmetry has to be introduced between awareness and knowledge (probably stronger that the one made by Fagin and Halpern, 1988).

ε reflects on total probability of the set W the margin of error the agents attribute to their ability of capturing within the set W all the possible states of the world. Thus $P(\Omega) = \varepsilon$ is the probability *a priori* that the agents attach to the possibility that any further state of the world will occur, although its description is unknown *ex ante*. Thus the probability that any generic $\omega_i \in \Omega$ will occur is ε.

Now let us put ourselves in the *ex post* perspective and assume that in the course of the game an unforeseen event occurs which – exhibiting a characteristic which is not included in any description $w_i \in W$ – implies the possibility of giving a series of further alternative descriptions of the state of the world, that is all the states $\omega_i \in \Omega$. It is then natural to take the total prior probability, assigned to the unexpected states, as distributed over the set Ω that we now can describe (it should be recalled that *ex post* this description is vague however, for many relevant aspects). Given that *ex post* we know that $|\Omega| = n$, let us assume that out of the n states $\omega_i \in \Omega$ the code establishes the inadmissibility of a^* for h of these. Let us further hypothesise that, analogously to the previous case, the prior probability of the states is concentrated *almost* entirely (less a negligible quantity η) on those that according to the code imply the inadmissibility of a^*. The prior probability of each unforeseen state among the relevant *h* would therefore be $p(\omega_i) = (1/h) (\varepsilon - \eta)$.

We may regard as unvarying both the *a priori* values of the probabilities of the *types* p, q and r, and the likelihood functions $p(a^c|\omega_i \cap \theta_j)$, now defined with reference to the unforeseen states $\omega_i \in \Omega$, since for the *types* $\theta 1$ and $\theta 3$ they nevertheless depend on the code, while $\theta 2$ implies a^* in all the states. It follows from the calculation of the conditional probabilities of the type $\theta 1$, given the observation a^c, that even in the presence of unforeseen events, the updating of the probabilities, in the light of the evidence of a^c when the code requires it, has the required dynamic property of belief-change such that $p(\theta 1|a^c) > p$ [8].

---

[8] This is true for each of the h states $\omega_i \in \Omega$ in which the code establishes the inadmissibility of a*

$$p(\theta 1|\omega_i \cap a^c) = \frac{p \times 1/h\, \varepsilon}{\Sigma^h_{i=1}(p \times 1/h\ \varepsilon) + \Sigma^h_{i=1} 0.25(r \times 1/h\varepsilon)}$$

8. ETHICAL DECISION-MAKING PROCEDURE

Therefore an adequate number of observations of the action a^c will make the expected utility of the action e sufficiently high for the player A_i, entering the game after an appropriate number of periods, to induce them to play (e), at least until they observe a period in which B plays $a*$ in a state in which the ethical code implies $a*$ to be inadmissible[9].

Let us call N the number of the periods that the players A_i use to update the conditional probabilities of the *types*, such as to generate a probability distribution over the actions of B that is sufficient to induce player A_{n+1} to enter. $M < N$ is the number of times in which the players A_i learn effectively, given that sometimes (precisely $N - M$ times) states may occur for which the code requires $a*$, and thus learning does not take place. Let us further suppose that for the N initial periods player B acted as if he were the *type* $\theta1$, that is, he used a^c in the M periods in which the code requires it and $a*$ in the remaining $N - M$ periods. According to the hypothesis about the rationality of the players A_i, they will have refrained from playing e until the period N, but from the period N + 1 they will begin to enter and continue as long as the their beliefs, updated according to the *Bayes rule*, allows it. Then, to choose his best reply player B will compare the expected payoffs from at least two strategies:

---

which, with the value of the parameters $\varepsilon = 0.1$, $h = 10$. $1/h\ \varepsilon = 0.01$, gives the result

$(\theta1|\omega_i \cap a^c) = 0.002 / 0.0275 = 0.072.$

Therefore the conditional probability of the type $\theta1$, after the observation of the action a^c in the hypothesis that any one of the states $\omega_i \in \Omega$ may occur, is - analogously to the previous case

$p(\theta1|a^c \cap \Omega) = \Sigma^h_{i=1} p(\theta1|\omega_i \cap a^c) = 0.72$

so that the total conditional probability that player B is of the type $\theta1$ in all the possible states, foreseen and unforeseen, therefore in the union of the sets W and Ω is

$p(\theta1|a^c) = \varepsilon \Sigma^h_{i=1} p(\theta1|\omega_i \cap a^c) + (1 - \varepsilon) \Sigma^h_{i=1} p(\theta1|\omega_i \cap a^c) = 0.75.$

[9] Let us suppose that the whole probability mass of the *a priori* probabilities is concentrated on the states for which the ethical code establishes that a* is inadmissible, since in the absence of updating of beliefs about the types the players A_i would never enter given this distribution *a priori*. Otherwise the players A_i could decide to enter even in periods preceding the game, in the light of the probability of the states in which $(e, a*)$ is dominant and the code regards $a*$ as admissible.

(i)   *strategy s1*: after having used a^c in all the first M periods in which the code established the inadmissibility of a^*, in the $N + 1^{th}$ period (or any of the succeeding periods) in which the code again requires the use of a^c, use instead a^*.

(ii)   *strategy s2*: after having used a^c in all the first M periods in which the code required it, from the $N + 1^{th}$ period and in all succeeding periods, when the code again requires it, continue to use a^c.

The strategy *s1*, after the initial series of N plays in which the payoff is zero, on a single occasion offers the expected payoff of the dominant action a^* of the stage game (calculated on the payoffs of a^* in each of the possible states for the probability of each state.) In the succeeding periods therefore it has zero as the expected continuation payoff (remember that we assumed the total probability of states where A_i's dominant action in the stage game is e to be near to zero, even if B chooses his action a^*). After N periods in which the payoff is zero, strategy *s2* obtains in each play of the remaining infinite succession, in which the ethical code requires the action a^c, the expected payoff of a^c calculated on the set of possible states $k + h$ in which a^* is inadmissible. This must be multiplied for their probability (it should be remembered that, according to the hypothesis on the probability of states, payer B predicts that in none of the remaining plays will a state occur which, according to the ethical code, requires the adoption of the action a^*). Therefore *s2* dominates *s1* simply if the continuation expected payoff of *s2* counterbalances the single occasion on which *s1* offers the payoff of the pair (e, a^*).

Fudenberg and Levine's theorems guarantee that, in fact, for a discount level of future payoffs $\delta \sim 1$, there exists an equilibrium of the repeated game that, except for an initial period of N plays, gives player B the stage game *Stackelberg's payoff* for the whole remaining duration of the repeated game and this is the equilibrium which offers B the highest total payoff. Obviously *Stackelberg's payoff* in each play, given the hypotheses on the probabilities associated with the states, coincides with the pair (e, a^c), since if B's binding commitment fell on a^* in all states with positive probability, A_i's best reply would be *non-e*, with the payoff 0 for B. Thus the optimal choice of binding commitments for a leader *á la Stackelberg* would always coincide with behaviour that conforms to the ethical code, or with the *type* $\theta 1$.

8. ETHICAL DECISION-MAKING PROCEDURE

Therefore, after the N plays devoted to accumulating reputation, player B is in a position to generate outcomes (e, a^c) for the entire continuation of the repeated game, since this combination is kept in equilibrium on the one hand by the expectations of the players A_i regarding player B's *types* and, on the other hand, by B's best reply. In fact, for $\delta \sim 1$, the strategy $s2$ dominates B's strategy $s1$, since it allows B to obtain an identical payoff in the N initial plays and a higher payoff in every continuation plays after N except one, while the advantage that can be obtained from $s1$ in that one play is more than balanced by the series of higher discounted payoffs in the continuation. Summing up, by adopting strategy $s2$ player B can generate an equilibrium in the game, apart from the initial period which is spent accumulating reputation, whose total payoff approximates the *Stackelberg payoff*; that is the same as he could obtain if the rules of the game permitted the announcement of binding commitments. We can therefore state the following:

PROPOSITION: *take a hierarchical transaction structured like the sequential PD non-cooperative game, repeated an infinite number of times between a hierarchical* superordinate *and an infinite series of* subordinates, *in the presence of unforeseen events which render contractual obligations ambiguous. Then an ethical code – conceived as a system of general principles whose domain of application are fuzzy sets and whose prescriptions are derived by default inferences – to which is associated with positive initial probability a 'compliant type' of the hierarchical* superordinate, *allows the* superordinate *to induce a profile of strategies* in equilibrium *in the repeated game, such that*
- *the total payoff of the hierarchical* superordinate *is identical to that which he would obtain if he were able to take on binding commitments* à la Stackelberg *about compliance with the ethical code, except for the payoffs obtained in N initial periods spent in accumulating reputation,*
- *in no period does the payoff of the hierarchical subordinates differ from that which conforms to the ethical code.*

Since the ethical code, in our definition, incorporates the same efficiency and fairness criteria as those of the social contract of the firm (discussed in chapter 1 and 2) we have therefore demonstrated that the firm, as an institutional order designed to regulate hierarchical transactions, can avoid the instability inherent in the reciprocal expectation of opportunistic behaviour by acting in conformity with a code that expresses the efficient/fair social contract. Furthermore it has an incentive to do so, since such behaviour is identified with the equilibrium behaviour that is most advantageous for the firm itself.

VII. Limitations and Final Remarks

Some apparently limiting assumptions are implicit in our result. *First*, it is assumed that two agents A_i and A_{i+1} who participate consecutively in the repeated game must share the same judgement regarding the observed action $a*$, i.e. whether it does or does not constitute an abuse given what the code says. When a state that was not specified *ex ante* occurs, their judgement regarding the compatibility of the state with the two conditions of admissibility must be the same, that is to say the vagueness of the relationship between the state and the two events $E1$ and $E2$ must be measured identically by the two players. This assumption is assured by interpreting vagueness as objective indeterminacy or as vague knowledge, but not as subjective belief. It should be noted that both vague knowledge and subjective belief (subjective probability) intervene, but at very distinct points of the argument: when the state ω_i occurs, its compatibility with the events $E1$ and $E2$ is the subject of vague evaluation but inter-subjectively invariable. Since the code contains a rule of default inference, the judgement about the admissibility of the action $a*$ observed *ex post* is neither vague nor uncertain, but univocal although not monotonic. If the action in such circumstances is inadmissible, B's behaviour is abusive. This behaviour is incompatible with the hypothesis that he is a *type* who respects the code. Only at this point does probability come into play: each A_i and A_{i+1} will have an initial belief expressed via a subjective probability distribution regarding the *types* of B. The *type* is established without any vagueness, since it coincides with the behaviour prescribed by the default inference or its negation. Each pure *type* (i.e the *ethical* and the *non*-ethical) chooses $a*$ when the conditions regarding the membership of states in the sets $E1_\alpha$ or $E2_\beta$ are respectively (1,1) or (1,0). The probability of the *type* varies with the evidence collected *ex post*. For any prior probability, an evidence with zero likelihood implies an *a posteriori* zero conditional probability. In particular the likelihood that B will choose $a*$ if the conditions are (1,0), under the hypothesis that B is the *type* that respects the code, is zero. Whatever the prior probabilities assigned by A_i and A_{i+1} to the *types* of B, after an observation $a*$, contrary to the requirements of the code, the conditional probability of the hypothesis that B is of the *type* that respects the code becomes zero.

Second, in order that B may be able to foresee and anticipate this evolution in the beliefs of the other players, based on their common evaluation of vague events *ex post*, it is necessary that B comes to the same vague judgement as they do regarding the compatibility of the state known *ex post* with the events $E1$ and $E2$. What is required is not that B has the same piece of information and therefore expresses the same judgement about the compatibility between the states and the sets $E1$ and $E2$. What is required is that B should have access to the common judgements expressed by A_i and A_{i+1}, since it is from these judgements that A_i and A_{i+1}'s short-run behaviour derives. Therefore the only relevant thing is the vague judgement in the state of information shared by A_i and A_{i+1}.

In general we might ask for something like a *common understanding* of the values and a common understanding of their application. The social contract ensures consensus on common values via agreement, regardless of any concrete situation. In addition there should be a common distribution of fuzziness regarding the membership of the concrete circumstances in the initial conditions of the normative model. Furthermore, this common distribution should be known by B (B must know the distribution of fuzziness shared by all the players A_i)[10]. As a matter of fact, however, this assumption would be excessive and not necessary. What we really need is much less than this: only any couple of players A_i and A_{i+1} must share the same fuzziness distribution on the unforeseen states which have already transpired when they participate in the game. This same distribution must be also known by B at stage i and i+1, without asking however that B agrees on it being an accurate representation of the vagueness at hand. On the other hand, player B has strong reasons for employing it when he is implementing the rules of the code. In fact, only if his behaviour conforms to what the code asks him in the light of reputation effects as seen by any couple of players

---

[10]   These assumptions are similar to those usually accepted in game theory according to which there exists a common *a priori* probability distribution that the players know (Harsanyi 1967/68, Harsanyi and Selten 1988, Binmore 1987/88). How appropriate this hypothesis can be in the context of incomplete information is debatable as it is in the original contexts. But it should be remembered that vagueness is here taken as an objective phenomenon (or perhaps inter-subjective), therefore inherent to some terms of our language and does not rely on subjective opinion.

A_i, A_{i+1}, he will benefit from the reputation effects that induce those players, participating in the stage games in the role of A, to "enter". To put it in other words, it is in B's best interest to take the fuzziness distribution assigned by any couple A_i and A_{i+1} for granted, in order to maintain the reputation effects mechanism at work.

Summing up: (i) ethical principles are constant, (ii) the conditions of application of the principles are constant, (iii) the criterion of maximum vagueness for inferring judgement is constant, (iv) the judgement of admissibility is therefore constant. What can vary from one case to another is the attribution of the weight of membership of the state in the event. If this attribution is completely subjective and relative to the agent the model does not work. If for each repetition the current players A_i and A_{i+1} reach the same judgement about membership then the model succeeds. There therefore has to be a cognitive local inter-subjectivity[11].

---

[11]   It is precisely this that an appropriate use of the theory of *focal points* – the objections outlined in chapter 4 notwithstanding – allows us to assume. From time to time individuals will tend to be attracted by the same contextual characteristics, which belong to the unforeseen states, so that they will tend to bring these characteristics within the domain of application of the same principles according to the *same* membership function, and furthermore they will tend to form the expectation that others too are attracted by the same contextual characteristics and that they will form membership judgements in the *same* way. This ensures a role for the psychological theory of focal points in our approach, without making the theory entirely dependent on the context, because what rests on contextual focal points are only the fuzzy judgement about the relationships between contextual features and principles, not the principles themselves. See moreover Sugden (1995, 1996).

References

ADELSTEIN R. P.: "Deciding for Bigness", *Constitutional Political Economy*, 2 (1991), pp.7-30.

AGHION P. and TIROLE J.: "Formal and Real Authority in Organisations" *Journal of Political Economy*, 105 (1997), pp.1-29.

ALCHIAN A. and H.DEMSETZ: "Production, Information Costs and Economic Organization", *American Economic Review*, 62 (1972), pp.777-795.

AOKI M.: *The Co-operative Game Theory of the Firm*, Oxford (Oxford University Press), 1984.

ARROW K.: *The Limits of Organization*, New York (WW. Norton), 1974.

ARROW K.: "Business Codes and Economic Efficiency", in Beuchamp T. and N Bowie (eds), *Ethical Theory and Business*, 3rd ed., Englewood Cliffs, N.J. (Prentice Hall), 1988.

ASFOR: *Il manager di fronte ai problemi etici*, Milano (IPSOA), 1989.

AXELROD R.: *The evolution of cooperation*, New York (Basic Books), 1984.

AUMANN R. and A.BRANDENBURGER, "Epistemic Conditions for Nash Equilibrium", *Econometrica*, 63, (1995), pp.1161-1180.

BACHARACH M.: "A Theory of Rational Decision in Games", *Erkenntnis*, 27 (1987), pp.167-190.

BACHARACH M.: "The Epistemic Structure of a Game", *Theory and Decisions*, 37 (1994), pp.7-48.

BAGWELL K.: "Commitment and Observability", *Games and Economic Behavior*, 8 (1995), pp.271-280.

BAIER K.: "Duties to One's Employer", in T.Regan (ed.), *Just Business, New Introductory Essays in Business Ethics*, New York (Random House), 1984.

BARCA F.: *Imprese in cerca di padrone*, Roma-Bari (Laterza), 1994.

BENSON G.C.S.: "Codes of Ethics", *Journal of Business Ethics*, 8, (1989).

BERNHEIM D.: "Axiomatic Characterisation of Rational Choice in Strategic Environments", *Scandinavian Journal of Economics*, 88 (1984), pp.473-488.

BERNHEIM D.: "A Theory of Conformity", *Journal of Political Economy*, 102 (1994), pp.841-877.

BEUCHAMP T. and N.BOWIE : *Ethical Theory and Business*, 3rd ed., Englewood Cliffs, N.J. (Prentice Hall), 1988.

BICCHIERI C.: *Coordination and Knowledge*, Cambridge (Cambridge University Press), 1994.

BILLOT A.: *Economic Theory of Fuzzy Equilibria*, Berlin (Springer), 1991.

BINMORE K.: "Modeling Rational Players, I and II", *Economics and Philosophy*, 3 (1987), pp.179-214, 4 (1988), pp.9-57.

REFERENCES

BINMORE K.: "Social Contract I: Harsanyi and Rawls", *The Economic Journal*, 99 (1989), pp.84-102.

BINMORE K.: "Game Theory and The Social Contract", in R.Selten (ed.), *Game Equilibrium Models in Economics, Ethics and Social Sciences*, Berlin (Springer) 1991.

BINMORE K.: *Playing Fair*, Cambridge Mass. (The MIT Press), 1994.

BINMORE K.: *Just Playing*, Cambridge Mass. (The MIT Press), 1998.

BLAIR M.M.: *Ownership and Control*, Washington D.C. (The Brookings Institution), 1995.

BOBBIO N.: *Sull'interpretazione giuridica*, Torino (Giappichelli), 1979.

BOOLOS G. and R.JEFFERY: *Computability and Logic*, Cambridge (Cambridge University Press), 1980.

BOWIE N. and E.R.FREEMAN: *Ethics and Agency Theory, An Introduction*, Oxford (Oxford University Press), 1992.

BOWIE N.: *Business Ethics*, Englewood Cliffs N.J.(Prentice Hall), 1981.

BRATMAN M.E.: *Intention, Plans and Practical Reason*, Cambridge Mass. (Harvard University Press), 1987.

BRAYBROOKE D.: "Justice and Injustice in Business", in T. Regan (ed.), *Just Business, New Introductory Essays in Business Ethics*, New York (Random House), 1984.

BROCK H.W.: "A New Theory of Social Justice Based on the Mathematical Theory of Games", in Ordeshook (ed.) *Game Theory and Political Science*, New York (New York University Press), 1978.

BROCK H.W.: "A Game Theoretical Account of Social Justice", *Theory and Decision*, 11 (1979), pp. 239-265.

BUCHANAN J.M.: *The Limits of Liberty, Between Anarchy and Leviathan*, Chicago (The Univ. of Chicago Press), 1975.

BUCHANAN J.M.: "The Gauthier's Enterprise", in E.Frankel Paul, F.D.Miller Jr., J.Paul. and J.Arhrens /eds.) *The New Social Contract, Essays on Gauthier*, London (Basil Blackwell), 1988.

BUCHANAN J.M.: *The Economics and the Ethics of Constitutional Order*, Ann Arbor (The University of Michigan Press), 1991.

BUCKLEY P. and J.MICHIE: *Firms, Organizations and Contracts, A Reader in Industrial Organization*, Oxford (Oxford University Press), 1996.

CALTON J.M. and L.J.LAD: "Social Contracting as a Trust Building Process of Network Governance", *Business Ethics Quarterly*, 5 (1995), pp. 271-296.

CASSON M.: *The Economics of Business Culture*, Oxford (Oxford University Press), 1991.

CENTER FOR BUSINESS ETHICS: "Are Corporation Institutionalizing Business Ethics?", *Journal of Business Ethics*, 5 (1986), pp.77-89.

CERNIAK C.: *Minimal Rationality*, Cambridge Mass. (The MIT Press), 1986.

CHELLAS B.F.: *Modal Logic*, Cambridge (Cambridge University Press), 1981.

COASE R.: "The Nature of the Firm", *Economica*, IV (1937), pp.386-405.

REFERENCES

COASE R.: "The Problem of Social Cost", *Journal of Law and Economics*, III (1960), pp.1-44.

COASE R.: *The Firm, the Market and the Law*, Chicago (The University of Chicago Press), 1988.

COLEMAN JAMES: *Foundations of Social Theory*, Cambridge Mass. (Belknap Press Harvard), 1990.

COLEMAN JULES: *Market Morals and the Law*, Cambridge (Cambridge University Press), 1988.

COLEMAN JULES: *Risks and Wrongs*, Cambridge (Cambridge University Press), 1992.

CONRY E. J.: "A Critique of Social Contract for Business", in *Business Ethics Quarterly*, .5 (1995), pp.187-212.

CREMER J.: "Corporate Culture and Shared Knowledge", *Industrial and Corporate Change*, 2 (1993), pp.351-386.

CROZIER M.: *Le Phénoméne Bureaucratique*, Paris (Editions de Seuil), 1963

CROZIER M.: "Perchè il gioco è una metafora più utile per la ricerca organizzativa", in L.Sacconi (ed.) *La decisione*, Milano (Franco Angeli), 1986.

DANIELSON P.: "Closing the Compliance Dilemma: How it's Ratioanl to be Moral in a Lamarkian World", in P.Vallentyne (ed) *Contractarianism and Rational Choice, Essays on David Gauthier's Morals by Agreement*, Cambridge (Cambridge University Press), 1991.

DANIELSON P.: *Artificial Morality*, London (Routledge), 1992.

DANLEY J.: "Ought Implies Can or The Moral Relevance of the Theory of the Firm", *Journal of Business Ethics*, 7 (1988), pp.23-28.

DANLEY J.: "Corporate Moral Agency: The Case for Anthropological Bigotry", in Hoffman M. and Mills Moore J. (eds.), *Business Ethics*, New York (McGaw-Hill), 1990.

DE GEORGE R.: *Business Ethics*, 4th ed., Englewood Cliffs N.J. (Prentice Hall), 1995.

DEMSETZ H. and R.LEHN: "The Structure of Corporate Ownership, Causes and Consequences", *Journal of Political Economy*, 93 (1985), pp.1155-1177.

DENZAU A. and D.NORTH, "Shared Mental Models: Ideologies and Institutions", *KYKLOS*, 47 (1994), pp.1-31.

DI NORCIA V.: "Mergers, Takeover and a Property Ethic", *Journal of Business Ethics*, 7 (1988), pp.109-117.

DONALDSON T.: *Corporations and Morality*, Englewood Cliffs, N.J. (Prentice Hall), 1982.

DUBOIS D. and H.PRADE: *Possibility Theory. An Approach to Computerized Processing of Uncertainty*, New York (Plenum Press), 1988.

DUBOIS D. and H.PRADE: "Non–Standard Theories of Uncertainty in Plausible Reasonong", G.Brewka (ed.) *Principle of Knowledge Representation*, (CSLI Publications), 1996.

217

REFERENCES

DUBOIS D. and H.PRADE: *Qualitative Possibility Theory and its Application to Reasonong and Decision under Uncertainty*, Toulouse (IRIT-CNRS discussion paper), 1997.

DUNFEE T. and DONALDSON T.: "Contractarian Business Ethics", *Business Ethics Quarterly*, 5 (1995), pp.167-172.

DWORKIN R.: *A Matter of Principle*, Cambridge Mass. (Harvard University Press), 1985.

EGGERTSSON T.: *Economic Behavior and Institutions*, Cambridge (Cambridge University Press), 1990.

ELSTER J.: *The Cement of Society, A Study of Social Order*, Cambridge (Cambridge University Press), 1989.

EOA NEWS: "US Sentencing Commission Survey", Spring, vol.3, n.1, 1996.

ERIN C.A.: "Who owns MO?", in Harris J. and Dison (eds.), *Ethics and Biotechnology*, London (Routledge), 1994.

FAGIN R. and J.HALPERN: "Beliefs, Awareness and Limited Reasoning", *Artificial Intelligence*, 34 (1988), pp.39-76.

FAGIN R., HALPERN J., MOSES Y. and M.VARDI: *Reasoning About Knowledge*, Cambridge Mass. (The MIT Press), 1995.

FAMA E. and M.JENSEN: "Agency Problems and Residual Claims", *Journal of Law and Economics*, XXVI (1983), pp.327-349.

FRANKEL PAUL E., PAUL J. and JR. F.MILLER (eds.): *Ethics and Economics*, London (Basil Blackwell), 1985.

FREEMAN R.E.: *Strategic Management: A Stakeholder Approach*, Boston (Pitman), 1984.

FREEMAN R.E. (ed.): *Business Ethics. The State of the Art*, Oxford (Oxfrod University Press), 1991.

FREEMAN R.E. and P.EVANS: "Stakeholder Management and the Modern Corporation: Kantian Capitalism", in Beuchamp T. and N.Bowie (eds.) *Ethical Theory and Business*, 3rd ed., Englewood Cliffs N.J. (Prentice Hall), 1988.

FUDENBERG D.: "Explaining Cooperation and Commitment in Repeated Games", in J.J.Laffont (ed.) *Advances in Economic Theory, 6th World Congress*, C Cambridge (Cambridge University Press), 1991.

FUDENBERG D. and E.MASKIN: "Folk Theorems for Repeated Games with Discounting or with Incomplete Information", *Econometrica*, 54 (1986), pp.533-554.

FUDENBERG D. and D.LEVINE: "Reputation and Equilibrium Selection in Games with a Patient Player", *Econometrica*, 57 (1989), pp.759-778.

FUDENBERG D., KREPS D. and E.MASKIN: "Repeated Games with Long-run and Short -run Players", *Review of Economic Studies*, 57 (1990), pp.555-573.

FUDENBERG D. and J.TIROLE: *Game Theory*, Cambridge Mass (The MIT Press), 1991.

FUDENBERG D. and D.LEVINE:, "Maintaining Reputation when Strategies are Imperfectly Observed", *Review of Economic Studies*, 59 (1991), pp.561-579.

218

REFERENCES

GALEOTTI G. and A.BRETON: "An Economic Theory of Politcal Parties", *KYKLOS*, 39 (1986), pp.47-65.

GAMBETTA D. (ed.): *Le strategie della fiducia*, Torino (Einaudi), 1989.

GÄRDENFORS P.: *Knowledge in Flux*, Cambridge Mass. (The MIT Press), 1988.

GAUTHIER D.: *The Logic of Leviathan*, Oxford (Clarendon Press), 1969.

GAUTHIER D.: "Rational Cooperation", *Nous*, 8 (1974), pp.53-65.

GAUTHIER D.: *Morals by Agreement*, Oxford (Clarendon Press), 1986.

GAUTHIER D.: "Economic Man and the Rational Reasoner", in J. Nichols and C.Wright (eds.) *From Political Economy to Economics And Back?*, San Francisco (ICS Press), 1990.

GAUTHIER D.: "Commitment and Choice" in F.Farina, F.Hahn and S.Vannucci (eds.) *Ethics, Rationality and Economic Behavior*, Oxford (Clarendon Press), 1996.

GEFFNER H.: *Default Reasoning, Causal and Conditional Theories*, Cambridge Mass. (The MIT Press), 1992.

GILBOA I.: "Expected Utility with Purely Subjective non-Additive Probabilities", *Journal of Mathematical Economics*, 16 (1987), pp.65-88.

GILBOA I. and D.SCHMEIDLER:. "Updating Ambiguous Beliefs", *Journal of Economic Theory*, 59 (1993), pp.33-49.

GOLDMAN A.H.: "Business Ethics: Profits, Utilities and Moral Rights", *Philosophy and Public Affairs*, 9, 3 (1980), pp.260-286.

GREIF A., MILGROM P. and B.R.WEINGAST: "Coordination, Commitment and Enforcement: The Case of Merchant Guild", *Journal of Political Economy*, 102 (1994), pp.745-776.

GRILLO M.: "Teoria economica dell'organizzazione", *Economia Politica*, 3, (1994).

GRILLO M. and. F.SILVA: *Impresa, concorrenza e organizzazione*, Roma (NIS); 1989.

GROSSMAN S. and O.Hart: "The Costs and Benefit of Ownership: A Theory of Vertical and Lateral Integration", *Journal of Political Economy*, 94 (1986), pp. 691-719.

HACKING J.: "Slightly More Realistic Personal Probability", *Philosophy of Science* 34 (1967), pp.311-325.

HAMPTON J.: *Hobbes and the Social Contract Tradition*, Cambridge (Cambridge University Press), 1986.

HANSMANN H.: "Ownership of the Firm", *Journal of Law Economics and Organization*, 4, 2 (1988), pp.263-304.

HANSMANN H.: *The Ownership of Enterprise*, Cambridge Mass. (Harvard University Press), 1996.

HARDIN R.: *Morality Within the Limits of Reason*, Chicago (University of Chicago Press), 1988.

HARDIN R.: "Ethics and Stochastic Processes", in E.Frankel Paul, F.D.Miller Jr. and J.Paul (eds.), *Foundations of Moral and Political Theory*, London (Basil Blackwell), 1990.

219

REFERENCES

HARE R.M.: *Reason and Freedom,* Oxford (Oxford University Press), 1963.

HARE R.M.: *Moral Thinking,* Oxford (Clarendon Press), 1981.

HARSANYI J.C.: *Rational Behavior and Bargaining Equilibrium in Games and Social Situations,* Cambridge (Cambridge University Press), 1977.

HARSANYI J.C. and R.SELTEN: *A General Theory of Equilibrium Selection,* Cambridge Mass. (The MIT Press), 1988.

HART H.L.A.: "Legal Rights", in ID. *Essays on Bentham,* Oxford (Clarendon Press), 1982.

HART O.: *Firms Contracts and Financial Structure,* Oxford (Clarendon Press), 1995.

HART O. and J.MOORE : "Property Rights and the Nature of the Firm", *Journal of Political Economy,* 98 (1988), pp.1119-1158.

HAUSMAN D.M. and M.MCPERSON: "Taking Ethics Seriously: Economics and Contemporary Moral Philosophy", *Journal of Economic Literature,* XXXI (1993), pp.671-731.

HAUSMAN D.M. and M.MCPERSON: *Economic Analysis and Moral Philosophy,* Cambridge (Cambridge University Press), 1996.

HAYEK VON F.: *Law, Legislation and Liberty,* London (Routledge), 1982.

HINICH M.J. AND M.MUNGER, *Ideology and the Theory of Political Choice,* Ann Arbor (the University of Michigan Press), 1994.

HOBBES T.: *Leviathan,* (ed. by C.B.Machperson), Harmondsworth (Penguin), 1968 (1651).

HOFFMAN M. and J.MILLS MOORE (eds.): *Business Ethics,* New York (McGraw Hills), 1990.

HOHFELD W.: *Fundamental Legal Conceptions,* New Haven (Yale University Press*)*, 1923.

HÖLMSTRON B. and J.TIROLE: "The Theory of the Firm", in Schmalensee R. and R.Willing (eds.), *Handbook of Industrial Organisation,* Amsterdam (North Holland), 1987.

HUANG P.H. and WU HO-MOU "More Order Without More Law: A Theory of Social Norms and Organizational Cultures", *Journal of Law, Economics and Organization,* 10 (1994), pp.390-406.

HUGES G.E. and M.J.CRESSWELl: *An Introduction to Modal Logic,* London (Methuen), 1968.

HUME D.: *A Treatise on Human Nature,* 2nd edition, Oxford (Clarendon Press), 1978 (1739).

JENSEN M. and E.FAMA: "Separation of Ownership and Control", *Journal of Law and Economics,* 26 (1983), pp.301-325.

JENSEN M. and W.MECKLING: "Theory of the Firm: Managerial Behavior, Agency Costs and Capital Structure", *Journal of Financial Economics,* 3 (1976), pp.305-360.

KACPRZYK J. and M.FEDRIZZI (eds.): *Multiperson Decision Making Models Using Fuzzy Sets and Possibility Theory,* Dordrecht (Kluwer Academic Press), 1990.

REFERENCES

KALAI E. and M.SMORODINSKY: "Other Solution to Nash's Bargaining Problem", *Econometrica*, 43 (1975), pp.880-895.

KANDORI M.: "Social Norms and Community Enforcement", *Review of Economic Studies*, 59 (1992), pp. 63-80.

KAUFMANN A.: *Introduction to the Theory of Fuzzy Subsets*, Dordrecht-Boston (Kluwer Academic Press), 1975.

KEELEY M.: *A Social-Contract Theory of Organization*, Notre Dame IN (University of Notre Dame Press) 1988.

KEELEY M.: "Continuing the Social Contract Tradition", *Business Ethics Quarterly*, 5 (1995), pp.241-256.

KLEIN D.B.: "The Microfoundation of Rules VS. Discretion" *Constitutional Political Economy*, 1 (1990), pp.1-19.

KOSKO B.: *Fuzzy Thinking: The New Science of Fuzzy Logic*, Hyperion, 1993.

KREPS D.: *A Course on Microeconomic Theory*, New York (Harvester Weatsheaf), 1990(a).

KREPS D.: *Game Theory and Economic Modelling*, Oxford (Clarendon Press), 1990(b).

KREPS D.: "Corporate Culture and Economic Theory" J.Alt and K.Shepsle (eds.), *Perspectives on Positive Political Economy*, Cambridge (Cambridge University Press), 1990(c).

KREPS D.: "Static Choice in the Presence of Unforeseen Contingencies", in P.Dasgupta, D.Rae, O.Hart, E.Maskin (eds.), *Economic Analysis of Markets and Games*, Cambridge Mass. (The MIT Press), 1990(d).

KREPS D.: "Markets, Hierarchies and (Mathematical) Economic Theory", *Industrial and Corportate Change*, 5 (1996), pp.561-595.

KREPS D. and R.WILSON.: "Reputation and Imperfect Information", *Journal of Economic Theory*, 27 (1982), pp.257-279.

KREPS D., MILGROM P., ROBERTS J. and R.WILSON: "Rational Cooperation in the Finitely Repeated Prisoner's Dilemma", *Journal of Economic Theory*, 27 (1982), pp.245-252 .

LAFFONT J.J. and J.TIROLE: *A Theory of Incentives in Procurement and Regulation*, Cambridge Mass. (The MIT Press), 1993.

LAKATOS I.: *Proofs and Refutations. The Logic of Mathematical Discovery*, Cambridge (Cambridge University Press), 1976.

LANGLOIS C.C. and B.B. SCHLEGELMILCH: "Do Corporate Code of Ethics Reflect National Character? Evidence from Europe and United States", *Journal of International Business Studies*, 21 (1990).

LEGRENZI P., GIROTTO V. and P.N. JOHNSON LAIRD: "Focussing in Reasoning and Decision Making" *Cognition*, 49 (1993), pp.37-66.

LEWIS D.: *Convention. A Philosophical Study*, Cambridge Mass. (Harvard University Press), 1969.

LOCKE J.: "Two Treatise on Government", in. *The Works of John Locke*, vv.II-III, pp.99-228, 1714.

221

REFERENCES

LUCE D. and H.RAIFFA: *Games and Decisions*, New York (J.Wiley & Sons), 1957.

LUCKASIEWICZ J.: *Selected Works*, Amsterdam (North-Holland), 1970.

MAGRI T.: *Contratto e convenzione*, Milano (Feltrinelli), 1994.

MAITLAND J.: "The Limits of Business Self-Regulation", in Beuchamp T. and N Bowie (eds), *Ethical Theory and Business*, 3rd ed., Englewood Cliffs, N.J. (Prentice Hall), 1988.

MANSUR Y.M.: *Fuzzy Sets and Economics*, Aldershot Hampshire (Edward Elgar), 1995

MARCH J.G. and H.SIMON: *Organizations*, New York (J.Wiley & Sons), 1958.

McCLENNEN E.F.: "Justice and the Problem of Stability", *Philosophy and Public Affairs*, 19 (1989), pp.3-30.

McCLENNEN E.F.: *Rationality and Dynamic Choice: Foundational Explorations*, Cambridge (Cambridge University Press), 1990(a).

McCLENNEN E.F.: "Foundational Explorations for Normative Political Economy", *Constitutional Political Economy*, 1 (1990b), pp.67-99.

McCLENNEN E.F.: "Rationality, Constitutions and the Ethics of Rules", *Constitutional Political Economics*, 4 (1993), pp.172-210.

McDERMOTT D. and J.DOYLE: "Nonmonotonic Logic I", *Artificial Intelligence*, 13 (1980), pp.41-72.

McDERMOTT D.: "Nonmonotonic Logic II. Monmonotonic Modal Theories", *Journal of the Association for Computing Machinery*, 29 (1982), pp.33-57.

McKENZIE R. (ed.): *Constitutional Economics*, Lexington Mass. (Lexington Books), 1985.

McMAHON C.: "Managerial Authority", *Ethics*, 100 (1989), pp.35-53.

McMAHON C.: "The Political Theory of Organisation and Business Ethics" *Philosophy and Public Affairs*. 24 (1995), pp.292-313.

McPERSON M.: "Efficiency and Liberty in the Production Entreprise: Recent Work in the Economics of Work Organization", *Philosophy and Public Affairs*, 12 (1982), pp.354-368.

MEYER M., MILGROM P. and J.ROBERTS: *Organizational Prospects, Influence costs, and Ownership Changes*, London (CEPR, discussion paper n.665), 1992.

MILGROM P. and J.ROBERTS: "Predation Reputation and Entry Deterrence", *Journal of Economic Theory*, 27 (1982), pp.280-312.

MILGROM P. and J.ROBERTS: "Bargaining and Influence Costs and the Organization of Economic Activity", in J.Alt and K.Shepsle (eds.) *Perspectives on Positive Political Economy*, Cambridge (Cambridge University Press), 1990.

MILGROM P. and J.ROBERTS: *Economics, Organization and Management*, Englewood Cliffs, N.J. (Prentice Hall), 1992.

MODICA S. and A.RUSTICHINI: "Awareness and Partitional Information Structures", *Theory and Decision*, 37 (1994), pp.107-124.

MOLANDER E.: "A Paradigm for Design, Promulgation and Enforcement of Ethical Codes", *Journal of Business Ethics*, 6 (1987), pp.619-663.

222

REFERENCES

MOSES Y.: "Resource Bounded Knowledge", in M.Vardi (ed.) *Theoretical Aspects of Reasoning about Knowledge*, San Francsco Calif. (Morgan Kaufman), 1988.

MUELLER D.C.: *Public Choice II*, Cambridge (Cambridge University Press), 1989.

NAGEL T.: *The View from Nowhere*, New York (Oxford University Press), 1986.

NASH J.: "The Bargaining Problem", *Econometrica*,18 (1950), pp.155-162.

NASH J.: "Non-Cooperative Games", *Annals of Mathematics,* 54 (1951), pp.286-295.

NASH J.: "Two Person Cooperative Games", *Econometrica*, 21 (1953), pp.128-140.

NORTH D.: *Institutions, Institutional Change and Economic Performance*, Cambridge (Cambridge University Pess), 1990.

ORDESHOOK P. C.: "Constitutional Stability", *Constitutional Political Economy*, 3 (1992), pp.137-176.

PREITE D.: *L'abuso della regola di maggioranza nelle deliberazioni assembleari delle società per azioni*, Milano (Giuffrè), 1992.

RAIFFA H.: "Arbitration Schemes for Generalized Two Person Games", in H.W.Kuhn and A.W.Tucker (eds.) *Contribution to the Theory of Games*, Princeton (Princeton University Press), pp.361-387, 1953.

RAWLS J.: "The Sense of Justice", *Philosophical Review*, 62 (1963).

RAWLS J.: *A Theory of Justice*, Oxford (Oxford University Press), 1971.

RAWLS J.: *Political Liberalism*, New York (Columbia Univ. Press), 1993.

RAZ J.: "Authority and Justification", in *Philosophy and Public Affairs*, 15 (1985), pp.3-29.

REITER R.: "A Logic for Default Reasoning" , *Artificial Intelligence,* 13 (1980), pp.81-132.

RIOLO F.: *Etica degli affari e codici etici aziendali*, Milano (Edibank), 1995.

ROEMER J.: *Theories of Distributive Justice*, Cambridge Mass. (Harvard University Press), 1996.

ROUSSEAU J.J.: *Il contratto sociale*, (G.Petricone ed.) Milano (Mursia), 1971 (1762).

SACCO P.L. and S.ZAMAGNI, "An Evolutionary Dynamic Approach to Altruism" in F.Farina, F.Hahn and S.Vannucci (eds.), *Ethics, Rationality and Economic Behaviour*, Oxford (Clarendon Press), 1996.

SACCONI L.: *Teoria dei giochi, contratto sociale e giustizia distributiva*, Milano (Politeia, discussion paper n.7), 1986.

SACCONI L.: "Teoria dei giochi un approccio adeguato al problema della giustizia sociale", *Teoria politica*, II, 3 (1986), pp.73-96.

SACCONI L.: *Etica degli affari. Inividui, imprese e mercati nella prospettva di un'etica razionale*, Milano (Il Saggiatore), 1991.

SACCONI L.: "Equilibrio e giustizia (I):la stabilità del contratto sociale", *Il giornale degli economisti*, vol.LII, N.S. (1993a), pp.479-528.

SACCONI L.: "Equilibrio e giustizia (II):la selezione del contratto sociale, *Il giornale degli economisti*, vol.LII, N.S. (1993b), pp.529-575.

REFERENCES

SACCONI L.:"Etica degli affari", in S.Zamagni (ed.) *Politica Economica. Enciclo-pedia dell'impresa*, Torino (UTET libreria), 1994(a).

SACCONI L.:. "Codici etici e cultura di impresa", in S.Zamagni (ed.) *Politica Economic. Enciclopedia dell'impresa*, Torino (UTET libreria), 1994(b).

SACCONI L.: "Etica e impresa", in S.Zamagni (ed.) *Politica Economica. Enciclo-pedia dell'impresa*, Torino (UTET libreria), 1994(c).

SACCONI L.: "Considerazioni sulla possibilità del vincolo morale razionale", in S.Maffettone and S.Veca (eds), *Filosofia, Politica , Società, Annali di etica pubblica n.1*, Roma (Donzelli), 1995.

SACCONI L.: *Economia, etica organizzazione*, Roma-Bari (Laterza), 1997.

SACCONI L.: *Etica della pubblica amministrazione*, Milano (Guerini), 1998.

SACCONI L.: "Codes of Ethics as Contractarian Constraints on the Abuse of Authority within Hierarchies: A Perspective from the Theory of the Firm", *Journal of Business Ethics*, 21 (1999), pp.189-202.

SACCONI L.: "Ethics, Corporate Culture and Economic Modelling" in P.Koslowski (ed.) *Historismus as Challenge to Economic Ethics*, Proceedings of the 5th Conference on Economic Ethics and Philosophy, Berlin (Springer), forthcoming.

SAMUELSON L.: *Evolutionary Games and Equilibrium Selection*, Cambridge Mass. (The MIT Press), 1997.

SAVAGE J. L.: *The Foundation of Statistics*, New York (Dover), 1972.

SAYRE MCCORD G.: "Deception and Reasons to Be Moral" in P.Vallentyne (ed.) *Contractarianism and Rational Choice, Essays on David Gauthier's Morals by Agreement*, Cambridge (Cambridge University Press), 1991.

SCHMEIDLER D.: "Subjective Probability and Expected Utility Without Additiv-ity", *Econometrica,.*57 (1989), pp.571-587.

SCHOTTER A.: *The Economic Theory of Social Institutions*, Cambridge (Cambridge University Press), 1981.

SEN A.: *On Ethics & Economics*, London (Basil Blackwell), 1987.

SEN A.: *Moral Codes and Economic Success*, London (LSE, ST-ICERD discussion papers n.49), 1993.

SEN A.: *On Economic Inequality. Expanded Edition*, Oxford (Clarendon Press), 1997.

SHAPLEY L.S.: "A value for N-Person Games", in H.W.Kuhn and A.W.Tucker (eds.), *Contributions to the Theory of Games*, Princeton (Princeton University Press), 1953.

SHELLING T.: *The Strategy of Conflict*, Cambridge Mass. (Harvard University Press), 1960.

SIMON H.: "A Formal Theory of Ownership Relationship", *Econometrica*, 19 (1951), pp.293-305.

SIMON H.: "Theories of Bounded Rationality", in C.B. McGurie and R.Radner (eds.), *Decision and Organisation, Studies in Honor of J.Marshack*, Amster-dam (North-Holland), 1972.

REFERENCES

SIMON H.: "From Substantive to Procedural Rationality", in C.B. McGurie and R.Radner (eds), *Decision and Organisation, Studies in Honor of J.Marshack*, Amsterdam (North-Holland), 1972.

SIMON H.: "Organizations and Markets", *The Journal of Economics Perspectives*, 5 (1991), pp.25-44.

SIMS R.R.: "The Institutionalisation of Organizational Ethics", *Journal of Business Ethics*, 10 (1991), pp.493-506.

SKYRMS B.: *The Dynamics of Rational Deliberation*, Cambridge Mass. (Harvard University Press), 1989.

SKYRMS B.: *Evolution of the Social Contract*, Cambridge (Cambridge University Press), 1996.

SMITH H.M.: "Two-Tier Moral Codes", in E.Frankel Paul, F.D.Miller Jr. and J.Paul (eds.), *Foundations of Moral and Political Theory*, London (Basil Blackwell), 1990.

SMITH H.M.: "Deriving Morality from Rationality" in P.Vallentyne (ed.) *Contractarianism and Rational Choice, Essays on David Gauthier's Morals by Agreement*, Cambridge (Cambridge University Press), 1991.

SUGDEN R.: *The Economics of Rights, Co-operation and Welfare*, London (Basil Blackwell), 1986.

SUGDEN R.: "Contractarianism and Norms", *Ethics*, 100 (1989), pp.768-786.

SUGDEN R.: "A Theory of Focal Point", *Economic Journal*, 105 (1995).

SUGDEN R.: "Rational Co-ordination" in F.Farina, F.Hahn and S.Vannucci (eds.) *Ethics, Rationality and Economic Behaviour*, Oxford (Clarendon Press), 1996.

SUNSTEIN C.: "Norms in Surprising Places: The Case of Statutory Interpretation", *Ethics*, 100 (1990), pp.803-820.

TAN T. and S.R.WERLANG: "The Bayesian Foundation of Solution Concepts in Games", *Journal of Economic Theory*, 45 (1988), pp.370-391.

TAYLOR M.: *Anarchy and Cooperation*, London (J.Wiley & Sons), 1976.

TIROLE J.: "Hierarchies and Bureaucracies", *Journal of Law, Economics and Organization*, 2 (1987), pp.235-259.

TIROLE J.: *The Theory of Industrial Organization*, Cambridge Mass. (The MIT Press), 1988.

TIROLE J.: "Collusion and The Theory of Organization", in J.J. Laffont (ed.), *Advances in Economic Theory*, 6th World Congress, Cambridge (Cambridge University Press), 1991.

TRIMARCHI P.: "Commercial Impracticability In Contract Law: An Economic Analysis", *International Review of Law and Economics*, 11 (1991), pp.63-82.

ULLMAN MARGALIT E.: *The Emergence of Norms*, Oxford (Clarendon Press), 1977.

VAMBERG V.J.: "Organizations as Constitutional Order", in *Constitutional Political Economy*, 3 (1992), pp.223-255.

VAMBERG V.J.: *Rules & Choice in Economics*, London (Routledge), 1994.

VELASQUEZ M.G.: *Business Ethics*, Englewood Cliffs N.J. (Prentice Hall), 1982.

REFERENCES

VERCELLI A.: *Hard Uncertainty and Environment*, Milan (FEEM discussion paper), 1994.

WEIBULL J.W.: *Evolutionary Game Theory*, Cambridge Mass. (The MIT Press), 1995.

WILLAMSON O.: *Market and Hierarchies*, New York (The Free Press), 1975.

WILLAMSON O.: *The Economic Institutions of Capitalism*, New York (The Free Press), 1986.

WILLAMSON O.: "Calculativeness, Trust and Economic Organization" *Journal of Law & Economics*, 36 (1993), pp.453-500.

WILLAMSON T.: *Vagueness*, London (Routledge), 1994.

YAARY M.E.: "Remarks on Rationality and Morality", in F.Farina, F.Hahn e S. Vannucci (eds.) *Ethics, Rationality and Economic Behaviour*, Oxford (Clarendon Press), 1996.

ZADEH L.A.: "Fuzzy Sets", *Information and Control*, 8 (1965), pp.338-353.

ZADEH L.A.: "The Concept of Linguistic Variable and its Application to Approximate Reasoning, I, II, II", *Information Science*, 8 (1975), pp.199-257, pp.301-357, 9, pp.43-80.

ZADEH L.A.: "Fuzzy Sets As a Basis for the Theory of Possibility", *Fuzzy Sets and Systems* 1 (1978), pp.3-28.

ZADEH L.A.: "The Role of Fuzzy Logic in the Management of Uncertainty in Expert Systems", *Fuzzy Sets and Systems*, 11 (1983), pp.199-227.

ZIMMERMAN H.J.: *Fuzzy Set Theory and Its Applications*, 2nd revised ed., Dordrecht-Boston (Kluwer Academic Press), 1991.

Names Index

227

Studies in Economic Ethics and Philosophy

Printing: Weihert-Druck GmbH, Darmstadt
Binding: Buchbinderei Schäffer, Grünstadt